CHEF TELL
Tells All

A gourmet guide from the market to the table

By Tell Erhardt and Hermie Kranzdorf

Schiffer Publishing Ltd

Box E, Exton, Pennsylvania 19341

Library of Congress catalog card number: 79—52440

ISBN: 0-916838-27-7

Printed in the United States of America

Dedication

To Max:

Max is very tall, very handsome and very proud. He was determined his son was not to become a chef, not in a family of the 'right type' professionals.

His son is very proud. Proud that he inherited his tenacity, determination and aggressive traits. All of which enabled him to go so far in the 'right' profession ... a chef. Thanks Papa.

To Giesela:

Growing up in post-war Germany often meant weeks of meatless meals and very little of most foods to go around. My Mother, Giesela, took this constant problem as a challenge and always made innovative, exciting and original meals from very little.

From my Mother, I learned the sensuality and creativity of food at a very tender age. I still use many of her timeless recipes with love, appreciation and warm memories of a gentle and loving lady who has long been with the angels.

Acknowledgements

To our photographer, William Hyland, Jr., for the excellent job he did on the illustrations for this book.

A special thanks to Christl Eggstein for her help with the napkin folding section.

Our thanks to Herbert Engelbert, wine consultant, for allowing us to include his Wine and Food Affinities charts in this book.

Our thanks to the National Live Stock and Meat Board for allowing us to use their meat charts.

And thank you to all of the staff of Tell Erhardt's International Cuisine who helped in preparing the food for the illustrations for this book.

Prologue

People always ask me if I have ever cooked for anyone famous and if so, what they are really like. The first celebrity I ever cooked for was John F. Kennedy. He was visiting Berlin back in 1964. I wasn't a chef then, just one of the cooks in a large outfit that catered all the food for this visit. There were constant clearances and checks, but one day JFK wandered into the kitchen and asked us how we were doing. He wanted the experience of trying new things, so he let us cook him some really hefty German food. He was a nice friendly man and a real pleasure to cook for.

In 1966, Queen Elizabeth visited Berlin for four days. She was there in the middle of November and insisted on having a cocktail every night with a fresh mint leaf in it. It's difficult to get fresh mint in Germany, period. But at that time of year, it was even more impossible. We finally located some fresh mint in Israel. It was brought to the airport in Tel Aviv and from there flown to Berlin. But the Berlin Airport was fogged in, so the plane had to land in Hamburg. We got the mint delivered just as the dinner was starting. It looked horrible, because it had not been kept in water, but we used it anyway.

None of our staff was allowed near the Queen, as she had a personal valet who served all her food. He also had to taste everything first. Three times a day we had to prepare three identical meals for the Queen, but we never knew which one of the three she actually ate. It was exciting, but also a lot of trouble.

I also cooked for her sister, Princess Margaret, when she stayed at the Barclay Hotel in Philadelphia. She was much easier to work for, no tasters or anything. The only thing she wanted was a special tea which we had to buy in New York. Other than that, she liked all kinds of food.

Yul Brynner was another celebrity that was extremely difficult. He only ate one special kind of apple grown in Washington state and we had to get these apples for him. He also wanted special meals cooked late at night, sometimes as late as 4:00 A.M. He was difficult for the hotel staff, also. His shades had to be drawn at all times. He demanded sixty foot extension cords on all his phones, so he could walk from one room to the other while he was talking.

One day, when Peter Ustinov was at the Barclay Hotel, he walked into the kitchen. He said the menu had looked European and thought that perhaps I was German. When I said that I was, he immediately began to speak in German and continued to do so for the next three weeks. He was playing at a local theatre in Philadelphia at this time. Peter used to come into the kitchen and ask me to cook European dishes for him. The man was a pleasure to cook for and a thoroughly nice person.

One morning, while I was still at the Barclay, I was on the elevator when Henry Fonda got on. He saw I was the chef and suggested that we have breakfast together. It was a real thrill because here was a man I had seen all my life in the movies and on television. Imagine having breakfast with Henry Fonda!

I think the most spectacular thing I have ever done was a 500 pound birthday cake in the shape of a baby grand piano for Arthur Rubinstein's 89th birthday. Beginning one week before the party, my pastry chef and I started baking lots and lots of sheetcakes. We assembled the whole cake on the stage of the Academy of Music. For the base we used an actual stand made to hold a baby grand piano. We assembled all of the sheetcakes on top of the stand and covered the whole thing with marzipan. The keyboard was made out of pure marzipan. There are 110 white keys and 55 black keys and we were one black key short. I kept hoping the maestro wouldn't notice because we were clean out of marzipan. When we wheeled the cake on stage, he was so overwhelmed by its size that he made us take a bow. He couldn't believe that the cake was real until he felt one of the keys and then licked his fingers. I still keep the pictures of this cake on the wall of my restaurant.

Introduction

Beginnings often happen because of a stroke of luck or a quirk of fate. There are two beginnings that I am always asked about, no matter where I go. First, how did I become a chef and second, how I got my start in television. I'd like to tell you about both of these.

I became a chef because of my mother's influence. I have dedicated this book to her since she was the part of my life that made me love good cooking. I grew up in post war Germany where, besides Care packages, there was not much food around. But somehow my mother was able to make delicious meals out of nothing. I was always in the kitchen with her, perhaps because I was always hungry or because I was interested, I don't know.

At any rate, my first job was not as a chef, but as a hairdresser. I didn't like this job much because I always had to clean up after everyone else. So after six months, I left and went back to the National Employment office. There were two jobs available at that time for someone my age. One of them was for a butcher's apprentice and the other was for a chef's apprentice. To be a chef in Germany you have to serve an apprenticeship of three years. Naturally, I decided on the second job.

I left home when I was thirteen and a half years old. When you serve an apprenticeship such as that, you have to live where you work. The hotel I worked in was sixty miles from my own home. I worked for eighteen hours a day, six days a week. On my day off, on Monday, I just slept. You never dared complain that there was too much work, because there were always five people waiting to take your job. The hotel provided me with room and board, but my father had to pay twenty dollars a month for a year in order for me to keep this job. The second year they pay you twenty dollars a month and the third year you got a raise to forty dollars a month. So for three years you make very little money. After serving this time you then take an examination. If you pass, you are given a certificate that says you graduated and that you are a cook, not a chef.

From this point on you begin your learning again. I worked in restaurants all over Europe. The better the hotel or restaurant, the less money you make. However, you are always provided with room and board, so any money you do make is free and clear. There's not much time to spend your money, anyway. You work a split shift in most European restaurants, from 7:00 A.M. to 2:00 P.M. and from 5:00 P.M. to 10:00 P.M. You usually keep each job for six or eight months and take a vacation between jobs. I did this for several years until I finally ended up working as executive chef at the Kronin Hotel in the Black Forest for eleven years. Then I came to America and now that I am here, I love it!

My first appearance on television began with a funny story. Back somewhere around 1971 or 1972, I was working for the Marriott as a chef-trainee. I was put into this position, even though I had my master-chef's degree from Europe, so that I would learn some English and also the Marriott procedures.

Channel 29 called the Marriott and asked them to send one of their chefs to do a public appearance on a television show. The executive chef, who was also German, refused to go because he wouldn't perform on television unless he got paid. He asked me if I wanted to go and of course, I said yes, I would love to be on television.

I went down to Channel 29, a local Philadelphia television station, to perform on a show called "Smalltalk", to do a segment for the Weight Watchers of Greater Philadelphia. It was so long ago, the show was filmed in black and white. I have no idea how people could have understood my English then. I've been on television for many years and some people still have trouble understanding me even now. But I did the show and they got so much response that they asked me to come back again. I did five or six demonstrations for the Weight Watchers. While I was on this show, someone from Channel 6 saw me.

They had a morning show called "Dialing for Dollars" with Connie Roussin and Jim Mac Lane, who was on even before Jim O'Brien had started. They asked me if I would do a cooking demonstration. Naturally, I said, "Yes, of course, I would." The Marriott provided the food for this show and "Dialing for Dollars" gave us airtime. Both the Marriott and I got lots of publicity so it worked well for all of us. The first time I was on the show, I received 800 letters. I was asked to perform once a month, then twice a month and then, finally, once a week. I was on this show for about three years.

When "Evening Magazine" decided to do a show in Philadelphia, they asked me to do an audition for them. It was 9:00 A.M. on a Monday and I wasn't feeling too well. This audition took place in the park across the street from the KYW building. I had to perform in front of a camera and just talk, they wouldn't let me hold anything in my hands. I thought it was an absolutely horrible audition. But three weeks later I got a call from the station. They had hired me as a local tipster on the "Evening Magazine" television show. And from there, things just snowballed. I'm now syndicated in thirty cities and have millions of viewers. I fly all over the country to do personal appearances on a variety of shows, shopping centers, and so on. And I love it, I just love it!

Table of Contents

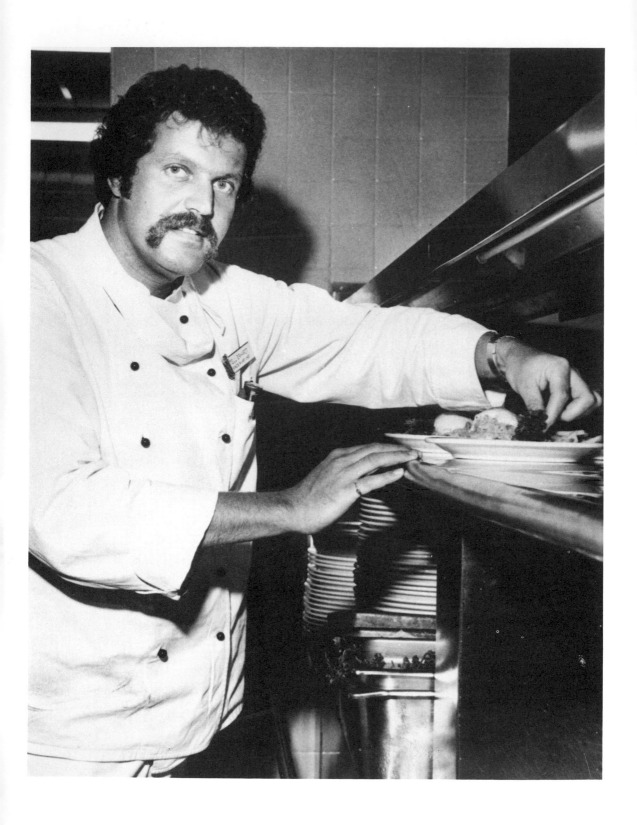

Tips From Tell - Chapter 1

Tips:
How To Buy a Knife
Sharpening Knives
Selecting Knives
Pots and Pans
Double Boilers
How to Season a Pan
Wooden Spoons
Getting out Ingredients
Weighing Ingredients
How to Chop an Onion
Blanching
Breading
Cooking with Wine
How to Clarify Butter
Garlic Paste
How to Squeeze a Lemon
Seasoning Food

Recipes:
Clarified Butter
Garlic Oil

How To Buy A Knife

There are several things to consider when buying a knife. First, make sure it's a stainless steel knife. Carbon knives will discolor when you cut lemon or any fruits that contain acid. They will then, in turn, discolor anything they cut. Make sure the knife actually says "Stainless Steel" on the blade, not "no stain". Sometimes there are carbon knives that are highly polished. It must say stainless steel to be stainless steel.

Second, it should be a German knife. We still do make the best cars, the best steel and the best knives. Make sure the steel that forms the blade runs all the way through the handle as well. It should not stop two-thirds of the way down. The rivets holding the handle together should be of the same material as the knife blade itself. Brass or copper rivets do not hold as well as steel ones.

Make sure the handle of the knife begins with a steel ridge rather than wood. It's more sanitary because no dirt can get stuck between the blade and the handle if the handle begins with steel.

Weight is very important in a knife. It should be well balanced. The weight of the handle should be the same as the weight of the blade. Try balancing the knife in your hand to see if this is so.

Do buy good knives, for they will last you a lifetime. My idea of a good knife is a stainless steel German knife.

Sharpening Knives

You should sharpen your knives everytime you use them. Buy a steel for this purpose when you buy your knives. It looks like a big iron rod with a handle. To sharpen a knife, hold the steel in your left hand and, at an angle of 45 to 65 degrees, draw the knife across the steel, towards your hand. **Illustration 1.** *Do this several times, alternating the sides of your knife.* **Illustration 2.** *These directions only apply if you are right-handed. If you are left-handed reverse the instructions.*

Selecting Knives

I would recommend that you start out by buying three knives. **Illustration 3.** *First, a chef's knife, anywhere from 8 to 12 inches long with a wide blade. You would use this knife for chopping, mincing and dicing.*

You should also have a shorter knife, anywhere from 5 to 8 inches long with a narrower blade. They are usually called slicing knives. This is a good size for filleting fish, boning some meats and cutting fruits.

Last, everyone needs a little paring knife. Use it for coring fruits and peeling vegetables. It will have a million uses in your kitchen.

Illustration 1.

Illustration 2.

Illustration 3.

Pots and Pans

The kinds and number of pots and pans that you need in a kitchen depends on the size of your family and the amount of cooking you do. I believe that you can cook anything in any pot as long as you start with good ingredients and a recipe that works. You can cook chinese food in a french copper pot or french food in a wok. You don't have to buy special equipment to cook ethnic foods. If your pot doesn't care what nationality it is, why should you!

Double Boilers

A double boiler is one of the most unnecessary pieces of equipment you can buy for your kitchen. Anytime a recipe asks for a double boiler, try doing this ... Half fill a pot with boiling water and put it on the stove. Place a metal bowl on top of the pot. Use a bowl that is large enough to stay on top and not fall in. Also make sure the bowl is metal, not plastic that will melt. It is much easier to stir or beat ingredients in a rounded bowl than in a pot. This set up will work even better than a double boiler.

How To Season A Pan

I always season my pans before I cook in them. The reason for this is that seasoning prevents food from sticking to the bottom of the pan when you cook. You can season any pan so long as it does not have a coating, such as teflon, on its surface.

Place a layer of salt in the pan, approximately one cup for a medium sized frying pan. Put the pan on your stove and heat it, using a high flame, until it gets very hot. The salt will start to turn brown and burn. This should take anywhere from twenty to thirty minutes.

Spread out several layers of newspaper on a work surface. Carefully place the pan on the paper and let it cool for a few minutes. Take some more newspaper and crumble it into a ball. Then rub the inside of the pan with this newspaper, using a rotating motion. Really rub the salt into the pan. Be careful when you do this as the salt is very hot. The newspaper will turn very black. Dump the salt out of the pan.

Then add about ½ cup of vegetable oil to the pan. Heat the pan again so that the oil reaches the smoking point. Tilt it so that the oil films the whole inner surface of the pan. Let it cool a little. Pour the oil out carefully. Then wipe out your pan with a towel. Your pan is now seasoned.

There are some rules you should follow for using a seasoned pan. First, always heat the pan before you add any food to be cooked. Second, after cooking, wipe the pan out with a dry towel and put it away. Never, never wash a seasoned pan out with soap and water.

Your pans should be re-seasoned once a year. If your pan happens to burn before this time, then wash it out well and season it again. You don't have to wait for the year to be up. If you have an iron pan that rusts, just rub in a little bit of oil everytime you finish with the pan, before you put it away. You will never have trouble with food sticking to your pans if you follow these instructions.

Wooden Spoons

I like to use wooden spoons when I cook. If a wooden spoon hits the side of a stove or a hot pot, it will not melt like a plastic spoon does. If you use a metal spoon to stir something hot, the spoon itself will get too hot to handle. Wooden spoons don't get too hot or too cold and they don't develop a flavor or smell, unless you never wash them, of course.

Getting Out Ingredients

Being organized when you cook is half the work. Always get all your ingredients out before you start to cook or bake. There are lots of reasons for doing this. First, this way you will know that you have everything you need. You won't have to run all over the neighborhood looking for a cup of sugar while your egg whites get overbeaten. Borrow the sugar before you begin. You don't have to run around the kitchen with floury fingers opening cabinets and hunting for that new container of baking powder you knew you put somewhere last week. You already found it while your fingers were clean. Also you will never leave out an ingredient if everything is in front of you. Your actual preparation time will be much shorter if you do this my way.

Weighing Ingredients

In Europe we usually weigh our ingredients rather than measure them. It's a much more accurate way to both cook and bake. For example, high humidity may make your flour more compact in the summer, while it is dryer and lighter in the winter. If you measured out three ounces of flour, it would be a different weight, according to the season. But if you weighed them, three ounces weighs three ounces, summer or winter. Once this country changes to metrics, we'll all be weighing ingredients. It's much easier and much more accurate.

How To Chop An Onion

Everyone knows how to chop an onion, but most people don't know how to do it the easy way. "How to chop an onion" is usually the first show requested when I am introduced into a new city on television. People are amazed at how fast it can be done and how easy I make it look. You need two things to chop an onion ... a very sharp knife and, of course, an onion.

*There are three steps to chopping an onion the right way. First you have to peel the onion. Make sure you don't cut off the root end, you want the onion to stay together. Then you slice the onion in half, lengthwise. Lay it on your chopping board with the cut side down. Then cut through the onion at one-quarter inch intervals, vertically, about two-thirds of the way down to the root end. **Illustration 4.** Slice the onion once or twice horizontally, also being careful not to cut through the root. **Illustration 5.** Then chop, from top to bottom, using your index finger as a guide for your knife as you go along. **Illustration 6.***

People always ask what to do when they chop an onion so that they don't cry. It's easy for me not to cry when I chop onions, because I'm so tall. I'm at least three feet from the onion. However, what you can do is to breathe through your mouth, not your nose, while chopping. This will work most of the time. Sometimes even I cry if the onion is very juicy. Just think about the nice clear eyes you'll have afterwards.

Illustration 4.

Illustration 6.

Blanching

When a recipe says to blanch something it means you have to precook your food for a short amount of time. You do this by bringing some water to a boil in a pot. Add your food and wait for the water to come back to a boil. Drain the food and run some cold water over it to stop the cooking action.

Parboiling is almost the same thing, but the food is cooked in the boiling water for a little longer period of time. Follow the same procedure as above, but start counting the cooking time the recipe specifies from the time the water comes back to the second boil.

Blanched foods usually keep a little longer than raw food. This technique was often used in Europe when there was little or no refrigeration to preserve foods for any length of time.

Breading

Do you ever bread pork chops and find that you have more breading on your fingers than on your chops? There is a way to bread food without having such a mess.

First, set out everything that you will use. You will need some flour, and egg wash, which is two eggs beaten with a teaspoon or two of water, and some breadcrumbs. *Illustration 7.*

First, dredge all of your food in the flour. Then, using one hand, dip your food into the egg wash. Remove the food and set it into the pan containing the breadcrumbs. Then with your other hand, turn and pat the breadcrumbs into place. One hand always stays wet in the egg wash and one hand always stays dry in the crumbs.

This way you don't rebread your fingers everytime you bread another pork chop. You don't have to stop and wash your hands all the time and you'll use much less breadcrumbs.

Illustration 7.

Cooking With Wine

Lots of my recipes call for cooking with wine. There are several reasons for this. Wine contains acid. When you cook meats this acid acts as a tenderizer. Wine also makes your sauces taste much better.

Don't use the so called "cooking wines" if you can possibly avoid them. They contain a lot more salt than regular wine and will throw off the balance and the taste of your sauce. If you must use them, be very careful about adding seasonings and definitely use less salt then your recipe calls for.

Don't go down to your husband's wine cellar and take the oldest bottle you can find to use for cooking. Your food might taste great, but your husband will be very angry. Always ask before you open a bottle from the cellar.

The best thing to buy are two bottles or gallon jugs of table wine to keep for cooking, one white and one red. Almost all vineyards put out an inexpensive table wine that will suit this purpose. The wine will keep for a long time for cooking purposes, as long as you keep it refrigerated.

How To Clarify Butter

I always use sweet butter in my restaurant. I don't like the taste of salted butter. Salt is used as a preservative to keep the butter from going rancid and to give it a longer shelf life. You call always tell when sweet butter is fresh by the taste and the smell. It's not as easy to tell if salt butter is good or not.

For cooking, I always use clarified butter. Clarified butter is butter which has been cooked to remove the water content and the sediment.

Clarified butter has a much higher burning point than regular butter. This fact enables you to cook your food at a much higher temperature than you could if you used regular butter. Your food will also cook much faster at this higher temperature, and you have less chance of burning anything.

Here is how to make clarified butter:

Clarified Butter

Using as much butter as you require, place it in a small saucepan and melt the butter on a high heat. As it bubbles, a foam will come to the surface. When this foam subsides, the water has been removed and the butter is clarified.

Garlic

Garlic Paste

Did you ever taste some food and find that you have bitten into a hidden hunk of garlic? The taste can be pretty awful, even if you love garlic. This will never happen if you use garlic paste when you cook. Now don't go out to your local store and look for a brand of paste that contains garlic, you won't find any. Garlic paste is made with salt and garlic cloves. The salt absorbs the moisture from the fresh garlic and enables you to mash it into a fine paste.

*To make garlic paste, just put a teaspoon or two of salt on your chopping board and place a clove or two of garlic on the salt. With a broad chef's knife, begin to chop the garlic. When the garlic is chopped into fairly small pieces, turn your knife sideways and with the flat part of the blade, begin to mash the garlic into the salt. You should have a fine paste in just a few minutes. **Illustration 8.** You can use this paste whenever your recipe calls for crushed garlic. Just remember to use less salt, as the garlic paste already contains salt.*

Illustration 8.

Here is another great way to get the flavor of fresh garlic in your food without ever biting into a piece of garlic.

Garlic Oil

1 Cup Oil
6-7 Cloves of Garlic, Peeled

Add the garlic to the oil and keep in a jar with a screw top in the refrigerator. After 2 days, you will have a garlic flavored oil which will add flavor to all your dishes. This way you don't have to peel and dice a garlic clove every time you need one. It will keep for 1 to 2 months in your refrigerator.

Lemons

Before you cut a lemon in half to use it for juice, make sure you roll the lemon on a tabletop and bear down with your hand while rolling. This will break down the cell structure inside the lemon. It will be easier to squeeze and will yield much more juice.

Also when you squeeze a lemon half, keep two of your fingers in front of the lemon the way I do to catch the seeds as you are squeezing. It's easier than picking them out of your dish afterwards.

Seasoning Food

You should season your food at three different stages of cooking. First, add one-third of the seasoning when you begin to cook. Second add another third about mid-way through the cooking process. And last, just before serving time, correct the seasoning.

If you cook food without adding any seasoning at the beginning, your food will not develop the proper taste or flavor. But don't add all the seasoning the recipe calls for at the beginning either, for sometimes as the liquid reduces down, you may find that you have used way too much. Remember you can always add more seasoning, but it's hard to remove it once it is there.

The best way to season food is to add a little bit at the beginning to develop flavor. Add a little more half-way through the cooking time. Then taste your food right before you serve it and make any final adjustments you need.

If, for some reason, you have added too much seasoning to a stew or a sauce, there are a few ways to try to save your dish. One way is to drain off half the liquid and add water in its place. Your dish will be thinner, but it will taste better. Don't throw away the sauce you have removed, save it to use another time.

If you have overseasoned a stew or a soup, then another thing you can try is to add potatoes. Potatoes tend to absorb the extra seasoning. If you've really overdone the seasoning, you can try both remedies.

Tips:

Boiling Guide	Cauliflower
Asparagus	Celeraic
Avocados	Corn
Beets	Cucumbers
Belgian Endive	Green Peppers
Brocolli	Leeks
Brussels Sprouts	Mushrooms
Cabbage	Spinach
Sauerkraut	Tomatoes
Carrots	

BOILING GUIDE FOR FRESH VEGETABLES

Vegetable	Boiling time (minutes)	Vegetable	Boiling time (minutes)
Asparagus, whole	10 to 13	Okra	12 to 14
Beans:		Onions, mature:	
Lima	25 to 27	Whole	11 to 15
Snap, 1-inch pieces	13 to 15	Quartered	10 to 14
Beets, whole	38 to 40	Parsnips:	
Broccoli, heavy stalks, split	9 to 12	Whole	20 to 40
Brussels sprouts	15 to 17	Quartered	8 to 15
Cabbage:		Peas	10 to 14
Shredded	6 to 8	Potatoes:	
Wedges	10 to 13	Whole, medium size	25 to 29
Carrots:		Quartered	15 to 17
Whole	20 to 22	Spinach	8 to 12
Sliced or diced	18 to 20	Squash:	
Cauliflower:		Acorn, quartered	18 to 20
Separated	8 to 12	Butternut, cubed	16 to 18
Whole	20 to 24	Yellow, crookneck, sliced	11 to 13
Celery, sliced	15 to 19	Zucchini, sliced	13 to 15
Collards	15 to 20	Sweetpotatoes, whole	28 to 35
Corn:		Turnips:	
On cob	5 to 7	Cut up	10 to 12
Whole kernel	6 to 8	Whole	30 to 38
Kale	15 to 20		

Vegetables - Chapter 2

Recipes:

Asparagus

A good way to tell if asparagus is fresh is to check the bottoms of the stalks. If they are moist, the asparagus should be fresh. However, many markets store asparagus with their stalks in water. So the old reliable test is not always very reliable. What you should do is to check the stalks to see if they are nice and firm. If the asparagus looks like a bunch of limp flowers, don't buy them.

I don't like thin asparagus. When I cook asparagus, as you can see in the following recipes, I recommend that you peel the stalks. If you peel thin asparagus, there is nothing left to eat. So I prefer the thick stalks, even if they cost a little bit more.

To prepare asparagus for cooking, cut off the last inch from the bottom of each stalk. Then place the stalk on a chopping board and peel with a potato peeler two-thirds of the way down from the tips to the bottom. Illustration 9. This makes the asparagus much easier to eat and the stalks taste very tender this way.

How To Cook Asparagus

I like to use a large frying pan to cook my asparagus. Fill it two-thirds of the way with water. Add one teaspoon of salt and one teaspoon of sugar and bring the water to a boil. Add a few spoons of butter and then place the peeled asparagus into the boiling water so that they are lying down. I like to cover my asparagus with a folded towel so that they all remain under water. Simmer until tender. This will take about six to eight minutes. Serve the asparagus when they are nice and fresh and hot. Very simple, very easy and very delicious. Good plain or even better with hollandaise sauce.

Illustration 9.

Artichokes Grand-Duc

8 canned artichoke bottoms
salt, pepper
few spoons butter

1 pound asparagus
1 teaspoon sugar
1 recipe hollandaise sauce, page 74

You will only use the tips of the asparagus for this recipe. Trim the asparagus so that the tips are all the same length, about three inches. Don't throw out the stalks, use them to make asparagus soup. Peel the stalks and cook the asparagus as described in the previous recipe. Be careful not to overcook the tips as they take less time than the stalks.

Place the canned artichoke bottoms into a buttered baking pan. Place a few of the asparagus tips into each bottom. Cover with the hollandaise sauce and heat in the oven until warm. Serve immediately.

Avocados

An avocado is ripe when it's dark green in color. Sometimes there will even be some black spots on the skin. Most important, it should feel soft and pulpy in your hand. If an avocado is light green with shiny skin and feels very hard to the touch, then it's not ripe enough to eat.

An avocado should be ripened by leaving it out at room temperature. Depending on how green it is when you buy it, this sometimes can take up to a week or two.

However, there is a trick to ripening an avocado immediately. Bring a small pot of water to a boil. Put the avocado into the boiling water, turn off the heat and let it stand. The color of the skin will turn black immediately and the fruit will ripen in about ten to fifteen minutes. Remove it from the hot water and use it right away. Avocados ripened in this way cannot be refrigerated or stored, they must be used immediately.

Guacamole

1 avocado, peeled and chopped
½ tomato
1 chili pepper, finely chopped

2 tablespoons finely chopped onion
juice ½ lemon
salt, pepper

Peel, seed and dice the tomato. Combine all the ingredients and mix well. Serve with crackers or corn chips.

Avocado Salad

2 large ripe avocados   ¼ head iceberg lettuce
1 cup cocktail sauce, page 77   cooked shrimp, optional

Make the cocktail sauce. Finely shred the lettuce. Place some of the lettuce into each of 6 serving plates or glasses.

Cut the avocado into dice. Mix the avocado with the sauce and spoon over the lettuce.

Top with one or two cooked shrimp or a parsley sprig, if desired. Serves 6.

Beets

To keep beets red, always cook them with the skins on, just scrub them well with a vegetable brush. Leave the root end on and also about one inch of the tops. Place the beets in boiling salted water and cook until they are tender. This can take from thirty to sixty minutes or longer, depending on the size of the beets. Drain, then cool the beets under cold running water. When they are cool enough to handle, just slip the skins off.

You can then slice, dice or julienne your beets. They are good sauteed in a little butter, seasoned with salt and pepper. Or try this recipe for a cold beet salad.

Beet Salad

1-2 bunches beets   ½ onion, sliced
½ teaspoon caraway seeds   1 bay leaf
⅓ cup wine vinegar   ⅓ cup oil
salt, pepper   dash sugar

Wash the beets well, but do not peel them. Place them in a pot with the onion, bay leaf and caraway seeds. Cover with water and boil until the beets are tender. Place the beets under cold water to cool. Peel when they are cool enough to handle. Slice.

In a small saucepan, heat the vinegar, oil, salt, pepper and a few caraway seeds. Pour the hot vinagrette over the sliced beets. Cover and cool in the refrigerator. Mound on a plate at serving time. Serves 8.

Belgian Endive

Most people don't like Belgian endive because they're not used to its mildly bitter taste. It's expensive, but since almost all of it is edible, there is very little waste.

To select fresh Belgian endive, the bottom end should look very white and the tips should be a light green or yellow-green in color. If they look brown and shriveled, then the endive is old.

There is a trick to taking much of the bitterness out of Belgian endive when you use it raw. First cut the endive in half, lengthwise. You will see a triangular shaped root at the bottom of the stalk. This has to be removed, for it's the most bitter part of the plant. Cut it out and then soak the leaves in warm water for about one-half hour. Drain the endive well. *Illustration 10.* Then you can separte the leaves or slice or dice the endive. It goes very well with any number of dressings and makes a most interesting and unusual salad.

Illustration 10.

Belgian Endive and Orange Salad

4 to 6 endive   2 oranges
juice of 1 lemon   ½ cup heavy cream
salt, pepper   optional garnish: chopped parsley

Slice the endive in half lengthwise. Cut out the center core. Soak the endive in lukewarm water for about ½ hour. Drain.

Skin the oranges and cut them into sections.

Place the oranges and the endive into a bowl.

Whip the cream lightly and mix in the lemon juice, salt and pepper to taste. Pour over the salad, toss and serve. Garnish with chopped parsley if you like. Serves 8.

Endive Salad

4 Belgian endive   bib or boston lettuce leaves

Salad Dressing:
    ¼ cup red wine vinegar   salt, pepper
    ½ cup salad oil   dash nutmeg
    1 clove garlic, crushed   1 teaspoon mustard (dijon)
    2-3 tablespoons chopped parsley

Slice endive in half lengthwise and cut out the core. Soak the endive in lukewarm water for about ½ hour. Drain well and slice. Mix the ingredients for the dressing together, pour over the sliced endive and toss well.

Serve the endive salad mounded on individual lettuce leaves. Serves 6.

Brocolli

When you buy brocolli, make sure the stalks are very firm and crisp looking. The tops, or blossoms, should be very green and tightly formed together. If they look like yellow flowers that are about to open, the brocolli is too old.

A piece of wire usually holds two or three bunches together. Remove the wire and peel off some of the outside leaves. Cut off some of the bottom of the stem. If you cook brocolli until the bottoms of the stalks are done, then the tops will be overcooked. Don't throw the bottoms away, you can make a nice soup out of them.

How To Cook Brocolli

Separate the brocolli bunches into large stalks. Cut off the tough bottom portions of the stalks.

Place the brocolli, lying down, into a large pan.

Add one teaspoon of salt and one teaspoon of sugar. Cover with hot water and add a few spoons of butter.

Bring to a boil and simmer for about 8 minutes, or until the brocolli is tender.

Brocolli And Cauliflower Mix

1 head cauliflower   1 bunch brocolli
salt, pepper   1-2 tablespoons oil

Cut both the cauliflower and the brocolli into florets. Parboil both vegetables separately in lots of boiling salted water. Drain and refresh both vegetables.

At serving time, saute both vegetables together in the hot oil. Season to taste and serve. Serves 8 to 10.

Tomato Halves With Brocolli

½ tomato per person   brocolli
salt, pepper   mustard sauce, page 77

Cut the tomatoes in half. Scoop out the pulp using a melon ball cutter. Hold the tomato firmly in your hand while using the cutter so that you don't make a hole on the outside. Sprinkle the inside of the tomato with salt and pepper.

Cook brocolli according to the directions given under brocolli. Place the tops of a bunch of brocolli in the tomato half. Serve cold with mustard sauce.

Brussels Sprouts

Brussels sprouts should be bright green in color and firm to the touch. Try to select sprouts that are all the same size, they'll cook more evenly this way. Trim the base of the sprouts and cut a small cross into the bottom with a paring knife. This helps the stems to cook faster. If you cook Brussels sprouts without doing this, the tops will be overcooked before the bottoms are done.

Braised Brussels Sprouts

2 boxes Brussels sprouts   4 strips bacon
1 onion, chopped   salt, pepper
chopped parsley

Cook sprouts in boiling salted water until they are about three-quarters done. Refresh in cold water.

Saute the bacon and drain off most of the grease. Add the chopped onion to the pan and saute until golden. Add the sprouts and saute until they are finished cooking.

Season with salt and pepper and garnish with the chopped parsley. Serves 4 to 6.

Sautéed Brussels Sprouts

1 box Brussels sprouts   2-3 Tablespoons butter
salt, pepper

Clean the Brussels sprouts. Cook them in boiling salted water until barely tender. Refresh under cold water and drain.

When ready to serve, melt the butter. Saute the sprouts in the butter for a few minutes, seasoning with salt and pepper. Serve hot. Serves 4 to 6.

Cabbage

To core a head of cabbage, place it stem up, on a chopping board. Use a medium sized knife and make a round, rotating cut around the core at an angle about 4 to 5 inches deep. It's much easier if you hold your knife still and rotate the cabbage while cutting. The core should come out in one cone shaped piece. Illustration 11.

Illustration 11.

Austrian Cabbage Salad

2 cups raw cabbage, shredded
4 slices bacon, diced
½ cup onion, diced
2-3 tablespoons oil

dash caraway seeds
salt, pepper
2-3 tablespoons vinegar

Saute the onion with the bacon. Mix in the caraway seeds, salt, pepper, vinegar and oil.

Pour the dressing over the shredded cabbage and toss well.

Serve on a lettuce leaf garnished with a tomato wedge.

Sautéed Cabbage

1 small head cabbage
1 to 2 cups chicken or beef broth
salt, pepper
3 tablespoons butter or oil

1 large onion, diced
2 teaspoons sugar
1 potato, grated
3 slices bacon, optional

Slice the cabbage thinly. Dice the onion.

Saute the onion in the butter or oil until soft. If you are using the bacon, eliminate the oil and saute the onion and the diced bacon together.

Add the sugar, the cabbage, the salt and pepper and stir. Add the broth and cook, stirring often, until the cabbage is almost tender. Grate the potato and add it to the cabbage mixture. Cook until thick and dry, stirring often. This should take about 20 minutes. Serve hot. Serves 8.

Red Cabbage Salad

1 small head of red cabbage, sliced or shredded
1 small onion, sliced thinly
1 apple peeled, cored and shredded
¼ cup of red wine vinegar
½ cup of red wine
¼ cup of oil
sugar, cinnamon and salt to taste

Mix all ingredients together in a large bowl and let sit for at least one to two hours, to develop a nice flavor. This salad goes very well with all pork and fowl dishes.

Red Cabbage

1 head red cabbage
1 onion, chopped
1 cup red wine
1 cup water
½ cup sugar
salt, pepper

2 apples
½ cup red wine vinegar
1 potato
2 tablespoons oil or duck fat
1 teaspoon cinnamon

Peel and core the apple. Slice thinly. Shred the cabbage.

Saute the apple and the onion in the oil or duck fat for a few minutes. Add the cabbage, the vinegar, wine, sugar, cinnamon, salt, pepper and half the water.

Cook, covered, for 1 to 1½ hours, stirring occasionally. Add more water if necessary, so that the cabbage does not stick and burn.

Twenty minutes before the cabbage is done, peel and grate the potato. Stir it into the cabbage mixture. Stir and cook until thick and dry. Adjust the seasonings and serve hot with fowl. Serves 8 or more.

Sauerkraut

Sauerkraut is cabbage which has been preserved in a brine or salt solution. If you eat it or cook it with the liquid in which it is packed, it will have a very strong taste.

I like to blanch my sauerkraut before I use it. To do this, bring a large pot of unsalted water to a boil. Add the sauerkraut to the boiling water and bring it to a boil again. Then drain the sauerkraut well and proceed with your recipe. It will have a much nicer flavor.

Sauerkraut

2 pound package sauerkraut, drained
2-3 apples
2 cups white wine
1 bay leaf

2 onions, chopped
2 tablespoons butter or oil
1 raw potato, peeled and grated
salt, pepper, cloves

Blanch the kraut in boiling water for about 5 minutes and drain. Peel, core and chop the apples. Saute the onion and apples in butter until they are tender. Combine with the sauerkraut. Add the bay leaf, salt and pepper. Cover with wine and simmer for an hour or two, stirring occasionally. Add the grated raw potato and continue cooking until desired degree of dryness is reached.

Serve hot with sliced meats. Serves 8 or more.

Carrots

If you are using carrots for a recipe, such as a soup or sauce that will be strained, it is not necessary to peel them. Just wash them well and cut off the green tops and a little bit of the root end.

When used as a vegetable or in a salad, do peel them. I always like to cook my carrots with a pinch of both sugar and salt.

Carrot Salad

4 carrots	juice of 1 lemon
1-2 tablespoons honey	1 apple
1 tablespoon chopped parsley	¼ cup toasted almond slices

Peel the apple, cut into quarters and core. Peel the carrots. Shred the carrots and the apple using the julienne blade of a food processor. Mix with the lemon juice and the honey. Serve chilled, on a lettuce leaf garnished with the chopped parsley and the almonds. Serves 6 to 8.

Glazed Carrots

1 pound carrots	2-3 tablespoons butter
1 cup water	1-2 tablespoons sugar
pinch salt	

Peel and slice the carrots. Melt the butter. Add the sugar and salt and cook for a few minutes. Add the carrots and stir well.

Cover with the water and cook slowly until the liquid is evaporated and the carrots are tender and glazed. Serves 6.

Vichy Carrots

1 pound carrots	1 onion, chopped fine
1 tablespoon sugar	salt
2-3 tablespoons butter	water

Peel the carrots and slice them into thin rounds. Saute the onion with the butter and the sugar. Add the sliced carrots, the salt and a little water. Cover with a lid and cook for about 8 to 12 minutes, until the carrots are tender and the water has evaporated. Serve hot. Serves 6.

Cauliflower

I like to cook cauliflower whole, rather than to separate it into rosettes. It looks much nicer this way. To clean the cauliflower, just trim off all of the outer green leaves. If you have the time, soak the whole head, stem side up, in a bowl of cold salted water for about thirty minutes. This will remove any dirt or bugs that are caught between the rosettes.

Just be sure not to overcook your cauliflower as it tastes best when it is still crisp, not soft and mushy. If you want to keep the cauliflower very white, you can add the juice of half a lemon to the cooking water.

Cauliflower Polonaise

1 head cauliflower, cleaned
2-3 ounces of fine dry bread crumbs
1 hard boiled egg, chopped

3 ounces butter
¼ cup chopped parsley
salt, pepper

Cook the whole cauliflower in boiling salted water until it is done, but still crisp. Remove and keep warm.

Saute the breadcrumbs in the butter until they are golden. Season and add the chopped egg and the parsley. Cook just to heat and pour over the cauliflower. Serve immediately. Serves six to eight.

Cauliflower With A Cream Sauce

1 head cauliflower, cleaned
salt, pepper
water to cover

3 tablespoons butter
3 tablespoons flour

Cook the whole cauliflower in boiling salted water, to cover. Remove from the water when done but still firm enough so that it remains together. Keep warm. Reserve two cups of the cooking water.

Make a roux with the flour and the butter. Remove the roux from the heat and let it cool for a few minutes. Heat the two cups of the cauliflower liquid you saved to the boiling point. Add this boiling liquid to the cooled roux, stirring. Season with salt and pepper and let the sauce simmer for about fifteen minutes to remove the floury taste.

To serve, pour the sauce over the head of cauliflower. Serves 6 to 8.

Celeraic

Celery root or celeraic is the root of a plant used widely in Europe for salads. It is found more readily in the fall of the year. It can be stored for long periods of time, as can most root vegetables.

The greens on top of the celeraic are very strong and cannot be used in the same way as regular celery leaves. Most of the time they are already cut off the plant before you but it.

To use celeraic, cut the greens off, if they are still there. Wash or brush the dirt off the root. Then peel off the skin with a paring knife. The white celery root will turn color when it is exposed to the air. One way to avoid this is to squeeze some lemon juice over the peeled root or rub it well with a lemon half.

Waldorf salad in Europe is not made with apples and nuts as it is here, it is made with celeraic. Here is a recipe for true European Waldorf salad.

Waldorf Salad

2 apples
½ cup pineapple juice
1 cup mayonnaise
1 teaspoon MSG

2 celery roots (celeraic)
juice ½ lemon
1 cup slivered almonds, roasted

Thinly slice the apple and the celery root.

Mix all ingredients and let stand for a few hours in order to tenderize the celery root. Serve on a bed of lettuce leaves. Serves 8.

Salad Belle Helene

4 cups celeraic, julienned
6 to 8 black olives, sliced
2 hard boiled egg yolks
¾ cup oil
1 tablespoon chopped parsley

1 large canned beet, sliced into crescents
walnut halves
1 raw egg yolk
1 tablespoon vinegar
salt, pepper

Place the egg yolks (both kinds) into a blender or food processor. Add the salt, pepper and vinegar, blend.

Add the oil slowly until a thick dressing is formed. Mix in the parsley.

Pour the dressing over the celeraic.

Shape into a mound in a bowl. Decorate the sides of the salad with the beet crescents. Place the olive slices in the center of the beets. Place the walnuts on top of the salad. Serves 8 to 10

Corn

When you buy corn, one way to tell if it is fresh is to look at the husks. If they are light green in color and not dried out looking the corn has probably been picked recently. Pull down a little of the husk and look at the kernels of corn. They should be nice and shiney and light in color. If you prick one with your thumbnail, the juice should pop right out. If it doesn't the corn is old and dry.

Try to use fresh corn as soon as possible after you buy it, as it is sweetest and best right after it is picked. If you have to store it for a day or two, put the unhusked ears, covered, into the coldest part of your refrigerator.

Cook corn in boiling water with a pinch of both sugar and salt added. Just be careful not to overcook it, as fresh corn takes only a few minutes to cook.

Here are some recipes for any corn you might have left over.

Fresh Corn Salad

½ cup onion, finely chopped
¼ cup diced pimento
¼ cup oil
salt, pepper

2 cups corn, cooked or canned
¼ cup diced green pepper
¼ cup vinegar

Mix all the ingredients together. Serve chilled, on a lettuce leaf. Serves 8.

Corn Fritters

3 eggs, separated
1½ cups corn, fresh or canned
½ cup flour

½ teaspoon salt
pepper
oil

You can use up leftover cooked corn on the cob for this recipe. Remove the pulp from the cobs by slitting each ear down the center line of the kernels. Scrape out the pulp and juice. Alternately, canned cream style corn can be used.

Beat the egg yolks until light. Add the corn. Add the seasonings and the flour. Beat the egg whites until light with a pinch of salt. Fold into the corn mixture.

Heat a little oil in a frying pan. Drop the batter, by tablespoons, into the hot oil. Cook until brown, turning once. Drain the fritters well and serve hot. Serves 6 to 8.

Cucumbers

Cucumbers usually come with a wax layer on their outside skin. It is almost impossible to wash this layer off, so I would suggest that you peel your cucumbers.

Cut off both ends of the cucumber before you peel the skin. Sometimes one of the ends is bitter and if you peel off the skin before you cut off the ends, the whole whole cucumber will taste bitter.

You can slice the cucumber in half lengthwise and remove some of the seeds with a teaspoon, if the seeds bother you.

Cucumber Dill Salad

2 cucumbers   salt, pepper
½ cup sour cream   1 tablespoon lemon juice
chopped fresh dill   few spoons finely chopped onion

Peel the cucumbers. Slice thinly and place in a bowl with salt. Let sit at least 30 minutes. Drain off the accumulated liquid. Add the sour cream, lemon juice, pepper, and additional salt, if needed. Add minced dill to taste, and onion.

Chill until ready to serve. Serves 6.

Stuffed Cucumbers

2 cucumbers   8 ounces cream cheese
3 tablespoons onion, finely chopped ½ teaspoon paprika
salt, pepper   chopped parsley

Cut the cucumbers into one and one-half inch segments. Peel half of the outside skin in stripes. Hollow out the center of the sections about two-thirds of the way through, leaving the bottom intact.

Whip the cream cheese until soft. Add the onions, paprika, salt and pepper and mix well. Form into small balls and roll in chopped parsley. Place one ball in each cucumber hollow. Serve very cold. Serves 6.

Tomato and Cucumber Salad

2 cucumbers
½ cup sour cream
chopped parsley
2 tomatoes

salt, pepper
1 tablespoon lemon juice
few spoons finely chopped onion, (optional)

Peel or score skins of cucumber as desired for decorative effect. Slice thinly and place in a bowl with salt. Let sit for at least 30 minutes. Drain off accumulated liquid. Add tomato slices or wedges. Add the sour cream, lemon juice, pepper and additional salt if needed. Add fresh chopped parsley and onion if desired. Chill until ready to serve. Serves 6.

Green Beans

Sauteed Green Beans

1 pound string beans
1 clove garlic, chopped
salt, pepper

1 small onion, chopped
3-4 tablespoons butter

Trim the string beans and cook them in a large pot of boiling salted water until they are al dente. Refresh them under cold water. Saute the onion in the butter until it is golden. Add the garlic. Add the beans and saute them until they are hot and well coated with the butter and the onion mixture. Season to taste and serve. Serves 4 to 6.

Bouquet Of Green Beans

1 pound string beans
bacon strips, raw

salt, pepper
butter

Cut the beans evenly, so that they are the same length. Cook them in a large pot of boiling salted water until they are cooked but still firm. Refresh under cold water.

Form into small bunches. Roll a strip of bacon around the middle of each bundle. Heat in a little butter when ready to serve. Serves 4 to 6.

Green Bean Salad

1-2 cups string beans
1 teaspoon chopped parsley
salt, pepper

⅓ cup wine vinegar
⅓ cup oil

Cook the beans in boiling salted water until al dente. Reserve ⅓ cup of the cooking water. Drain and refresh the beans. Mix the cooked beans with the rest of the ingredients, including the reserved cooking liquid. Let marinate for about 45 minutes. Serve on lettuce leaves. Serves 4.

Green Pepper

Green pepper is a very interesting vegetable because of its nutritional value. It is very high in vitamin content, especially vitamins A and C. When you slice raw green pepper, make sure you slice it skin side down. It's much easier to handle this way.

Removing the skin from the pepper will make it a little easier to digest. You can broil the peppers to loosen the skins or dip them into hot fat for a few seconds. You can also parboil them until the skins loosen. Rinse in cold water and then peel.

Green pepper is green because it is unripe. When peppers ripen, they turn red and develop an even sweeter taste. Paprika powder is made out of ground dried red peppers.

Green Pepper And Tomato Salad

1 or 2 tomatoes
1 to 2 tablespoons mayonnaise
honey, to taste

1 green pepper
lemon juice

Peel, seed and dice the tomato. Dice the green pepper. Mix together with the mayonnaise. Add lemon juice and honey to taste. Serve chilled on a lettuce leaf. Serves 3 or 4.

Grilled Pepper Salad

4 large green peppers
2 tablespoons wine vinegar
½ teaspoon oregano
2 tablespoons olive oil
garnish: anchovies

1 clove garlic, minced
salt, pepper
½ teaspoon basil
few spoons red wine
tomato wedges

Grill the green peppers until the skin chars. Remove and let sit covered a few minutes to steam. Peel off skin, cut and remove seeds. Save any juice and add it to the salad dressing. Pour the rest of the ingredients over the peppers and mix well. Let sit at room temperature for at least an hour to develop flavor. Garnish with anchovy fillets.

Do not refrigerate this salad. Serves 4 to 6.

Leeks

Leeks are a member of the onion family often overlooked in cooking in this country. In Europe leeks are often called "the poor man's asparagus" since they are, or at least were, inexpensive. They are very nice used in soups or even as a cooked vegetable.

Leeks tend to be very sandy and dirty. To clean them, cut off the very tops of the green leaves in a triangular shape. Then cut off some of the root end, but be careful to leave enough so that the leaves stay together, it's easier to wash that way. Then split the leek lengthwise, the whole way down. Hold the leek under running water and with your fingers, separate the leaves, so that the water washes out all of the sand and soil. Illustration 12.

Illustration 12.

Leeks And Bacon

2 leeks   6 slices bacon
salt, pepper   water

Wash leeks well and cut into two inch slices. Place half the bacon in the bottom of an oven proof pan. Place the leeks, crosswise, on top of the bacon. Sprinkle with salt and pepper.

Cover the leeks with the rest of the bacon slices. Put a little water in the pan. Cover and place in a hot oven for about 30 minutes, or until the leeks are tender. Serves 4.

Leeks - Beurre Noisette

leeks, 1 per person   sliced ham or butter for pan
water or broth   salt
½ cup butter

Wash the leeks well and cut into two inch lengths. Line a pan with the sliced ham or butter well. Place the leeks, crosswise into the pan. Add the broth or water and bring to a boil. Simmer until tender.

In a separate pan, heat the ½ cup butter. Continue to cook until it turns a light brown color and has a nutty smell. Pour over the leeks and serve immediately.

Mushrooms

Mushrooms should be nice and white in color and have a fresh smell. The caps should be closed around the stems tightly. If the caps are open and the gills are dark brown or black in color, the mushrooms are old.

You shouldn't wash mushrooms or soak them in water. Just rinse them off quickly before you are ready to use them. Mushrooms should be kept refrigerated. Once they are sliced they tend to turn dark. Use them as soon as possible after they are sliced.

Artichoke And Mushroom Salad

2 packages frozen artichoke hearts, thawed	bay leaf
5 cups mushrooms	1 cup water
1 cup white wine	½ cup olive oil
juice of 2 lemons	salt, pepper
	pinch thyme or oregano

Place the water, wine, oil, lemon juice and seasonings into a saucepan. Bring to a boil and reduce a little.

If the mushrooms are very large, quarter them. If small, leave whole. Add the artichoke hearts to the marinade and cook for 5 minutes. Add the mushrooms and continue to cook for another 3 minutes.

Remove from the heat and cool the vegetables in the marinade. Serve at room temperature. Serves 8 to 10.

Spinach

If you want to make a spinach salad, you have to use fresh spinach. But for cooking, it's perfectly alright to use frozen spinach. Make sure you use frozen leaf spinach, not the chopped kind, for chopped is mostly stems and water. Blanch the spinach in boiling salted water and then proceed with any cooked spinach recipe.

Here is my favorite way to cook spinach. The anchovies dissolve during cooking and you can't tell that they are there. They just give the spinach a very pleasant taste. I also like to use a little nutmeg whenever I cook spinach.

Spinach With Onion And Anchovies

2 pounds spinach	1 small onion, chopped
2-3 tablespoons butter	2-3 anchovy fillets
salt, pepper	pinch nutmeg

Blanch the spinach in boiling salted water. Refresh under cold water. Drain well and chop coarsely.

Saute the onion in the butter until soft. Add the anchovies and continue to saute. Add the spinach and cook, stirring often, for a few minutes. Season to taste and serve.

Spinach Timbales

two 10 ounce packages frozen
  spinach, or 2 packages fresh
  spinach
salt, pepper
2 eggs, plus 1 yolk
Mornay sauce, page 73

nutmeg, to taste
½ cup heavy cream
2-3 tablespoons butter

If using frozen spinach, thaw, blanch and drain well. Saute the spinach in the butter for a few minutes. Season with salt, pepper and nutmeg. Cool and coarsely chop.

Butter well 6 timbale molds. Press the spinach into the bottom of the molds.

Mix the egg yolks, the eggs and the cream together. Pour a little in each mold, over the spinach.

Bake the timbales in a 375° oven in a water bath for about 30 minutes, or until set and puffed. Let sit for a few minutes and turn out. Serve hot with mornay sauce. Serves 6.

Illustration   13.

Tomatoes

Many recipes ask for tomato concassee. This means tomato which has been peeled, seeded and diced.

There is an easy way to peel a tomato. Bring a small pot of water to a boil. Cut the core out of the tomato with a paring knife. Then turn the tomato upside down and cut a cross on the opposite side. Put the tomato into the boiling water and leave it there for a minute or two. The skin where you cut the cross will start to come loose. Remove the tomato from the boiling water and rinse under cold water. Then it is very simple just to peel off all the skin starting from the cross.

*Cut the tomato into quarters and squeeze out the seeds with your fingers or a spoon. I prefer to use my fingers, it's much easier that way. Then just chop up the tomato pulp and you have tomato concassee. **Illustration 13.***

Tomato, Apple And Melon Salad

1 cup diced cantelope or honeydew melon
1 large apple
juice of 1 lemon

1 tomato
1 cup shredded lettuce

Seed the tomato and cut into julienne strips. Peel and core the apple and cut into julienne strips also. Dice the melon and shred the lettuce. Mix the vegetables and fruits with the lemon juice. Serve chilled. Serves 4.

Tomatoes Provencal

4 tomatoes
2-3 tablespoons chopped parsley
salt, pepper

1 cup breadcrumbs
1 clove garlic, crushed
butter or oil

Cut the tomatoes in half and season with salt and pepper. Mix together the breadcrumbs, garlic and parsley. Spread a little of this mixture on each tomato half. Place in a buttered pan. Drizzle the tops of the tomatoes with a little melted butter or oil. Bake in a 375 degree oven for 15 to 20 minutes. Serves 8.

Zucchini

Julienne Of Zucchini With Carrots

2 zucchini   3 carrots
1 small onion, finely chopped   salt, pepper
4 tablespoons butter

Julienne the carrots and the zucchini in a food processor. Saute the onion in the butter for a few minutes.

Add the carrots and saute for a minute or two. Add the zucchini and continue to saute until tender. Season to taste. This wll take only a few minutes, do not overcook the vegetables, they should remain crisp. Serve immediately. Serves 7 or 8.

Sautéed Zucchini

3-4 zucchini   1 small onion, chopped
1 clove garlic, chopped   3-4 tablespoons butter or oil
salt, pepper   2 tablespoons chopped parsley

Scrub but do not peel the zucchini. Trim off the ends. Slice thinly. Saute the onion in the butter until golden. Add the garlic. Add the zucchini and saute, tossing for a few minutes until they are barely tender. Season with salt and pepper.

Add the chopped parsley and serve immediately. Serves 6.

Shredded Zucchini

2 cups shredded zucchini   2-3 tablespoons butter
½ onion, chopped   salt, pepper
1 tablespoon chopped parsley

Shred the zucchini using the julienne blade of a food processor. Saute the onion in the butter for a few minutes. Add the zucchini, salt and pepper. Cook and stir for a minute or two only. Sprinkle with chopped parsley and serve immediately. Serves 4 to 6.

Vegetable Combinations

Danish Salad

Any combination of vegetable salads that you like can be used. Just vary the colors and flavors so that they look pretty as well as taste good. Here are four salads that go very well together.

Cucumber Salad:

Peel and thinly slice one cucumber. Layer it with salt and let it sit for about 30 minutes. Drain well. Mix with pepper, oil, vinegar, and a spoon or two of chopped dill. Taste and add more salt if needed.

Radish Salad:

Clean one bunch of radishes and slice them thinly. Season with salt, pepper, oil and vinegar to taste.

Tomato Salad:

Thinly slice one large or two small tomatoes. Sprinkle with salt, pepper, oil, vinegar and a tablespoon of finely chopped onion.

Endive Salad:

Slice the endive in half lengthwise. Remove the core. Soak in lukewarm water for about 30 minutes. Drain well. Separate the leaves. Use a few leaves for each plate. Serve with a dollup of cocktail sauce, page 77 on top of the leaves.

Assembly:

For four salads, place cleaned bib or boston lettuce leaves on individual salad plates. Arrange each of the salads, divided among the plates. Garnish each plate with hard boiled egg slices and a sprig of parsley.

Stir-Fried Vegetables

2 tablespoons of butter
½ cup of diced onion
1 cup of broccoli rosettes
1 cup of cauliflower rosettes

1 yellow squash, sliced
4-5 mushrooms, cut in half
salt
few tablespoons of water

Melt the butter in a frying pan. Add the onion and saute for a few minutes. Add the rest of the vegetables and season. Add the water and cover the pan with a lid. Cook for a few minutes or until the vegetables are crisp.
Serve hot and enjoy!

Ratatouille

1 onion, sliced
2 eggplants, peeled and sliced
2 cloves garlic
salt, pepper

6 tomatoes
4 zucchini, sliced
chopped parsley
oil

Peel, seed and slice the tomatoes.
Heat the oil and saute the onions for a few minutes. Add the eggplant, zucchini and the tomatoes. Add the garlic, salt and pepper.
Simmer for about 30 minutes. Top with the chopped parsley. Can be served either hot or at room temperature. Serves 8 to 10.

Salad Nicoise

1 head bib or boston lettuce
12 radishes
1 cucumber, peeled
1 pound green beans
1 small can anchovies
black olives, optional
red wine vinegar

1 onion
2 or 3 tomatoes
1 green pepper
1 small can tuna fish (7 ounce)
2 hard boiled eggs, sliced
salt, pepper
salad or olive oil

Cook the string beans in lots of boiling salted water until al dente. Refresh under cold water. Drain and chill.
Thinly slice the onion, radishes, cucumber, tomatoes and green pepper. Drain and flake the tuna fish.
Clean the lettuce and break it into bite sized pieces. Place the lettuce in the bottom of a large salad bowl. Place all of the vegetables, tuna fish, anchovies,

eggs and olives, in layers, on top of the lettuce.

At serving time, sprinkle with salt and pepper. Add vinegar and oil to taste, toss together and serve. Serves 6 to 8.

Vegetable Relish

1 small onion	2 tomatoes
1 large or 2 small cucumbers	salt, pepper
2 tablespoons wine vinegar	2 tablespoons salad oil

Peel and chop the cucumber. Chop the tomatoes and dice the onion. Combine the vegetables and add salt and pepper to taste. Mix with the oil and vinegar. Serve on a lettuce leaf. Serves 6 to 8.

Chapter 3
Barley, Potatoes, Pasta, Rice and More

Tips:

Barley

Potatoes

Rice

Recipes:

Barley Casserole	East Indian Fried Rice
Mashed Potatoes	Rice Salad
Au Gratin Potatoes	Noodles with Shallot Butter
Pommes Berny	Pasta Primavera
Pommes William	Pasta with Zucchini
Pommes Boulangere	Pasta Verde with Prosciutto
Pommes Noisette	Spatzle
Potato Crisps	Apple Stuffing Loaf
Potato Pancakes	Stuffing Loaf
German Potato Salad	Bread Dumplings
Rice Pilaf	Farina Dumplings
Tomato Rice Pilaf	Glazed Chestnuts
Sultan's Rice	

Barley

Barley is a very starchy grain. If you add it directly to a soup or whatever recipe you are making, your dish will be very sticky and gummy.

Barley should always be parboiled. You do this by bringing lots of water with a little salt added to a boil. Add the raw barley, stir, and continue to cook for about 30 minutes. Then strain the barley through a sieve and wash it well under cold water so that most of the starch comes off. Drain and then proceed to use the barley in any recipe. It will taste much nicer this way.

Barley Casserole

1 ½ cups pearl barley	water
1 ½ cups stock	1 onion, chopped
3 tablespoons chopped parsley	1 cup mushrooms, sliced
4 tablespoons butter	salt, pepper

Bring a large pot of salted water to a boil. Add the barley and cook for 30 minutes. Drain and rinse the barley to remove the excess starch.

Cook the chopped onion in the butter until tender. Season with salt and pepper. Add the mushrooms and continue to cook for a few minutes. Add the barley and the stock. Bring to a boil, cover and place in a moderate (375 degree) oven for about 30 minutes or until the barley is tender. Stir in the chopped parsley and serve hot. Serves 8.

Potatoes

I like to use Idaho potatoes for cooking. As a matter of fact, it's the only kind we use in my restaurant. If you bake them, they become very dry and fluffy and will absorb lots of butter and sour cream. All purpose potatoes are cheaper and work very well for stews and potato salad. But to my taste, Idahos are the best.

Most people don't know how to make good mashed potatoes. They think they always come in powder form. Some people even think they grow that way. But when you taste them made fresh, my way, you'll never settle for the dry kind again.

Mashed Potatoes

4 potatoes   2 ounces butter
salt, nutmeg   1 to 1½ cups hot milk

Peel the potatoes and cut them into quarters. Cook them in boiling salted water until they are tender. Drain off the water. Put the pot containing the potatoes back onto the stove, without a lid, and continue to cook the potatoes for a minute or two until they are very dry.

Mash the potatoes by using a potato ricer or a food mill. Add butter, salt and a dash of nutmeg. Mix well. Gradually add the hot milk, stirring it into the potatoes until the desired consistency is reached. Serve immediately, and enjoy! Serves 4.

Pommes Au Gratin

                                        1 cup cream
4 potatoes   2 tablespoons butter
1 cup stock   ½ cup grated cheese, swiss or
salt, pepper   parmesan or mixture

Peel and slice the potatoes. Butter the bottom of a casserole. Place the potatoes into the dish, salt and pepper the layers. Pour the cream and the stock over the potatoes.

Sprinkle the cheese over the top of the casserole and bake in a moderate oven until the potatoes are tender and the cheese has formed a crust on the top, about one hour. Very simple, very easy and very good. Serves 8.

Pommes Berny

6 potatoes   2-3 tablespoons cornstarch, if needed
4 egg yolks   salt, pepper, nutmeg
1 cup flour   2 cups chopped toasted almonds
2 eggs, beaten with a little water

Boil the potatoes until they are still firm, but done. Rice them while still hot. Add egg yolks and seasoning. If they are not dry enough, add cornstarch and mix until they form a thick paste. Let cool for a few minutes.

Roll out into a long roll and cut into slices. Roll slices in your hand to form balls. Let balls cool on a pan dusted with cornstarch. Dip balls lightly in flour, then egg wash, then almonds.

Deep fry in hot oil a few minutes, until browned. Serves 12.

Pommes William

Use the same mixture as for Pommes Berny, but eliminate the almonds. Shape into pear shapes instead of balls. Coat the potatoes with breadcrumbs instead of nuts. Put a piece of raw spaghetti on top of the pear shape to form a stem. Then deep fry. Put a clove on the bottom of the pear and serve hot.

Pommes Boulangere

4 potatoes	1 onion, chopped
4 slices bacon, diced	1 cup stock
2 tablespoons butter	1 cup cream
salt, pepper	

Saute the onion and the bacon in a small frying pan until the onion is golden and the bacon is cooked.

Butter the bottom of a casserole. Peel and slice the potatoes and place them into the dish, with salt and pepper between the layers. Pour the cream and the stock over the potatoes.

Put the sauteed onion and bacon in a layer on top of the potatoes. Bake in a moderate oven until the potatoes are tender, about 1 hour. Serves 8.

Pommes Noisette

2-3 large potatoes	4-6 tablespoons butter
salt, pepper	½ teaspoon paprika

Peel the potatoes. With a melon ball scooper, cut out small rounds of potato. Cook the potato balls in boiling salted water for 10 minutes. Refresh. At serving time, melt the butter in a saute pan. Toss the potato balls in the butter to coat well. Season with salt and pepper.

Cook, tossing, until the potatoes are well browned on the outside and tender on the inside. Add the paprika to the pan and toss again. Serve hot. Serves 6.

Potato Crisps

Use boiled or baked leftover potatoes. Peel and slice potatoes ½ inch or so thick. Dip in melted butter, then breadcrumbs. Bake in a 375 degree oven until browned. (35 minutes).

Potato Pancakes

1 large potato
1 egg
salt, pepper

2 tablespoons flour
1 slice of onion
butter or oil

Peel and coarsely chop the potato.

Place the potato, flour, egg, slice of onion and some salt and pepper into a blender or a food processor. Puree until well blended.

Pour immediately into a hot frying pan which has been heated with a few spoons of butter or oil.

Cook until well browned on one side, then turn and cook the other side. Add more butter or oil to the pan if needed. Cut pancake into wedges and serve right away. Serves 4.

German Potato Salad

6 potatoes
1 ½ to 2 cups beef stock or
    chicken broth
⅓ cup wine vinegar

1 teaspoon caraway seeds
1 small onion, finely chopped
salt, pepper

Cook the potatoes with the skins on in boiling salted water with the caraway seeds. Keep firm, do not overcook.

While they are still warm, peel the potatoes and slice thinly. Place them in a bowl and add the minced onion, salt, pepper, vinegar and the warmed stock.

The potato salad should have a creamy consistancy. The potatoes will absorb the stock while they are still warm. Serve at room temperature. Serves 10 to 12.

Rice

I never wreck the rice. I have been cooking it this way for twenty-two years and my mother did it the same way for twenty years before that and she never wrecked it, either.

Here's how to cook it the right way. Chop up a little onion and saute it in a few spoons of butter. Then add 1 cup of raw long grain rice and stir it around so that you coat all of the grains individually with the butter. Then add two cups of stock, chicken stock, veal stock, whatever kind you like. Bring the stock to a boil. Stir the rice and cover it with a lid.

Now here comes the important part. Put in into a preheated 375° oven for 18 to 20 minutes. The heat of the oven comes from all four sides and the rice cooks much more evenly. This way it won't stick to the bottom of your pan or burn, unless, of course, you forget to take it out of the oven. This is an absolutely foolproof method and you will never wreck your rice.

Rice Pilaf

1 cup rice	2 cups chicken stock
1 small onion, chopped fine	2-3 tablespoons butter

Melt the butter and saute the chopped onion until it turns translucent. Add the rice, cook and stir for a few minutes to coat all the grains with the butter.

Add the stock and bring to a boil. Cover and bake in a 375° oven for about 18 minutes. Serves 4 to 6.

Tomato Rice Pilaf

1 cup rice	1 ½ to 2 cups chicken stock
2-3 tablespoons butter	1 cup tomato concassee
salt, pepper	1 tablespoon tomato paste or
1 small onion, chopped finely	puree, optional

Melt butter, saute the onion until tender. Add the rice and stir to coat the grains. Add the chicken stock and bring to a boil. Cover and bake the rice in a 375° oven for about 18 minutes.

Stir in the peeled, seeded, and chopped tomatoes. Correct seasoning. Serve with fish. Serves 4 to 6.

Sultans Rice

1 cup rice
1 ½ to 2 cups chicken stock
salt, pepper
½ cup raisins

1 small onion, chopped fine
2-3 tablespoons butter
½ cup toasted almond slices

Melt the butter. Saute the chopped onion in the butter until it turns trans-lucent. Add the rice, cook and stir for a few minutes to coat the rice with the butter. Add the stock and bring to a boil. Cover and bake in a 375° oven for about 18 to 20 minutes or until done.

Stir in the almonds and the raisins. Serve at once. Serves 6 to 8.

Here are some recipes for leftover cooked rice. They are so good, you might want to cook some extra rice to have leftovers, next time.

East Indian Fried Rice

2 cups cooked rice
½ small onion, chopped
¼ cup diced green pepper
2 teaspoons curry powder
1 small can diced pineapple, with juice
¼ cup raisins

2-3 tablespoons butter
½ cup diced bananas
¼ cup diced pimento
salt, pepper
¼ cup toasted almonds

Garnish: pineapple ring, canned fig, chopped parsley

Saute the onion and the green pepper in the butter. Add the curry powder and immediately add the liquid from the pineapple. Stir in the rest of the ingredients. Saute until hot. Correct the seasonings and serve hot decorated with the garnish.

Rice Salad

1 cup cooked rice
¼ cup diced pineapple
2 tablespoons raisins
salt, pepper

½ cup diced apple
2 teaspoons curry powder
2 canned figs

Garnish: ½ cup toasted almond slices, parsley sprig

Dice and mix ingredients together. Season to taste. Serve on a lettuce leaf decorated with the garnish.

Noodles With Shallot Butter

1 package egg noodles	2-3 tablespoons chopped parsley
3 tablespoons chopped shallots	4 tablespoons butter
salt, pepper	

Cook the noodles in boiling salted water until al dente. Drain well. Melt the butter and saute the shallots until they are golden. Add the noodles, toss well to heat, mix in the parsley, season and serve. Serves 8.

Pasta Primavera

1 pound package linguini	1 cup sliced zucchini
1 cup brocolli florets	1 cup string beans
1 cup peas	1 cup cauliflower florets
1 cup mushrooms, sliced	4 large tomatoes, seeded and cut
10 tablespoons butter	into cubes
2 cloves garlic, crushed	½ cup pine nuts
2 teaspoons dried basil or 2	salt, pepper
tablespoons fresh, chopped	2 tablespoons chopped parsley
½ cup grated parmesan cheese, or	1½ cups cream
more to taste	

Parboil the string beans in boiling salted water until they are crisp. Drain, refresh and reserve.

Heat 2 tablespoons of the butter in a large frying pan and saute the pine nuts until they are light golden. Remove from the pan and set aside.

Add the mushrooms, brocolli, peas, zucchini, string beans and the cauliflower to the pan and saute for a few minutes, stirring. Add a few spoons of water to the pan, cover with a lid, and steam for about five minutes. The vegetables should remain very crisp.

Add the tomatoes, garlic, parsley and basil to the pan. Add more butter, if needed. Saute for a minute or two. Add the pine nuts to the pan and correct the seasonings. Meanwhile, cook the pasta in boiling salted water until it is al dente. Heat the remaining butter in a very large pan. Add the pasta, tossing, to coat with the butter. Add the cream and the cheese, stirring. Add the vegetable mixture and toss well to incorporate all the ingredients. Serve immediately. Serves 8 to 10.

This recipe calls for whatever fresh vegetables are in season. Don't be afraid to substitute anything else you may prefer or leave out any vegetables you don't like.

Pasta With Zucchini

6 zucchini
1 clove garlic, crushed
½ cup grated parmesan cheese
½ to 1 cup cream

½ cup onion, chopped fine
salt and pepper
1 teaspoon dried basil or 1 tablespoon
    fresh
6 tablespoons butter
1 pound linguini or penne

Dice unpeeled zucchini and salt well. Let sit for about one-half hour. Rinse and drain well.

In half the butter saute the onion until soft. Add the garlic and zucchini, salt, pepper and basil. Saute, stirring often, until the zucchini is cooked.

Cook the pasta until it is al dente in lots of boiling salted water. Drain.

Melt the rest of the butter with the cream in a large skillet. Add the pasta and mix well. Add the zucchini mixture and the cheese, toss, correct the seasonings and serve immediately. Serve with lots of freshly milled black pepper and extra cheese, if desired. Serves 6.

Pasta Verde With Prosciutto

1 package spinach noodles
1 cup prosciutto, diced
salt, pepper
2-3 tablespoons butter
½ cup cream

3 eggs, beaten lightly
3 tablespoons parsley
½ cup grated parmesan cheese

Saute the diced ham in the butter for a few minutes in a large pan. Cook the pasta al dente in lots of boiling salted water.

Drain and add to the diced ham. Add the parsley and seasonings and toss well, while adding the cream. Make sure the mixture is very hot and remove from the heat. Add the eggs, tossing well. The heat of the pan is enough to cook the eggs.
Serve with lots of pepper and the cheese. Serves 6.

Spatzle

2 pounds flour   6-8 eggs
dash salt   1-2 cups water, enough to make a
                                      thick dough

Mix the ingredients in a large bowl and beat up and down with your hand to incorporate air while working out the gluten in the flour. Beat until large air bubbles form.

Let dough rest a little.

Bring a large pot of salted water to a boil.

Place a small amount of the dough on a board. With a flat spatula, shave off small strips of dough. To keep the dough from sticking to the spatula dip the spatula into the hot water from time to time.

Lift out the spatzle when they rise to the surface of the water. Refresh under cool water. Spatzle can be kept covered in the refrigerator for a day or two. At serving time, saute the spatzle in a little butter. Makes enough to serves 12 to 16.

Apple Stuffing Loaf

8 ounces stale bread or rolls   4-5 tart apples
1 small onion, chopped   juice of 1 or 2 lemons
3-4 eggs   1½ cups stock
4 ounces butter   dash sugar
salt, pepper   1 teaspoon cinnamon

Cut the bread or rolls into dice. Peel and core the apples, slice thinly.

Melt the butter and add the onion, and cook for a few minutes. Add the apples, lemon juice, salt, sugar and cinnamon and saute for a few minutes. Add the bread cubes and mix well.

Mix the eggs with the stock, pour over the bread mixture and toss well. Pour into a buttered baking dish. Bake in a moderate oven until crisp and golden on top, about 30 to 40 minutes. Serves 10 to 12.

Stuffing Loaf

2 loaves stale bread, diced
2 cups diced onion
poultry seasoning, thyme, rosemary
2-3 cups chicken stock

2 cups diced celery
butter
salt and pepper
5-6 eggs

Saute the onion and celery in butter until golden.
Heat the stock and pour it over the bread. Let sit for a while.
Mix onion, bread, celery, eggs and seasonings together.
Bake in a greased loaf pan for 1 to 1½ hours.
Turn out and slice to serve.

Bread Dumplings

6 ounces stale bread or rolls
1 onion, chopped fine
salt, pepper, dash nutmeg
2-3 eggs

3-4 slices bacon
1½ cups milk
2 tablespoons chopped parsley
3 tablespoons butter

Cut the stale bread into thin slices.
Dice the bacon. Saute in a frying pan with the chopped onion until golden brown. Add to the bread slices. Add the parsley, salt, pepper and nutmeg. Heat the milk and pour over the bread mixture, pressing the bread down into the liquid. Let sit for a while to absorb the milk.
Mix in the eggs. If the mixture is too thick to form dumplings, add a little more milk. If too thin, add breadcrumbs. Form into large balls. Bring a pot of salted water to the boil. Drop the dumplings into the water and simmer until they rise to the surface. Remove and drain.
At serving time, heat the butter and add the dumplings. Saute until hot and serve. Serves 8 to 10.

Farina Dumplings

4 tablespoons soft butter
4 ounces farina
boiling water

1 egg
salt, pepper, nutmeg

Beat the egg with the butter until foamy. Add the farina, salt, pepper and nutmeg. Cook spoonfuls of the mixture in a pot of boiling water for 10 minutes. Add 1 cup cold water to stop the cooking process. Let them stand this way for ten minutes. Drain and serve. Serves 4.

Glazed Chestnuts

2 pounds chestnuts   1 cup sugar
½ cup stock   ½ cup red wine vinegar

Cut a cross on the top of each chestnut with a sharp knife. Bake in a moderate oven for ½ hour. Cool a little and peel.

Place the sugar in a heavy skillet and heat until it turns light brown in color. Add the vinegar and the stock, carefully. Add the chestnuts and cook until they are tender. Shake the pan often to keep the nuts from sticking and to glaze them evenly.

Serve with fowl. They are especially nice with turkey. Serves 8.

Chapter 4
Spices And
Salad Dressings

Tips:
Spices and Herbs

Curry Powder

Goulash Spice Mix

Paprika

Parsley

Salad Dressings

Vinegar

Croutons

Recipes:

Chicken Curry Dinner*

Lamb Curry

Turkey with Curry Sauce

Szegedin Goulash

Herb Butter

Snail Butter

Snails en Croute

Hungarian Goulash

Fried Parsley

French Dressing

Italian Dressing

Russian Dressing

Cauliflower Vinagrette

Roquefort Dressing

Spinach Salad with Bacon Dressing

Spinach Salad with Hazelnut Dressing

Garlic Croutons

Oven Browned Croutons

* Indicates Dinner for One

Spices And Herbs

Most department stores sell beautiful looking spice racks. You buy one, take it home and fill it up. Then you hang it in a nice sunny place in your kitchen and it looks great. Beautiful, but wrong, totally wrong!

You should always buy your herbs or spices in the smallest amounts possible and replace them as soon as they go bad. Don't think that because your rack comes with 30 jars that it's necessary to keep all of them filled all of the time. Buy only what you can use within a period of 6 months to a year. Dried herbs don't keep their flavor longer than that.

You can tell if a dried herb is still good by the way it looks and the way it smells. If it looks very dry and smells like straw, throw it out, for it won't do your food very much good either. Try to store your spices and herbs out of direct sunlight in a cool dry spot. They will keep longer that way.

To get the most flavor and aroma out of a dried herb, try this trick before you add it your food. Place the herb in the palm of your hand. Use the thumb of your other hand and rub the herb well to crush it a little. This brings out the flavor and bouquet and your food will taste better.

Curry Powder

Curry powder is a mixture of many different spices. The most expensive spice it contains is saffron, which along with tumeric, gives it its characteristic yellow color.

Curry powder is a little bit tricky to handle. Some of the spices in the curry mixture contain a small amount of natural sugar. When this sugar sautees in a hot pan, it will start to carmelize and turn bitter. To prevent this, add some liquid to the pan immediately after adding the curry powder.

I prefer to use Madras curry powder. Madras is a region of east India which makes the best curry powder. Try to buy it in a metal can and store it away from sunshine.

Chicken Curry Dinner*

1 tablespoon butter	½ teaspoon curry powder
1 chicken breast (boneless, diced)	½ cup white wine
2 slices pineapple	¼ cup heavy cream
3 figs	toasted almonds
salt, pepper	

Heat butter. Saute the diced chicken at a high heat. Add 1 slice of pineapple diced, salt, pepper and curry powder. Add the white wine, reduce the liquid a little then add the cream. Serve over rice. Garnish with figs, pineapple slice and toasted almonds. Serves one.

Lamb Curry

2 large onions, chopped	oil
2 apples, chopped	1 tablespoon Madras curry powder
4 cups hot chicken or veal stock	salt, pepper
2 pounds lamb, shoulder or leg	½ cup heavy cream
1 cup flour	

Trim meat. Remove fat and cartilage and cut into ½ inch cubes. Saute the onion and apple in oil until they are light brown. Add the flour to form a roux. Add the curry powder and cook for a minute longer.

Add the hot stock, stirring. Season and bring to a boil.

Saute the meat in oil in a frying pan until browned. Add the meat to the sauce.

Bake in a moderate oven for 1 to 1½ hours, until tender. Remove the meat from the sauce. Strain the sauce, add the heavy cream.

Add the meat back to the sauce. Correct seasonings. Serve hot with rice and curry condiments, and chutney, if desired. Serves 6.

Turkey With Curry Sauce

To make sauce:

1 tablespoon diced onion	¼ cup flour
1 tablespoon diced apple	2 cups hot chicken stock
¼ cup butter	1 tablespoon Madras curry powder

Saute butter with onion and apple. Then add the flour to make a cream sauce base. Remove from the heat and let cool. Now add the hot chicken stock and curry powder. Let simmer and season to taste. Strain.

With Turkey:

½ cup rice pilaf (cooked)	sliced turkey
½ cup curry sauce	

Pour the sauce over the turkey and rice in a casserole dish. Bake in a 350° oven for 15 minutes or until hot. You can garnish with a pineapple ring, a fig, or use 2 tablespoons chopped, toasted almonds or fresh cranberries. Good luck with this recipe! Serves 2.

Goulash Spice Mix

Goulash spice mix adds a very nice flavor to soups and stews. This combin-ation of ingredients has a beautiful smell and a taste that is unique. Try using some the next time you make a Hungarian dish.

Spice Mixture:

3 garlic cloves	1 bay leaf
½ teaspoon caraway seeds	dash marjoram
rind of 1 lemon	salt, pepper

   Place all of the ingredients on a chopping board. With a sharp heavy knife, mince all the ingredients until they are chopped very finely. Mix may be stored in a covered container in the refrigerator for a few days.

Szegedin Goulash

1 pound beef cubes	1 pound onions, sliced
1 pound sauerkraut, washed	1 potato, peeled and diced
2 tablespoons tomato puree	2 teaspoons paprika
1 cup beef broth or water	2 tablespoons oil
1 recipe spice mixture	

   Use chuck, bottom round or flank steak.
   Heat the oil, add the cubed meat and saute until brown. Add the onion and the tomato puree and saute for another 5 minutes. Add the sauerkraut, the paprika and the potato. Add the spice mixture. Pour the broth over the meat. Cover with a lid and cook for about 45 to 50 minutes in a 400° oven, or until the meat is tender.
   The dish should resemble a stew. If it looks too dry, add more water or beef stock. Serves 4.

Herb Butter

1 pound butter	1 teaspoon salt
2 tablespoons chopped parsley	½ teaspoon pepper
juice of ½ lemon	1-2 cloves garlic, crushed

   Soften the butter well. Mix in the rest of the ingredients. Roll the butter onto parchment paper, forming into a roll with a palette knife. *Illustration 14.* Store in the refrigerator or freezer. If frozen, cut off a slice at a time, as needed. Excellent served with grilled meats such as steak, etc.

Illustration 14.

Snail Butter

To make snail butter, add a dash of pernod to the herb butter when mixing it together. proceed with the rest of the recipe.

Snails En Croute

1 or 2 cans snails	snail butter
1 recipe crust, see seafood quiche, page 104	1 egg beaten

Prepare the snail butter and refrigerate.

Prepare the crust and chill a little before rolling.

Place five or six snails in individual ramckins along with a little of the liquid from the can. Place a generous slice of snail butter on top of the snails.

Roll out the pastry and cut out rounds to fit the tops of the ramekins. Place the crust on top and seal well. Brush with beaten egg. Cut a slit in each top.

Bake the ramekins in a 425° oven until the crust is browned, about fifteen to twenty minutes. Serve hot. Serves 8.

Alternate: You can leave off the pastry top and just serve the snails plain. Reduce the baking time to half.

Paprika

Paprika is a ripe red pepper plant which has been dried and ground into a powder. In Europe there are many different varieties of paprika from mild to very hot and spicy. The variety depends on what type of pepper is used and whether the whole pepper is ground or the seeds and core are removed first.

Since it is made from ripe pepper, there is some natural sugar present in paprika. It therefore has to be handled the same way in which you would handle curry powder. Make sure you add some liquid to your pan when you add the paprika so that it doesn't burn and turn your dish bitter.

Try to buy your paprika in a metal can as it will keep much better. Here is an interesting goulash recipe that uses paprika powder.

Hungarian Goulash

1 pound beef, cubed
1 clove garlic, crushed
¼ cup tomato puree
1 cup beef stock
2-3 tablespoons oil

1 large onion, sliced
1 tablespoon paprika
1 tablespoon flour
salt, pepper

Saute the cubed beef in the oil until well browned on all sides. In another pan, saute the onion until golden. Add the garlic, salt, pepper, paprika and tomato puree to the pan containing the onion. Stir in the flour. Add the stock and bring to a boil. Add the sauteed meat to the pan and continue to cook until the meat is tender. Serves 2 or 3.

Parsley

When a recipe asks for parsley, always use fresh parsley. Since it is available all year round, there is no need to use the dried kind as it has much less flavor. Fresh is always better.

Most recipes ask for chopped parsley. The easiest way to chop a large bunch of parsley is to use a food processor. I chop very fast, but a processor is just as fast for the this job. Wash the parsley and trim off the stalks. Place the tops in a processor fitted with a steel blade. Turn it off and on a few times, and in just a minute or two you have beautiful chopped parsley. Don't forget to plug in your machine.

Storing chopped parsley for a few days can be a problem because of its chlorophyll content. Chlorophyll makes the parsley green. But an excess of chlorophyll will make your chopped parsley develop a bad smell.

The easiest way to get rid of this extra chlorophyll is to wash some of it away. Don't use a washing machine, but place your chopped parsley in a clean towel. Fold up the towel and hold it securely closed. Run some cold water over the towel and then squeeze hard to remove all the water. The liquid you squeeze out should be bright green in color. Then turn your parsley out onto a dish. It will be clean, dry, fluffy, and easy to handle. If kept refrigerated, it will also smell nice and fresh for a day or two.

You don't have to run out and buy a food processor just to chop parsley, although I think that they are great. You can use a sharp chef's knife. And yes, you can wash parsley that you chop by hand. As long as the parsley is chopped fine, it will work equally as well.

Fried Parsley

1 or 2 bunches parsley
oil for frying

salt

Wash the parsley sprigs and dry well. Heat the oil in a deep pan. Place the well dried parsley into the hot oil. Remove when crisp. This will only take a minute. Place on paper towels to drain. Sprinkle with salt and serve at once. Makes a great appetizer. Serve with fried Camembert cheese, page 103.

Salad Dressings

In my opinion, it's absolutely ridiculous to buy salad dressing. It costs much less to make your own and it will taste better, also. If you read the ingredients on the labels of bottled salad dressing and see what is put into them, I'm sure you will want to try making your own using some of these recipes.

Vinegar

I like to use wine vinegar in all my recipes. I grew up on wine vinegar and really like the flavor and the way it blends with food. Try it and I'm sure you'll like it as much as I do.

If you use too much wine vinegar in your recipe, you can always equalize it by adding a little bit of sugar. This doesn't work if you use a stronger or more acidic vinegar.

French Dressing

⅓ cup wine vinegar   ⅓ cup salad oil
⅓ cup water   salt, pepper
dash sugar

Mix all ingredients and let stand one hour to develop flavor. Pour over salad and toss at serving time.

Italian Dressing - Add 1 teaspoon of basil and 1 teaspoon of oregano to the French dressing.

Russian Dressing - Add 1 diced hard boiled egg and 1 tablespoon finely chopped onion to the above dressing.

Cauliflower Vinagrette

1 head cauliflower   salt, pepper, sugar
few spoons chopped parsley   ½ cup cooking water from the
vinegar, oil   cauliflower
½ cup chopped onion

Parboil the cauliflower in salted boiling water until cooked but still firm. Save ½ cup of the cooking liquid. Refresh the cauliflower under cold water. Separate the flowerlets. Add the chopped onion, salt, pepper, sugar and the ½ cup reserved liquid. Add oil and vinegar to taste and mix in the chopped parsley.

Roquefort Dressing

1. As shown on T.V.

Beat ½ cup of heavy cream until fairly stiff. Add the juice of one lemon and one cup of crumbled roquefort cheese.

2. Alternate method

Make a vinaigrette and then add the roquefort cheese.

Vinaigrette

½ cup red wine vinegar   sugar to taste
¼ cup oil   some choped onion
salt and pepper   some chopped parsley or chives

Spinach Salad With Bacon Dressing

3 tablespoons chopped onion
2 cloves garlic, chopped
salt, pepper

⅓ cup red wine vinegar
⅓ cup salad oil
3-4 slices bacon

Dice the bacon and cook until crisp. Drain well and cool.

Mix the onion, garlic, salt and pepper to taste with the vinegar. Stir in the oil and then the bacon.

Serve over spinach leaves.

Spinach Salad With Hazelnut Dressing

1 cup raw spinach leaves
1 apple
2 to 3 tablespoons ground hazelnuts

1 cup mushrooms
2 to 3 tablespoons honey
2 to 3 tablespoons orange juice

Toast the hazelnuts in a moderate oven for about ten minutes to loosen their skins. Remove the skins, let cool, and grind the nuts.

Cut the mushrooms and the apple into julienne strips. Cut the spinach into fine strips.

Mix all of the vegetables and fruit with the orange juice, nuts and honey to taste. Serves 2 to 4.

Croutons

Croutons are a nice addition to a salad. If you have any stale bread left over, just cube it and make it into croutons by using one of the following methods.

Garlic Croutons

Heat a frying pan on your stove. Cut a garlic clove in half and pierce it with a fork. Using the fork, rub the garlic around the sides and bottom of the pan. Be careful not to burn yourself. Remove the garlic and add 2 or 3 tablespoons of butter. Add the cubes of bread and shake them well in the butter. They will take on a garlic flavor as they cook. When they are golden you can add 1 tablespoon of chopped parsley, if you like, and toss well. Remove the croutons from the pan and use in salads or soups.

Oven Browned Croutons

Dice stale bread into cubes. Place the cubes on a baking sheet and bake in a 350⁰ oven until they are golden in color. Check while they are browning and turn if needed. Remove and use for salads or soups.

Chapter 5
Sauces

Tips:

How to Make a Cream Sauce Base

How to Deglaze a Pan

How to Thicken a Sauce

How to Degrease a Stock or a Sauce

Pesto

Hollandaise Sauce

Mayonnaise

Recipes:

Pesto Sauce

Barbeque Sauce

Brown Sauce Espagnole

Sauce Chausser

Sauce Madeira

Bechamel Sauce

Mornay Sauce

Sauce Alsacienne

Horseradish Sauce

Hollandaise Sauce

Sauce Bernaise

Sauce Mousseline

Mayonnaise in a Food Processor

Mayonnaise in a Blender

Mayonnaise by Hand

Sauce Andalouse

Cocktail Sauce

Dill Cocktail Sauce

Sauce Tartare

Mustard Sauce

Dessert Sauces:

Caramel Sauce

Chocolate Sauce

Raspberry Sauce

Vanilla Sauce

How To Make A Cream Sauce Base

In order to make a sauce, you have to start out with what is called a roux. Roux is a French word thtat means a butter-flour mixture. You need to use the same volume of butter or margarine as you do of flour. Melt the butter in a saucepan and add the flour. Stir and cook this mixture on a low flame for a few minutes, just until the roux starts to bubble up. Then remove it from the heat and let it cool down a little before you proceed with your recipe.

Now comes the trick that will make your sauce lump-free every time. Heat whatever liquid your recipe asks for to the boiling point. Then add the boiling liquid to the cooled roux and stir.

If your liquid is hot and your roux is cool, the sauce will never lump. Continue to cook your sauce for an additional 15 minutes. All sauces containing a roux must cook for at least 15 minutes so that they will lose their starchy taste.

How To Deglaze A Pan

When meats are sauteed, they leave a brown residue or deposit on the bottom of the pan. These brown particles are actually carmelized juices from the meat. There is a lot of flavor in this residue or glaze.

You want to lift this glaze from the bottom of the pan and incorporate it into your sauce. There is a very simple, very easy way to do this. Just remove your meat from the pan and set it aside to keep warm. If there is a lot of fat in the pan, pour off the excess. Then pour a little liquid, which can be either wine, stock, or even water, into the bottom of your pan. Scrape the glaze with a wooden spoon and it will dissolve into your sauce. Cook for a few minutes, adding more liquid if needed. Deglazing the pan will give your sauce both a better color and flavor.

How To Thicken A Sauce

If you've made a sauce that is too thin and you want to use it immediately, the fastest way to thicken it is by using cornstarch. Just dissolve a spoon or two of cornstarch in a little cold water. Bring your sauce to a boil and stir in some of the cornstarch mixture. It should thicken up in a minute or two. If it is still too thin, add more dissolved cornstarch.

If you used flour to thicken your sauce, you would have to cook it for at least ten to fifteen minutes to get rid of the starchy taste. Cornstarch has the advantage of thickening immediately without affecting the taste of your sauce very much.

Degreasing a Sauce or Stock

The easiest way to degrease a sauce or a stock is to remove the fat layer after it is chilled. Let your sauce cool down a little and then put it in the refrigerator. The fat will rise to the surface and harden. Just remove this fat layer and your sauce is greaseless. Very simple, very easy.

If you don't have the time to do this there is another method that will work. Use a small spoon or a ladle and, making small circles, remove the grease, a little at a time. You should be able to get most of it off this way. If there is any left, just brush the surface of the liquid with a paper napkin. The remaining grease should adhere to the napkin.

Pesto

Pesto is an Italian herb sauce which is made from fresh basil leaves. You can usually buy them in the springtime or you can grow your own.

Besides being fantastic on pasta you can use it to flavor lots of other dishes. I even like it spread on French or Italian bread and toasted in the oven.

Pesto can be made ahead of time and stored in the refrigerator in a covered jar. It will keep well for a few days.

Pesto Sauce

1 cup fresh basil leaves, washed and dried
6 sprigs fresh parsley
½ cup pine nuts
2 cloves of garlic, mashed
⅓ cup Parmesan cheese
⅓ cup Pecorino or Romano cheese
4 tablespoons oil
2 tablespoons softened butter
¼ teaspoon salt.

Pound all of the above ingredients in a mortar or blend briefly in a blender.

Barbecue Sauce

1 orange rind grated	½ cup ketchup
1 lemon rind grated	½ cup honey
¼ cup vinegar	¼ cup chopped onion
¼ cup oil	juice of 1 orange
	juice of 1 lemon

Mix together all ingredients and add dash of salt. Bring to a boil for 15-20 minutes till reduced to one-half volume. The color will change from light red to dark red.

Note: If you like it sweet add a little brown sugar.

Use sauce for barbequed chicken.

Just spread barbecue sauce on the chicken, place it in oven (350⁰) for 25-30 minutes, then place on fire.

Brown Sauce or Espagnole

2 pounds bones, beef, veal or pork
few cloves garlic
bay leaf, parsley, thyme
salt and pepper
beef stock to cover, page 80
3 ounces flour plus 3 ounces butter
     or oil

2 carrots, chopped
2 onions, chopped
2 stalks celery, chopped
4 tomatoes, chopped
oil for pan

Place the oil in a roasting pan, add the bones and brown well. Add the chopped vegetables, garlic and tomatoes and continue to brown. Deglaze the pan several times with water or stock.

Place all ingredients in a stockpot and cover with the beef stock. Simmer for about 5-6 hours. Strain.

Make a roux with the flour and the butter or oil. Add the stock. Cook until the floury taste is gone.

Chill and remove the fat layer.

Brown or Espagnole sauce can be used for meats, or as a base from which to make other meat sauces.

Sauce Chausser

½ cup chopped onion
½ cup sliced mushrooms
2 cups Brown or Espagnole sauce

2 tablespoons butter or oil
1 tablespoon chopped parsley

Cook the onion in the butter until translucent. Add the sliced mushrooms and saute them for a few minutes. Add the brown sauce and heat. When hot, add the chopped parsley.

Serve over pork, game or fowl.

Sauce Madeira

1 cup Madeira
1 teaspoon sugar
2 cups Brown or Espagnole sauce

½ cup finely chopped onion
2 tablespoons butter or oil

Place the Madeira in a saucepan and reduce to one-half cup.

Saute the onion in the butter or oil with the sugar until lightly browned. Add the Madeira and the brown sauce.

Serve over beef tenderloin, beef roasts or chicken.

Bechamel Sauce

4 tablespoons butter   1 cup milk
4 tablespoons flour   1 cup stock
salt and pepper

Make a roux by heating the butter with the flour until it bubbles. Remove from the heat and let cool a little.

Heat the milk and the stock to the boiling point. Add the hot stock to the cooled roux, stirring.

Season to taste and cook for about 15 minutes or until the floury taste is gone.

Mornay Sauce

2 cups Bechamel sauce   liason: 2 egg yolks plus ¼ cup heavy
1 cup grated swiss or parmesan cheese   cream, mixed together

Make the Bechamel sauce. Add the cheese to the hot sauce and stir to melt. Correct the seasonings.

Add the liason, stirring, right before you are ready to use the sauce. Do not reboil the sauce after adding the liason.

Sauce Alsacienne

4 ounces butter   4 ounces flour
2½ cups fish stock, page 80   ¼ cup julienned carrots
¼ cup julienned leeks   2 tablespoons finely chopped dill
2 egg yolks   ½ cup heavy cream

Melt butter, add flour. Cook for a minute or two and cool. Heat the fish stock and add it to the roux, stirring. Cook until the sauce thickens and floury taste disappears, about 15 minutes. Poach the leeks and carrots in boiling salted water. Refresh. Add them to the sauce.

Make a liason by mixing the egg yolks with the heavy cream. Add to sauce, stirring. Serve immediately.

Do not bring sauce to a boil again after having added the liason.

Excellent with poached, sauteed or broiled fish.

Horseradish Sauce

4 tablespoons butter
1 cup milk
juice ½ lemon
2-3 tablespoons grated horseradish,
    fresh or bottled

4 tablespoons flour
1 cup beef stock
salt, pepper
sugar to taste

Melt the butter and add the flour. Cook, stirring for a few minutes. Remove the roux from the heat. Bring the stock and milk to a boil. Add this mixture to the cooled roux, stirring. Simmer for about 20 minutes, or until the floury taste is gone. Add the grated drained horseradish root. Season with salt, pepper, lemon juice and sugar to taste. Serve hot with boiled beef.

Hollandaise Sauce

Hollandaise is a very nice sauce that can be used over almost any vegetable. The trick to making good hollandaise is to make sure that the egg yolk mixture and the clarified butter are both at the same temperature of about 140° when you combine them. You will have no trouble with your sauce if you remember this.

6 egg yolks
½ cup white wine

12 ounces clarified butter
salt, pepper

Beat the egg yolks and wine carefully over heat until thickened. If you are hesitant about doing this, use a bowl over a pot of boiling water to beat the mixture until thickened. Remove from the heat and continue to beat until the mixture cools a little.

Combine with the clarified butter, mixing constantly with a whisk. Season to taste with the salt and pepper.

Do not reheat the sauce. Keep warm by placing the bowl with the sauce over a pot of hot water.

Important - both the yolk mixture and the butter must be the same temperature (about 140°) to blend properly.

Always use clarified butter to make hollandaise sauce.

If your hollandaise sauce should break down and separate, it is because your ingredients were either too hot or too cold. The easiest way to tell which it is is to use your finger and feel the sauce. If the sauce feels too hot, put an egg yolk or a little cold liquid into a clean bowl and slowly beat in your hollandaise.

If the sauce feels too cold, add a little hot water to a clean bowl, and slowly beat in the sauce. Sometimes the addition of an acid such as vinegar or lemon juice, or even a little white wine, will help to restore the hollandaise.

This is an easy way to make a Bearnaise sauce. Try it "My way".

Sauce Bearnaise

½ cup white wine
2 chopped shallots
6 to 8 crushed peppercorns
2 cups hollandaise sauce

1 to 2 teaspoons dried tarragon
1 tablespoon fresh tarragon, chopped
1 teaspoon chopped parsley
¼ cup tarragon vinegar

Place the white wine, shallots, pepper, vinegar and dried tarragon into a small saucepan. Reduce until only one tablespoon of liquid remains. Strain, pressing well.

Add this liquid to the hollandaise sauce. Mix in the fresh parsley and tarragon. Wonderful served with meats, such as steak or roast lamb.

Sauce Mousseline

2 cups hollandaise sauce   ½ to ¾ cup heavy cream

Whip the cream. Combine it carefully with the hollandaise sauce. Serve immediately.

Excellent with cooked fresh asparagus.

Mayonnaise

As you have seen on television, I always make my own mayonnaise. It can be made in a blender or a food processor or even by hand. Real mayonnaise should contain eggs and oil. If you read the labels on the mayonnaise that you buy, you'd be amazed at some of the ingredients.

The first time your family eats homemade mayonnaise they probably won't recognize it, as the taste is that much different from the commercial variety. It's much cheaper to make and it is also much better for you. Homemade mayonnaise can be stored in a closed jar in the refrigerator for a week or two.

Mayonnaise will separate if you have added your oil too fast or if you have not beaten hard enough while adding the oil. It can be saved by starting over again with a clean bowl and one or two extra egg yolks. Beat the egg yolks a little, then slowly, beat the broken mayonnaise into the yolks and your emulsion should return.

There is another way to save mayonnaise that we sometimes use in Europe. You need to make a thick flour-water paste. Use 1 cup of water and ½ cup of flour. Stir and cook the mixture until it is very thick, then cool it off. Put this cooled paste into your blender or food processor and slowly and the broken mayonnaise. The mayonnaise will be very thick, but usable.

Mayonnaise In A Food Processor

1 whole egg
1 tablespoon wine vinegar
1½ cups oil

dash of salt, pepper, paprika
½ teaspoon dijon mustard

Place the egg, vinegar and seasonings in a food processor. Blend for a few seconds. With the motor on, add the oil slowly. Taste and correct seasonings, if needed.

Mayonnaise In A Blender

2 egg yolks
salt, pepper, paprika
½ teaspoon dijon mustard

1 cup oil
1 tablespoon vinegar

Place the egg yolks, the vinegar and the seasonings in a blender. Blend for a few seconds. With the motor on, slowly add the oil through the top of the machine. Correct seasonings.

Mayonnaise By Hand

Follow the same recipe as for mayonnaise made in a blender. Use a wire whisk to incorporate the oil. Just add the oil a drop at a time at first, increasing the volume as you go along.

Sauce Andalouse

½ cup mayonnaise
chopped onion
dash of salt

1 tomato (peeled, seeded and diced)
chopped parsley
dash of pepper

Mix together all the ingredients and use as a dressing for cold fish salad, chicken salad, meat salad, and hard boiled egg salad.

Cocktail sauce

1 cup mayonnaise
1 tablespoon horseradish
few drops Worchestershire sauce
1 ounce brandy (or less)

¼ cup ketchup
few drops lemon juice
salt, pepper
½ cup whipped cream

Mix all the ingredients together except the cream. At serving time fold in the whipped cream.

Dill Cocktail Sauce

1 cup mayonnaise
juice ½ lemon
salt, pepper
½ cup cream, whipped

¼ cup ketchup
few drops Worchestershire sauce
2 tablespoons chopped dill

Mix together all the ingredients except the cream. At serving time, fold in the lightly whipped cream. Serve with cold fish or crabmeat.

Sauce Tartare

1 cup mayonnaise
1 tablespoon chopped parsley or chives
1 tablespoon finely chopped onion

1 hard boiled egg, chopped
1 tablespoon chopped pickles (gerkins)

Mix all ingredients together with the mayonnaise and season to taste. Use as a dip for raw vegetables or with fried seafood.

Mustard Sauce

½ cup dijon mustard
3 tablespoons vinegar
1 cup oil
1 hard boiled egg, chopped

2 tablespoons mustard powder
4 tablespoons sugar
3 tablespoons chopped dill
3 tablespoons chopped parsley

Mix mustards, sugar and vinegar. Add the oil slowly, while beating. Fold in the herbs and the egg.

Dessert Sauces

Caramel Sauce

2 cups sugar   1 cup or more water
few drops lemon juice

   Melt the sugar, stirring, in a heavy pan until melted and brown. Very carefully add the water and continue to cook and stir until all the lumps of sugar
are re-dissolved. Remove from the heat and add the lemon juice. Store in a
covered jar in the refrigerator. Add water if the sauce thickens. Keep your
face out of the way when adding the water to the caramel, it will splatter.

Chocolate Sauce

   Use equal parts heavy cream and semi-sweet chocolate. Melt, stirring, in a
saucepan. This sauce is very rich and very delicious.

Raspberry Sauce

1 package frozen raspberries   ¼ cup confectioners sugar
1 tablespoon Kirsch

   Defrost the berries and puree them in a food mill. If you use a food processor or blender, strain to remove the seeds. Mix in the sugar and the Kirsch.
More sugar may be added to taste, if desired. Chill.

Vanilla Sauce

2 cups milk   ½ cup sugar
4 egg yolks   1 ounce cornstarch
dash vanilla or a piece of vanilla bean   rum, if desired or other flavorings

   Heat 1¾ cup milk to boiling. If using the vanilla bean, split and heat with
the milk. Mix the egg yolks, sugar and cornstarch in a bowl with the remaining
milk until smooth.
   Add to the hot milk and whisk over heat until thickened. Add vanilla extract,
if used, and flavorings. Strain the sauce to remove any lumps. Chill or serve
warm.

Chapter 6
Stocks And Soups

Stocks:
Beef Stock
Chicken Stock
Fish Stock

Recipes:
Hot:
Cream of Asparagus Soup
Cream of Brocolli Soup
Cream of Carrot Soup
Cream of Cauliflower Soup
Hungarian Goulash Soup
Lady Curzon Soup
Lentil Soup
Minestroni
Onion Soup
Potato Soup
Potage Leopold
Scotch Barley Soup
Vegetable Soup
Cold:
Cold Fruit Soup
Cold Zucchini Soup
Iced Cucumber Soup
Gaspacho
Vichyssoise

Beef Stock

3-4 pounds beef bones
1 onion, chopped
1-2 cloves garlic
parsley sprigs
water to cover

2 carrots, chopped
2 stalks celery, chopped
bay leaf, pinch thyme
salt, pepper

Put all the ingredients into a stockpot. Cover with water and bring to a boil. Simmer for 3 to 4 hours. Remove scum as it forms at the top of the pot. Strain and degrease the stock.

Chicken Stock

2-3 pounds bones and giblets
   from chickens
1-2 carrots
1 onion

salt and pepper to taste
1-2 stalks celery
parsley, bay leaf, thyme
water to cover

Bring all ingredients to a boil in a large pot. Simmer and skim pot occasionally for 2 or 3 hours. Strain stock. Remove fat when cool.

Fish Stock

3 pounds or more carcasses and heads
   of non-fat white fleshed fish
1 onion, chopped
1 stalk celery, chopped
1 to 2 cups white wine

water to cover
2 carrots, chopped
thyme, bay leaf, parsley, salt
fennel seeds, optional

Cut up carcasses. Combine all ingredients in a stock pot. Bring to a boil and simmer for about 30 to 45 minutes.

Remove scum and foam as it forms on the surface of the liquid. Strain stock. Reduce if desired.

Hot Soups

Cream of Asparagus Soup

1 pound asparagus
4 ounces butter or margarine
4 ounces flour
2 egg yolks

water to cover
salt and pepper
dash sugar
½ cup heavy cream

Peel and trim the asparagus. Cook the peelings and trimmings in boiling salted water.

Cook the asparagus stalks separately in water with a dash of sugar and salt added.

Make a roux with the butter and flour. Cool a little.

Strain the stock from the asparagus peelings and add this hot liquid to the cooled roux. Cook about 20 minutes longer.

When ready to serve, thicken the soup with a liason made from the egg yolks and the cream.

Garnish the soup with some pieces of asparagus. Serves 8.

Cream Of Brocolli Soup

2 bunches brocolli
2 quarts water
4 ounces butter or margarine
4 ounces flour
½ cup heavy cream

½ onion, chopped
juice of 1 lemon
salt and pepper
2 egg yolks

Separate the brocolli rosettes from the stems. Heat the water and add the lemon juice. Cook the brocolli rosettes until they are about half way done and remove them. Reserve the cooking liquid.

Make a roux with the butter and flour, add the chopped brocolli stalks and the onion and cook for a few minutes. Cool.

Add the hot reserved liquid to the roux, stirring and cook for 30 minutes. Season to taste and strain the soup.

Thicken the soup by adding a liason made by mixing the egg yolks with the cream. Add more butter, if desired. Garnish the soup with the brocolli rosettes and serve hot.

Cream Of Carrot Soup

4 tablespoons butter or margarine
1 pound carrots
salt, pepper
½ onion, chopped
2 egg yolks

4 tablespoons flour
8 cups chicken stock
dash sugar
½ cup heavy cream

Peel the carrots. Reserve 2 of them for the garnish and chop the rest. Melt the butter and add the flour to make a roux. Add the chopped onion and the chopped carrots. Stir and cook for a few minutes. Remove from the heat and cool a little. Heat the chicken stock. Add the hot stock to the cooled roux, stirring. Let simmer for about 45 minutes. Puree the soup in a food processor or blender. Season to taste.

Julienne the two remaining carrots and cook them in boiling water with a pinch of sugar and salt added for just a few minutes, until they are barely tender. Refresh under cold water, drain and reserve.

Both soup and garnish may be prepared ahead to this point and refrigerated. Right before serving, heat the soup to the boiling point. Mix the egg yolks with the cream. Add to the hot soup, stirring. Add the julienned carrots to heat. Serve immediately. Do not reboil the soup after adding the liason. Serves 10 to 12.

Cream Of Cauliflower Soup

1 head cauliflower
3 quarts water
4 ounces margarine or butter
4 ounces flour
½ cup cream

½ onion
juice of 1 lemon
salt and pepper
2 egg yolks

Heat water, add lemon juice. Cook the cauliflower until it is about half way done and remove. Reserve liquid.

Make a roux with the butter and the flour. Add chopped outer green leaves from the cauliflower and the onion and cook a little. Cool.

Add the hot liquid from the stock to the roux and cook for ½ hour. Season to taste.

Make small flowerlets from the cooled cauliflower.

Strain the soup into a clean container, thicken with a liason made by mixing the egg yolks with the cream. Add butter if desired. Garnish soup with the pieces of cauliflower and serve hot. Serves 10 to 12.

Hungarian Goulash Soup

1 pound chuck, flank steak or bottom
    round of beef
2 pounds onions, diced
2 cups potatoes, peeled and diced
1 tablespoon goulash spice mix
    page 64
1 cup tomato puree

salt and pepper
water to cover
1 cup sauerkraut, washed and drained
2 tablespoons paprika
2 cloves garlic
1 green pepper, diced
1 tablespoon oil

Dice the meat into small cubes.

Heat the oil and saute the meat for about 5 minutes, stirring. Add the onions and continue to cook until the onions are golden brown. Add the garlic, the tomato puree, paprika and goulash spice. Fill the pot with water to cover.

Bring to a boil and add in the potatoes, green pepper and sauerkraut. Simmer for 1½ to 2 hours. Season to taste and serve with bread.

Lady Curzon Soup

4 tablespoons butter
one 7-ounce can turtle soup
Garnish: ½ cup lightly sweetened
    whipped cream

1½ to 2 teaspoons curry powder
liason: 2 eggs yolks plus ¼ cup heavy
    cream

Melt the butter and add the curry powder, cook for just a few seconds. Add the soup and bring the mixture to a boil. Remove from heat and add the liason. Pour into demi-tasse cups.

Pipe a little whipped cream on top of each cup and serve immediately. Will yield about 6 servings.

Lentil Soup

1 onion, chopped
whites of 2 leeks, diced
1 cup dried lentils
1 large potato, diced
¼ cup vinegar

2 carrots, diced
2-3 slices bacon, diced
5 cups chicken stock
salt, pepper

Saute the diced bacon and the onion for a few minutes.

Add the diced carrots and leeks and continue to saute for a few minutes longer. Add the chicken stock and the lentils and simmer for about one and one-half hours.

Add the diced potato and cook until done.

Season the soup to taste. Add the vinegar and serve hot. The vinegar will cut the heaviness of the lentil soup. Serves 8.

Minestroni

whites of 2 leeks, chopped
2 stalks celery, diced
3 tablespoons butter or oil
2 cloves garlic, crushed
½ cup tomato puree
6 cups beef or chicken stock
2 tablespoons chopped parsley
salt, pepper

2 carrots, diced
1 onion, chopped
½ head cabbage, shredded
3 tomatoes, peeled, seeded and diced
1 cup cooked noodles
1 can kidney beans, optional
½ cup grated parmesan cheese

Saute the onion and garlic in oil or butter. Add the leeks, carrots, celery, cabbage and tomatoes. Season and saute for a few minutes. Add the stock and cook for about 30 minutes or until the vegetables are tender.

Add the optional kidney beans and the cooked noodles.

When the noodles are hot, add the parsley and the cheese and serve. Serves 8.

Onion Soup

2-3 cups sliced onions
3 cups light beef stock (or chicken stock)
2 tablespoons butter
1 clove garlic

1 cup croutons
1 cup grated Parmesan and Gruyere cheese mixed
salt and pepper
½ cup white wine (optional)

Saute the onion in butter until golden. Add the white wine, garlic, salt, and pepper to taste. Cook for a few minutes to reduce the wine to half. Now add the stock and simmer for an additional 20-30 minutes.

Pour soup into crocks and top with croutons. Add cheese and top with dots of butter. Then bake in oven till golden brown. Serves 4 to 6.

Potato Soup

1 pound leeks, sliced
2 pounds potatoes, sliced
6 cups chicken stock
salt, pepper, marjoram
chopped parsley

½ onion, chopped
3 tablespoons butter or margarine
2 cups cream
4 egg yolks
bread croutons

Melt butter, saute onions and leeks until tender. Add chicken stock, salt, and pepper. Simmer until potatoes are tender. Puree. Add liason made by mixing cream with egg yolks. Correct seasonings. Serve hot garnished with marjoram, chopped parsley and bread croutons. Serves 8.

Potage Leopold

½ cup cream of wheat
4 cups chicken stock
salt, pepper, dash nutmeg
5-6 lettuce leaves, julienned

2-3 tablespoons butter
2 eggs
2 tablespoons chopped parsley

Melt the butter in an ovenproof pan and stir in the cream of wheat. Spread the cream of wheat out in the bottom of the pan and toast in a 375⁰ oven for about 15 to 20 minutes or until the cream of wheat is lightly browned. Remove from the oven and stir in the chicken stock. Bring the mixture to a boil. Simmer the soup for 35 to 40 minutes.

In a separate bowl beat the eggs with the salt, pepper and nutmeg. Add the eggs to the hot soup, stirring constantly.

Serve garnished with the lettuce leaves and the chopped parsley. Serves 6.

Scotch Barley Soup

¾ pound lamb, with bones
2 leeks, cut into julienne
6 stalks celery, diced
1 teaspoon oil
1 cup precooked barley
½ cup heavy cream, or half and half
3 quarts water

6 carrots, 2 chopped, 4 peeled
    and diced
salt, pepper, bay leaf
2 large onions, diced
3 cloves garlic, crushed
½ cup chopped parsley

Use either the shoulder or leg of lamb for this soup. Cut the meat off the bones and dice it into small cubes. Reserve the meat.

Make a lamb stock by heating the water to boiling. Add the lamb bones and any meat scraps, the green part of the leeks, 2 carrots, 2 stalks celery the bay leaf and some salt and pepper. Cook for one hour, skimming occasionally. Strain.

In a clean pot, saute the cubed lamb in the oil. When brown, add the rest of the carrots, leeks, celery and the onion and saute for a few more minutes.

Add the precooked barley (see section on cooking barley), the garlic and the strained lamb stock. Simmer for about 45 more minutes.

Remove the soup from the heat and add the cream. Pour into serving dishes and sprinkle with the chopped parsley. Serves 8 to 10.

Vegetable Soup

½ cup chopped or diced carrots
½ cup chopped or diced celery
½ cup chopped or diced onion
½ cup chopped or diced turnip
½ cup diced and peeled tomatoes
1 tablespoon butter
2-3 cups of chicken stock (or canned broth)
(optional, additional or other vegetables may also be used)

Saute all the vegetables in the butter for approximately 3 minutes. Then add the chicken stock and season to taste - be careful if you are using canned broth - it's always very salty. Simmer for approximately 20 minutes or until the vegetables are cooked. Serve piping hot and enjoy!

Cold Soups

Cold Fruit Soup

4 cups water
piece cinnamon stick
rind of 1 lemon
1 cup white wine or champagne
3 cups fruit, blueberries, plums, peaches, pears, apples, etc. ·
Garnish: whipped cream

½ to 1 cup sugar
cloves
1 tablespoon cornstarch dissolved in
    ¼ cup cold water

Bring the four cups of water and the sugar, cloves, lemon rind and cinnamon stick to a boil. Simmer for about 30 minutes. Strain. Thicken the soup with the dissolved cornstarch and cook for a few more minutes.

If using apples, pears or peaches, peel and dice them. Skin can be left on plums, if desired.

Add the fruits to the soup and bring to a boil. Remove from the heat and chill.

At serving time, stir in the wine or champagne and serve cold with a dollup of whipped cream for garnish. Serves 10.

Cold Zucchini Soup

2 pounds zucchini
2 tablespoons butter
2 tablespoons flour
salt, pepper
chopped parsley

3 cups chicken stock
1 teaspoon marjoram
2 cups milk
1 cup heavy cream

Wash and slice the zucchini. Cook in the chicken stock until tender. Add the marjoram and puree. Melt the butter and add the flour. Stir and cook for a few minutes and remove from the heat.

Heat the milk. Add the boiling milk to the cooled roux. Stir and cook for about 15 minutes.

Add the pureed zucchini mixture to the white sauce. Season to taste and chill. Mix the cream into the cooled soup. Serve garnished with the chopped parsley. Serves 6 to 8.

Iced Cucumber Soup

2 cucumbers, peeled and seeded
½ cup yogurt
1-2 tablespoons chopped dill

1 clove garlic
1 cup sour cream
salt, pepper

In a blender or food processor, add the cucumbers, garlic, yogurt, sour cream and half of the dill. Puree well and season with the salt and pepper to taste. Chill. At serving time, garnish with the remaining dill.

Gaspacho

Soup:
1 cup tomato juice
1 small cucumber
1 small onion
¼ cup wine vinegar
1 egg
juice of ½ lemon
¼ cup half and half

1 whole tomato
1 small green pepper
1 clove garlic
¼ cup olive oil
salt and pepper
dash tobasco

Garnish:
 chopped green pepper
 chopped red pepper
 chopped parsley
 diced tomato
 chopped cucumber

Blend all of soup ingredients in a blender or food processor. Cover and refrigerate. Serve ice cold.

I like to serve this soup from a tureen with plates of chopped vegetables on the side. This way each person can help themselves to whatever garnish vegetables they prefer. Serves 5 or 6.

Vichyssoise

whites of 3 or 4 leeks
1 onion, diced
salt, pepper, bay leaf, cloves
1 cup heavy cream

4 cups chicken stock
4 potatoes, peeled and sliced
2 cups half and half
garnish, chopped parsley or scallions

Wash the leeks well (see section on leeks) and slice them.

Combine the leeks, onions, potatoes and seasonings and the stock in a pot. Bring to a boil and simmer until the vegetables are tender, about 30 minutes. Cool.

Puree the cooled soup base in a food processor or blender. Refrigerate overnight.

Before serving, thin the base with the half and half and the cream. Correct the seasonings. Garnish with the chopped parsley or scallions and serve ice cold. Serves 8 to 10.

Chapter 7
Eggs, Cheese, Quiches and Pastry Appetizers

Tips:

How to Break an Egg
Boiling Eggs
Chopping Hard Boiled Eggs
Omelettes
Poaching Eggs
Cheese
Quiches
Cheese Swans
Strudel leaves

Recipes:

Egg Salad Hawaii
Russian Eggs
Stuffed Egg Platter
Herb Omelette
Mushroom Omelette
Spanish Omelette
Jelly Omelette
Noodle Omelette
Farmers Breakfast
Poached Eggs Provencal
Poached Eggs with Mustard Sauce
Easter Soufflé
Leftover Cheese Balls
Cheese Spread

Fried Camembert
Cottage Cheese Salad
Cottage Cheese with Herbs
Seafood Quiche
Quiche Lorraine
Zucchini Quiche
German Onion Tart
Cheese Swans
Strudels:
    Mushroom Strudel
    Spinach and Cheese Strudel

How To Break An Egg

I always use extra large eggs in all my recipes. There are two ways to break an egg, the right way and the wrong way. The wrong way is to crack the egg on a sharp surface, such as the edge of a bowl. The reason this is wrong is that you can get many small slivers of shell in your food which are hard to both see and remove. If your friends come to dinner and they bite on a piece of eggshell, they'll know you used fresh eggs. Why don't you just tell them you did.

The proper way to break an egg is to hit it on a flat surface and then open the shell. This way, if a piece of shell falls in your food, at least it will be a large one. It will be much easier to both see and remove. Illustration 15, 16, 17 and 18.

Illustration 15.

Boiling Eggs

If you want to hard boil eggs, remove them from the refrigerator ahead of time and bring them to room temperature. There is less chance of their cracking this way. Bring a pot of water to a boil and add your eggs in very carefully. The best way I have found to do this is to use a large spoon or ladle and lower them gently into the water, one at a time. When the water comes back to a boil cook the eggs for exactly ten minutes.

If some of your shells start to crack while cooking, add a little vinegar to your water immediately. The action of the vinegar will keep the whites from running all over the place.

After ten minutes, remove the pot from the heat and run some cold water over the eggs. Continue to do so until they are cool and then peel your eggs. They can be stored in salted water in the refrigerator for two or three days.

Chopping Hard Boiled Eggs

*Here is a way to chop a hard boiled egg without making a mess of your chopping board. Get yourself an egg slicer and a hard boiled egg. Make sure the egg is peeled before you put it in the slicer. Slice it one way. **Illustration 19.** Lift out the whole egg, keeping the slices together, and turn it the opposite way in the slicer. Then slice the egg in the opposite direction and you have a chopped egg. **Illustration 20.** No messy board and no messy knife.*

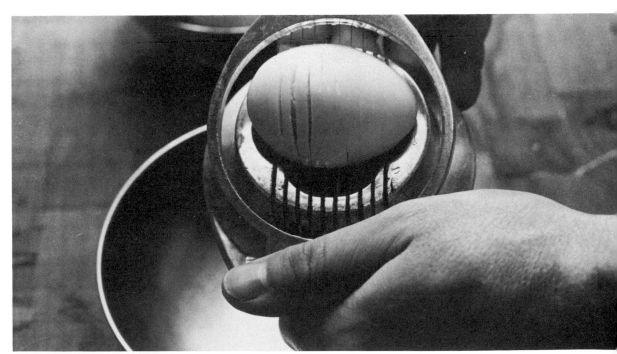

Illustration 19.

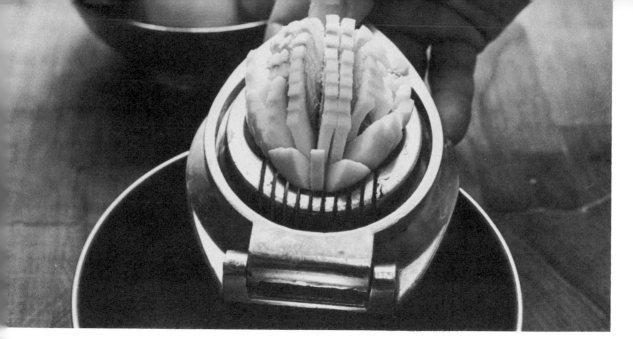

Illustration 20.

Egg Salad "Hawaii"

6 hard boiled eggs, sliced
3 slices pineapple, diced
1 pickle, diced (gerkins)
2 apples, diced
2 whole tomatoes, cut in small wedges
½ cup mayonnaise or Miracle Whip
½ cup tomato ketchup
1 tablespoon Worchestershire sauce, salt and pepper
Garnish: lettuce leaf, parsley sprig and tomato wedge

Mix all the ingredients except the eggs together and spice to taste. Fold eggs gently under so they don't fall apart. Put over lettuce leaf and garnish. Serve with toast or rye bread. Serves 4.

Russian Eggs

hard boiled eggs   cold ham salad, page 164
lettuce leaves   tomato wedges
caviar   parsley sprigs

Prepare the cold ham salad. Cut the hard boiled eggs in half. For each serving, place a mound of salad on a lettuce leaf. Place the hard boiled egg on top. Place a teaspoon of caviar on the eggs. Garnish with a tomato wedge and a parsley sprig.

Stuffed Egg Platter

To hard boil eggs, place eggs carefully into a pot of boiling salted water. Bring the water to a second boil and simmer for 10 minutes. If the eggs are cracked, add a spoon or two of vinegar to the water. Place the eggs under cold running water to let them cool off. Peel when cool. Store in a container of water in the refrigerator if not used immediately. Each recipe indicated on this page will be enough filling for 8 egg halves.

Base Mixture

yolks of 4 hard boiled eggs   2 ounces cream cheese

Mash the egg yolks and whip in the cream cheese until very soft and smooth. Mix with desired garnish and place in a pastry bag fitted with a star tube (3/8 to 1/2 inch).

Paprika Eggs

1 base mixture   1 green pepper
1 teaspoon paprika   salt, pepper

Roast the green pepper in a hot oven for about 20 minutes. Peel the pepper and puree the flesh. Mix half the paprika and the pepper puree into the egg base. Season. Pipe into 8 egg white halves. Sprinkle with remaining paprika.

Caviar Eggs

caviar   ½ cup heavy cream, whipped
dash lemon juice   1 base mixture
salt, pepper

Fold the whipped cream, lemon juice and some of the caviar into the egg base. Season. Pipe into 8 egg white halves. Garnish each one with a dollop of caviar.

Strassbourg Eggs

2 ounces foie gras   1 base mixture
salt, pepper   crushed black peppercorns

Break up the liver parfait and mix into the base mixture. Season. Pipe into 8 egg white halves. Garnish with crushed black peppercorns.

Shrimp Eggs

1 base mixture   cooked shrimp
salt, pepper   lemon juice

Puree 2 or 3 of the shrimp with the egg base. Add lemon juice and season. Pipe into 8 egg white halves. Garnish each one with a whole piece of shrimp.

Eggs With Avocado

1 ripe avocado   lemon or lime juice
salt, pepper   1 base mixture

Puree half the avocado with the egg base. Add lemon or lime juice and season. Pipe into 8 egg white halves, filling each one only half full. Place a slice of avocado in the center of the filling. Pipe the rest of the egg mixture on top.

Horseradish Eggs

1 base mixture   2 tablespoons grated fresh horseradish
salt, pepper

Season and pipe egg base into egg white halves. Place a small amount of grated fresh horseradish on top of each half.

Eggs With Onion Stuffing

1 base mixture   1 small onion, finely chopped
1-2 tablespoons butter   salt, pepper

Saute the chopped onion in the butter until soft and golden. Season. Reserve a spoon or two of the onion. Puree the rest with the egg base. Pipe into 8 egg white halves. Garnish the tops with a little sauteed onion.

Tomato Eggs

1 tomato   1 base mixture
salt, pepper

Peel, seed and dice the tomato. Squeeze out in a towel to remove all the moisture. Reserve a little for garnish. Mix the rest of the tomato with the egg base. Season. Pipe into 8 egg white halves. Place a piece of tomato on top of each for garnish.

Omelettes

The first rule for making omelettes is to always use a seasoned pan. You don't need to go out and buy a special omelette pan. Any frying pan will do, so long as it is well seasoned. If you don't use a seasoned pan, your eggs will stick and you will have scrambled eggs, not an omelette.

*I like to make my omelettes with three eggs. Being 6'3", this seems like a reasonable amount to eat. Beat the eggs lightly with a pinch of salt. Heat your frying pan and when it is hot, add a tablespoon or two of butter. When the butter is melted, pour in your eggs. **Illustration 21**. Let them sit for just a few seconds. Then, with a fork, begin to stir the eggs in a circular motion. **Illustration 22**.*

With your other hand, hold onto the handle of the pan, and shake it back and forth while tilting it away from you a little. You have to use both hands to do both things at the same time. It may feel awkward at first, but with a little practice, I'm sure you'll do just fine. The eggs will congeal towards the far end of the pan, opposite the handle, if you are shaking it properly.

*It takes less than a minute to cook an omelette. Place your filling, if you are using any, across the center of the eggs. Now you have to fold your omelette into thirds. With a fork or palette knife, loosen the edges of the omelette. Tilt the pan away from you and give it a few sharp raps. The far edge of the omelette should extend over the side of the pan a little. **Illustration 23**. Lift the edge nearest you and fold it over, one-third of the way. **Illustration 24**. Then fold over the far edge and your omelette should be neatly folded into three, like an envelope.*

*Hold your serving plate against the edge of the pan. Tilt the pan and turn the omelette out, upside down, onto the plate. **Illustration 25**. Garnish and serve immediately. Just remember, it takes much longer to read about how to make an omelette than it does to make one.*

Illustration 21.

Illustration 22.

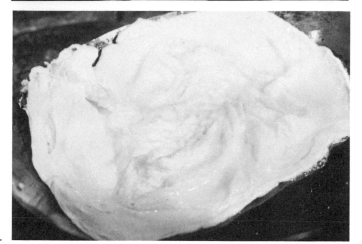

Illustration 23.

Illustration 24.

Illustration 25.

Herb Omelette

3 eggs
1 teaspoon fresh thyme
1 teaspoon fresh tarragon
salt and pepper

2 tablespoons oil
1 teaspoon chopped parsley
1 teaspoon fresh sorrel, chopped

Use whatever fresh herbs are available for this type of omelette. Chop them well and mix them with the eggs. Beat with a fork until mixed. Pour the omelette in the hot oil in the pan. Shake the pan so that the eggs run back. When all the liquid is gone, fold over the omelette. Turn upside down onto a serving plate.

Mushroom Omelette

1 cup mushrooms, sliced
1 tablespoon chopped parsley
1 three egg omelette

¼ cup white wine
salt, pepper

Cook the mushrooms in the wine until all the liquid is evaporated. Season and sprinkle with parsley.

Prepare the omelette. When firmed up, pour in the mushroom filling before you fold over the omelette.

Spanish Omelette

3 eggs
2 tomato slices
2 green pepper rings
parsley sprig

2 tablespoons oil
2 mushrooms, sliced
salt, pepper

Heat the oil in the pan. Mix the eggs. Pour the eggs into the hot pan. Set the vegetables on the eggs decoratively. Sprinkle with salt and pepper. Cook until the bottom of the omelette is brown, about 4 to 5 minutes. Turn the omelette and let it cook for a few minutes on the other side. Serve garnished with a parsley sprig.

Jelly Omelette

3 eggs (beaten)
2 tablespoons butter
2 tablespoons of your favorite jelly
¼ cup sugar

Heat the butter in an omelette pan and pour in the beaten eggs. Stir occasionally. Then lift up the pan and roll the eggs to one side of the pan. Add the jelly. Then turn the omelette onto a plate (the jelly should be on the inside - if not, try again!) Sprinkle the sugar on top of the omelette and using a very hot (glowing) piece of metal or steel, mark the sugar. Do this very quickly as the sugar will burn immediately. Don't Burn Your Fingers!

Noodle Omelette

This is a great way to use leftover noodles.

2 eggs, lightly beaten
2 slices ham, diced
salt, pepper

2 tablespoons butter
1 cup cooked noodles
2 tablespoons grated cheese

Saute the diced ham in the butter for a few minutes. Add the cooked noodles, season and continue to saute for a few minutes. Add the grated cheese and scrape the mixture to one edge of the pan.

Pour the eggs into the other side of the pan. Stir until thick. Turn the edge of the omelette over the cooked noodles. Turn out onto a serving plate and serve immediately.

Farmers Breakfast

2-3 eggs, beaten
1 large potato, cooked and sliced
3 tablespoons diced ham

2 tablespoons butter
2 tablespoons diced onion
salt, pepper

Heat the butter in a frying pan. Add the onion, potatoes and ham. Saute, stirring occasionally for 5 to 6 minutes. Push all of the ingredients to one side of the frying pan.

Pour the beaten eggs into the empty side of the pan. Shake the pan while the eggs are setting.
Turn the eggs over on themselves as you would for an omelette, turn out of the pan and serve. Season to taste with salt and pepper.

Poaching Eggs

In this country, most people poach their eggs in a wide flat pan in boiling salted water. In Europe we use a deep pot and I think it works better. Use 3 cups of water to ½ cup of wine vinegar. Bring the liquid to a boil and then turn down your heat so that the water simmers. Break your eggs open and drop them into the pot, one at a time and poach them for three to five minutes. Do not add salt to your poaching liquid for salt tends to break down the structure of the egg.

Eggs have a much nicer shape if you poach them in vinegar water. They will not taste from the vinegar, either. You can spinkle your eggs with salt when you serve them.

If you want to poach eggs and then keep them for reheating later, poach them for only three minutes. Store them in the refrigerator in cold salted water. Then to warm them, drop them into boiling salted water for just a minute or two to heat them through.

Poached Eggs Provencal

1 large tomato, skinned, seeded and diced	butter
1 small onion, chopped	1 clove garlic, chopped
1 tablespoon chopped parsley	4 raw eggs
salt, pepper	4 tablespoons heavy cream

Saute the onion in butter until soft. Add the garlic and the tomato and cook for a few minutes. Season with salt and pepper and add the parsley.

Butter well 4 individual ramekins. Place a spoonful of the tomato mixture in the bottom of each dish. Break a raw egg carefully into each ramekin. Cover with a tablespoon of cream.

Bake covered in a bain marie, either on top of the stove or in a moderate oven for about 8 minutes or until the eggs are set. Serve at once.

Poached Eggs With Mustard Sauce

Per person: ½ tomato	Garnishes: lettuce leaves
1 poached egg	chopped hard boiled egg white
mustard sauce, page 77	white
vinegar water for poaching	parsley, chopped

Hollow out the tomato halves and drain.

Poach the eggs in the vinegar water, for about 5 minutes. See the section on poaching eggs for the proper way to do this. Drain them well and trim off any extra white.

Place the egg in the tomato shell and place on top of a lettuce leaf. Top the egg with the mustard sauce. Sprinkle with chopped hard boiled egg whites and chopped parsley. Serve cold.

Easter Soufflé

prepare triple the amount of the recipe for spinach with ancovies and onions, page 42.

3 tablespoons butter	8 poached eggs, page 100.
3 tablespoons flour	1½ cups milk
salt, pepper	4 egg yolks
½ cup grated swiss cheese	5 egg whites
	¼ cup plus 2 tablespoons grated parmesan cheese

Butter a 1½ quart glass souffle dish. Place the spinach on the bottom of the dish. With a spoon, make indentations in the spinach to form a bed for the eggs. Place a poached egg into each hollow.

Prepare the souffle base by making a roux with the butter and the flour. Remove from the heat and let cool a little. Heat the milk and add the hot milk to the cooled roux, stirring. Cook until thickened.

Remove from the heat and add in the egg yolks, one at a time. Season and stir in the grated swiss cheese and the ¼ cup parmesan cheese. Let cool.

Beat the egg whites stiffly and fold into the souffle base mixture. Pour over the spinach and eggs in the souffle dish and sprinkle with the remaining parmesan cheese. Bake in a 375⁰ oven for about 20 minutes. Serves at once. Serves 8.

Cheese

When you serve a cheese platter to your guests try to limit the selection to just a few kinds, perhaps two or three. If you fill the plate with 5 or 6 cheeses, you'll have a lot of bits and pieces left over. People tend to eat only one kind of cheese when they see so many, rather than tasting two or three of them.

What I would serve, and do in my restaurant, is a selection of three cheeses. First a brie, then a goat cheese and one other kind.

Brie is one of my favorite cheeses. There are several ways to tell if a brie is ready to eat. The rind should be white with no dark or moldy spots on the outside. The inside of the cheese should be a solid ivory color. There should not be a white line through the middle of the cheese. A white core means the brie was not ripened enough before it was cut. Smell the cheese, if it has a strong, or ammonia like odor, it is overripe.

There are usually 10 or 15 different goat cheeses available in a good cheese store. Ask to taste a few of them if goat cheese is unfamiliar to you. Some are very mild and some are very sharp or "goaty" in flavor. What you buy all depends on what you like. Chevre is the french word for goat. If the label has "chevre" on it, then you know you are buying a goat cheese. I personally like boucheron and montrachet, but you might prefer another kind.

I would serve one other kind of cheese, a little bit sharper in flavor than the other two. Here are some suggestions ... a muenster, a beaumont, an essrom or even a stilton. Don't be embarrassed about asking for a taste of cheese before you buy. I can understand the owner saying no if you ask to taste 15 or 20 cheeses. But, most of the time, they are happy to help you learn about cheese, for it helps their business, too.

In order to bring out the flavor of any cheese, serve it at room temperature. If it is too cold, it will not taste right. Take it out of your refrigerator at least an hour before serving time. And don't forget to serve it with some nice french bread or crackers and a good bottle of wine.

The best way to store whole pieces of cheese is to wrap them individually in plastic wrap and store them in the refrigerator. We have included a few recipes for those bits and pieces of cheese you may have left over, so that they won't go to waste.

I also like to grate my own cheese for cooking. This way you know exactly what you have and do not have to depend on labels that aren't always clear as to the contents of the container. Store your grated cheese in a covered jar in the refrigerator.

Leftover Cheese Balls

Use any leftover cheese and cut into small pieces, about 1¼ inch. Run through food processor. If all the cheeses are hard, you may add a little butter at room temperature. When mixture is a nice paste, remove from the food processor and mold into small balls. Roll cheese balls in chopped walnuts or any other nuts, or even crumbled pumpernickle bread. Refrigerate until ready to serve. I hope you enjoy this recipe!

Cheese Spread

1 cup hard cheese	½ cup soft cheese
½ cup butter	2-3 tablespoons brandy

Chop the hard or stale cheese into large pieces. Place in a food processor or blender. Grind until finely chopped.

Add the soft cheese, such as cream cheese or any leftover soft or semisoft cheese. Add the butter and the brandy and blend until a paste is formed. Refrigerate until very firm.

Form into balls and roll in chopped nuts or parsley.

Fried Camembert

1 not too ripe wheel of camembert
2 eggs beaten with 1 tablespoon
    water
oil for frying

flour for dredging
breadcrumbs for dredging

Cut the cheese into slices. Dip first into the flour, then the egg wash and then the breadcrumbs. Chill the coated cheese.

Heat the oil. Add the coated cheese slices carefully, turning once to brown. They will take only a minute or two to cook, do not overcook. Drain well on paper towels and place on a serving platter. Serve immediately. Serve with fried parsley.

Cottage Cheese

Americans love cottage cheese perhaps because they always think of it as diet food. It is low in calories and very nutritious. In case you get tired of your cottage cheese on a lettuce leaf surrounded with fruit as it always seems to be, here are a few interesting recipes for you to try.

Cottage Cheese Salad

1 carrot, julienned
1½ cups cottage cheese
juice of ½ lemon

¼ cup toasted almond slices
2-3 tablespoons honey

Mix all the ingredients together and serve on a bed of lettuce. Served chilled. Serves 2 to 3.

Cottage Cheese With Herbs

½ green pepper, diced
2 tablespoons chopped parsley
salt, pepper

1 pimento, diced
1 cup cottage cheese

Mix all ingredients and season to taste. Serve, chilled, on a lettuce leaf. Serves 1 to 2.

Quiches

Quiche can be eaten as an appetizer at dinnertime or as a main course for lunch. I even like to eat them for breakfast or brunch, especially with a glass of wine.

There are an infinite variety of quiches that you can make. I would, however, suggest that you bake your crust blind for most of them. Baking a crust blind does not mean that you should put it in the oven and then close your eyes. It means you pre-bake your empty crust part way so that it doesn't see the oven. Place a layer of aluminum foil over the unbaked crust and then fill it with some weights. Bake it for 10 to 15 minutes, just until the crust sets. Remove the crust from the oven and take off both the foil and the weights.

Then fill your crust and proceed with your recipe. Pre-baking your crust this way will prevent it from becoming soggy.

Seafood Quiche

Crust:

1¼ cups flour	½ cup butter
pinch of salt	2-3 tablespoons cold water

Mix the flour and the salt with the butter until small crumbs are formed. Add in enough water to form a dough. Chill. Roll out the dough and place in a floured and buttered quiche pan with a removable bottom. Bake blind in a 375⁰ oven for 15 minutes. Remove from the oven and let cool.

Filling:

1 cup cooked shrimp	3-4 ounces scallops, cooked
3-4 ounces cooked fillets of sole	1¼ cups heavy cream
3 eggs	salt, pepper
½ cup grated swiss cheese	

Cut the fish and seafood into bite sized pieces. Arrange the seafood around the bottom of the pastry. Mix the eggs, salt, pepper and cream together. Pour into the shell over the seafood. Sprinkle the top of the quiche with the grated cheese. Bake in a 375⁰ oven for 30 minutes or until the filling is set. Serve warm. Serves 10-12.

Quiche Lorraine

1 recipe piecrust (same as seafood quiche)	1¼ cups heavy cream
	chopped parsley
½ cup diced bacon	1 cup diced onion
½ cup grated swiss or parmesan cheese	3 eggs
	salt, pepper

Saute the bacon and the onion together. Drain and place in the bottom of the pre-baked crust. Mix the eggs, cream, parsley and salt and pepper together. Pour into the crust. Sprinkle with the grated cheese.

Bake in a 375⁰ oven for 30 minutes or until the filling is set. Serve warm and enjoy. Serves 10 to 12.

Zucchini Quiche

1 crust recipe, see seafood quiche
6 medium zucchini
2 eggs plus 1 egg yolk
salt, pepper

2 tablespoons butter
1 cup heavy cream
1 heaping teaspoon marjoram

Wash but do not peel the zucchini. Put through the large blade of a mouli-julienne or the julienne blade of a food processor. Salt in layers in a bowl. Let sit for 30 minutes. Squeeze out the moisture very well. Saute the zucchini in butter for 3-4 minutes, or until dry. Mix together eggs, yolk, cream and seasonings. Add the sauteed zucchini, stir well. Fill crust and bake in a 400° oven for about 35 minutes or until set. Let sit for a few minutes before slicing.

Both the filling and the crust may be prepared ahead of time if desired. Pour the filling into the partially baked crust and finish baking just before serving. Serves 10 to 12.

German Onion Tart

Crust:

2½ to 3 cups flour
1 teaspoon salt
1 egg

1 teaspoon baking powder
½ cup butter
3 tablespoons sour cream

Mix two and one-half cups of the flour with the salt and the baking powder. Work the butter into the flour mixture until crumbly.

Mix together the egg and the sour cream. Work this into the dough. If more flour is needed to make a firm dough, use the additional one-half cup. Chill the dough.

Roll the dough into a rectangle and place on a buttered jelly-roll pan or 2 nine inch pie tins.

Filling:

1½ pounds onions, sliced finely
½ cup sour cream
salt, pepper, caraway seeds
2 tablespoons flour

1 egg plus 1 egg yolk
3-4 tablespoons butter
4 slices diced bacon

Heat the butter in a large frying pan. Add the bacon, onions, salt, pepper and caraway seeds. Cover and steam until the onions are very tender.

Sprinkle the flour over the onions and mix in. Stir together the sour cream, egg and egg yolk and add to the onion mixture. Cook and stir for a few minutes. Correct the seasonings.

Pour into the crust and bake in a 400° oven for 30 minutes or until the crust is done and the top is browned.

Serve hot or at room temperature. Serves 12 to 16.

Cheese Swans

The cheese swans in this recipe are made out of pate a choux. Pate a choux, or cream puff dough, is really very easy to make and can be used for lots of desserts and appetizers.

When you make the swans, just be sure to make some extra necks. The reason for this is that the necks break very easily. You'll have trouble serving twelve swans if you only have ten necks.

If you want to use the swans for dessert, just leave the swiss cheese out of the dough and ingrease the sugar to one tablespoon. The swans can be filled with sweetened whipped cream and make a very pretty dessert.

Cheese Swans

1 cup flour	4 ounces butter
pinch sugar, pinch salt	4 eggs
1 cup water	1 to 2 ounces grated swiss cheese

Pate a choux:

Place the butter and the water in a saucepan and heat until boiling. Add the flour, sugar and salt all at once. Stir over heat for a few minutes until the dough forms a ball and is dry.

Remove the pot from the heat and beat in the eggs, one at a time. Beat well after each egg is added. Beat in the swiss cheese.

You will need two pastry bags, one fitted with a small round tip (¼ inch) and the other fitted with a star tube (½ inch). Divide the dough, placing two-thirds into the bag fitted with the star tube and one-third into the other bag. With the star tube, pipe small oval shapes for the bodies onto a greased baking sheet. Pipe S shapes for the heads and necks, using the small round tube. **Illustration 26**. Remember to make a few extra necks. Bake in a 400⁰ oven until puffed, brown and dry. The necks will bake faster than the bodies. Remove them when they are done.

When cool, cut the bodies in half lengthwise. Cut the top piece into quarters, these will be the wings. **Illustration 27**. Pipe the filling into the bodies of the swans. Place the two wings facing towards the back and the neck onto the front of the swans. Makes ten to twelve swans.

Filling

16 ounces cream cheese	4 tablespoons finely chopped scallions

Whip the cheese in a mixer until it is light and fluffy. Fold in the finely chopped scallions. Use a pastry tube to fill the swans.

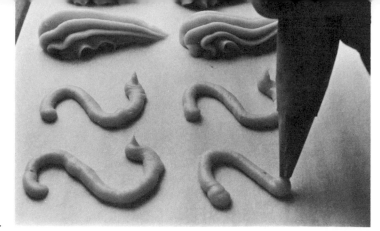

Illustration 26.

Illustration 27.

Strudel Leaves

You can buy strudel or filo leaves in almost any cheese or gourmet food store. They come in refrigerated packs and will keep well for a few weeks if properly wrapped. Open the box and look at the leaves before you buy them. If they look dried out, they are too old and will be very difficult to handle. They should look soft and pliable. Try not to buy the leaves frozen, as they will be much harder to handle.

There are a few tricks to handling these leaves so that they won't give you any trouble. First, you must keep the leaves covered at all times. When they remain in the air for even just a few minutes, they will dry out and crumble apart. The best way to do this is to spread out a clean dry towel. Open the package and spread the leaves onto this towel. Then cover them with a second dry towel. If you put back this top towel after you remove each leaf, they shouldn't dry out on you.

If you like your strudel to have a nice crunchy taste, use four layers of leaves. Spread each layer with a little melted butter (use a pastry brush, it's the easiest way) and sprinkle with some toasted breadcrumbs. This will keep the layers separate as they bake and make them taste crisper. You won't know the bread-crumbs are there after the strudel is baked.

There is an easy way to roll strudel, but you have to dirty another towel. Put a clean dry towel in front of you and layer the leaves onto this towel. Place *your filling about two inches from the top of the leaves, lengthwise. Fold over the top flap, tuck in the ends and roll, using the towel as leverage to pull the dough towards you. Your roll will be nice and tight this way. Place on a buttered baking sheet and brush with lots of melted butter.*

There is one more trick we have discovered in our cooking classes. We pre-cut the strudel a little before baking. It is then much easier to slice the strudel into serving portions after it is baked. Use a sharp serrated knife and gently slice through the top of the leaves, about one-third of the way down. The filling does not come out and the leaves stay together better.

You can get your strudel filled and completely ready to bake a few hours ahead of time. Just make sure you keep your baking pans well covered so that the dough does not dry out.

If you have any leaves left over, don't throw them out. You can keep them in the refrigerator for two or three weeks. Roll the leaves back up and wrap them well with clear plastic wrap. Then place them in a plastic bag and seal. Strudel or filo leaves can also be frozen. Again, wrap them well. To use the leaves, defrost them for twenty-four hours in the refrigerator. They will be a little harder to handle once they have been frozen, buy they are usable.

Mushroom Strudel

1 small onion, chopped fine	1 pound mushrooms, chopped fine
one 8 ounce package cream cheese	1 cup melted butter
salt, pepper	1 cup toasted breadcrumbs
8 strudel or filo leaves	

Cook the onion in 2 tablespoons of butter for a few minutes. Add the mushrooms and salt and pepper to taste. Cook, stirring occasionally, until the mixture is dry. Let the mushrooms cool for a few minutes, then mix in the cream cheese.

Spread out the strudel dough, keeping it covered with a towel. Place one layer in front of you on a clean towel. Brush with melted butter and sprinkle with breadcrumbs. Repeat 3 more times, for a total of 4 layers, leaving the top layer plain.

Make a row with one-half of the mushroom mixture about 2 inches from one side of the leaves. Roll the small flap over the filling. Fold in the sides and roll up the rest of the leaves, using the towel as leverage to put the strudel together. Place on a buttered baking sheet and brush with melted butter. Slice the strudel one-third of the way down into serving sized pieces. Repeat with the rest of the leaves and the filling.

Bake in a 400° oven until brown and crisp, about 25 to 30 minutes. Slice and serve warm. Serves 12.

Spinach And Cheese Strudel

1 onion, finely chopped
2 tablespoons butter plus melted
    butter
2 eggs
½ cup grated gruyere cheese
1-2 tablespoons flour, if needed

one 15 ounce container ricotta cheese
one 10 ounce package frozen spinach
dried breadcrumbs
salt, pepper, nutmeg
8 sheets filo or strudel leaves

Parboil the spinach in boiling salted water. Refresh, drain and squeeze dry. Chop very fine.

Cook the onion in the 2 tablespoons of butter. Season. Add the spinach and cook until dry.

Mix the spinach into the ricotta cheese. Add the eggs and the gruyere cheese and mix. Correct the seasonings. If the mixture seems runny, stir in a little flour.

Spread out the filo leaves. Keep covered with a towel.

Place one layer in front of you on a clean towel. Brush with melted butter and sprinkle with a thin layer of breadcrumbs. Repeat 3 more times for a total of 4 layers. Leave the top layer plain.

Make a row with one-half of the filling about 2 inches from one side of the leaves. Roll up the bottom of the filo over the filling. Fold in the sides and roll up the rest of the dough, using a towel as leverage to pull the roll tight.

Place on a buttered baking sheet. Brush the top of the roll with melted butter. Slice as described in section on strudel leaves.

Repeat process with the rest of the leaves and the filling.

Bake in a 400° oven until brown and crisp, about 25 to 30 minutes. Serve warm, in slices. Serves 12 to 16.

TIMETABLE FOR COOKING FISH

Cooking method and market form	Approximate ready-to-cook weight or thickness	Cooking temperature	Approximate cooking time in minutes
BAKING			
Dressed	3 pounds	350° F.	45 to 60
Pan-dressed	3 pounds	350° F.	25 to 30
Fillets or steaks	2 pounds	350° F.	20 to 25
Portions	2 pounds	400° F.	15 to 20
Sticks	2¼ pounds	400° F.	15 to 20
BROILING			
Pan-dressed	3 pounds		10 to 16[1]
Fillets or steaks	½ to 1 inch		10 to 15
Portions	3/8 to ½ inch		10 to 15
Sticks	3/8 to ½ inch		10 to 15
CHARCOAL BROILING			
Pan-dressed	3 pounds	Moderate	10 to 16[1]
Fillets or steaks	½ to 1 inch	Moderate	10 to 16[1]
Portions	3/8 to ½ inch	Moderate	8 to 10[1]
Sticks	3/8 to ½	Moderate	8 to 10[1]
DEEP—FAT FRYING			
Pan-dressed	3 pounds	350° F.	3 to 5
Fillets or steaks	½ to 1 inch	350° F.	3 to 5
Portions	3/8 to ½ inch	350° F.	3 to 5
Sticks	3/8 to ½ inch	350° F.	3 to 5
OVEN—FRYING			
Pan-dressed	3 pounds	500° F.	15 to 20
Fillets or steaks	½ to 1 inch	500° F.	10 to 15
PAN—FRYING			
Pan-dressed	3 pounds	Moderate	8 to 10[1]
Fillets or steaks	½ to 1 inch	Moderate	8 to 10[1]
Portions	3/8 to ½ inch	Moderate	8 to 10[1]
Sticks	3/8 to ½ inch	Moderate	8 to 10[1]
POACHING			
Fillets or steaks	2 pounds	Simmer	5 to 10
STEAMING			
Fillets or steaks	2 pounds	Boil	5 to 10

[1] Turn once.

Chapter 8

Fish

Tips:

Timetable for cooking fish.

Cooking en papillote

Sautéed fish

Recipes:

Hot

    Fish and Vegetables en papillote

    Fish with Asparagus en papillote

    Bluefish on a grill

    Sautéed Fish*

    Sautéed Scallops

    Baked Fish with Vegetables*

    Baked Stuffed Fish

    Fish Timbale

    Fish - Nouvelle Cuisine

    Fish Mousse

Cold

    Cold Fish Salad

    Cold Crabmeat Salad

    Herring Salad

    Tuna Salad

    Tuna Spread

Fish

If fish has a fishy smell, it is not fresh. Really fresh fish does not have a fishy odor, it has a rather sweet smell.

When you buy whole fish there are several ways, besides the smell, to tell if it is fresh or not. The eyes should be clear and not cloudy or glazed looking. The scales should also have a shine to them. Check the gills, they should be bright red in color. If they are very dark or brownish looking, your fish is old.

When you buy a fillet of fish, much the same rules apply. First, it should smell good. The color of the flesh should be iridescent, not dull. If you are able to touch the fillets, they should feel very firm and resistant to the gentle pressure of your fingers. If they are very soft and fleshy to the touch, chances are the fillets have been around for a while.

The best way to eat fish is to have a fisherman in the family … catch and eat it the same day. Just make sure the fish is gutted as soon as it is caught. Don't store it for more than two or three hours or freeze it with the guts still inside, for they will change the taste of the fish.

To keep fish in your refrigerator, either whole fish or fillets, wrap it in plastic wrap and store it in the coldest part of your box. Even better, put it into a container filled with ice cubes. Just make sure the fish is wrapped first or it will become waterlogged and have no flavor at all when cooked.

Cooking En Papillote

Cooking en papillote, or in a pocket, is a nice way to prepare meat or fish. You can even use this method for poaching a whole fish and you won't need to buy a fish poacher. This technique is used more frequently is Europe than in the United States. Most recipes call for parchment paper to wrap the food. This is a very thick treated paper which is sometimes hard to find. I have found that a piece of heavy duty aluminum foil works just as well.

Start with a nice large piece of foil, maybe three times the size of what you intend to wrap. Place your fish or meat on the first third of the foil. Add vegetables, wine, lemon juice, seasonings, whatever you desire to the meat or fish. If you want to use a vegetable that has to cook for a long amount of time, just make sure that you parboil it first.

*Then fold your foil over, much like a pocket and roll the edges up tight. To do this, place the long ends of the foil together and fold them over once to form a tight seal. **Illustration 28.** Repeat this folding and rolling two more times. **Illustration 29.** Then fold the two sides in the same way, sealing them tightly. **Illustration 30.** Make sure you don't puncture the foil, for your package has to be airtight in order to work. When you place your papillote in a hot oven, steam will be generated inside the packet and soon it will begin to blow up like a balloon. What actually takes place is a simultaneous steaming and* *poaching process, which emanates from the little bit of liquid that is trapped.*

Cooking en papillote works equally well on a barbeque or or outdoor grill as it does in the oven. It's a great way to keep your kitchen cool in the summer and you'll have no pots or pans to wash after dinner.

Be very careful when you slit open the packet to serve the contents. The steam inside is very hot and can burn. So remember to keep your face out of the way when you first open the papillote.

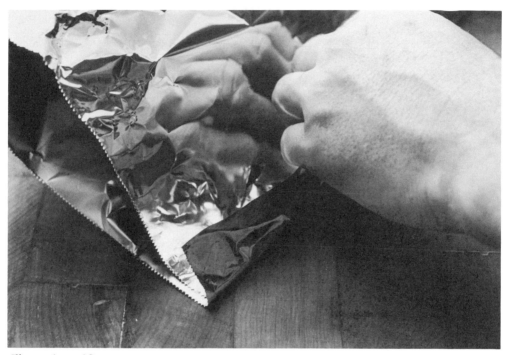

Illustration   28.

Illustration   29.

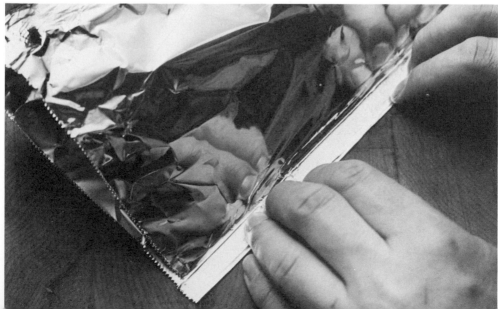

Illustration 30.

Fish And Vegetables En Papillote

6 flounder fillets	juice of 1 lemon
1 carrot, sliced	1 stalk celery, sliced
parsley sprigs	2 tomatoes, peeled, seeded and diced
salt and pepper	few spoons white wine

Spread out a large piece of aluminum foil. Place the fish on the foil and add the vegetables, seasonings and wine. Fold over the long end of the foil and seal the edges very well by folding several times, page 112. Place on a baking sheet and bake in a 350⁰ oven for 35 to 45 minutes. The packet should swell up about 10 minutes before the fish is done.

Alternate method: Place packet in a frying pan with a little oil in the bottom and cook on top of the stove. Cook for about 15 minutes, or until the packet is well puffed.

Fish With Asparagus En Papillote

6 fillets of flounder	juice of 1 lemon
2 tomatoes, peeled, seeded and diced	6-8 asparagus spears
salt, pepper	few sprigs parsley
3 tablespoons white wine	4 tablespoons melted butter

Spread out a large piece of aluminum foil and butter the middle. Roll the fish, skin side in, and place on the buttered foil.

Place the asparagus and tomato around the fish. Sprinkle with the white wine, season, and drizzle some melted butter on top. Fold the foil and seal well, page 112.

Place on a baking sheet and bake in a 350⁰ oven for 35 to 45 minutes. The packet should swell up about 10 minutes before the fish is done.

Alternate method: Pour a little oil in the bottom of a frying pan. Place the foil packet in the pan and cook on top of the stove for about 15 minutes, or until well puffed.

Bluefish On A Grill

1 fillet of bluefish
1 clove garlic, sliced thin
2 parsley sprigs
salt, pepper

6 onion rings
4 slices carrot
juice of 1 lemon

Tear off a large sheet of heavy aluminum foil. Place the fish at one end of the foil. Cover the fish with the vegetables. Sprinkle on the lemon juice and season with salt and pepper. Fold over the long end of the foil and seal the edges very well by folding in several times. Cook for 25 minutes on a grill, seam side up. The packet should swell up about 10 minutes before the fish is done.

Remove fish and vegetables from the packet and serve. Be careful when you cut open the foil, as there is a lot of steam inside and you don't want to get this in your face.

Sautéed Fish

Many times, in this country, people tend to overcook their fish. A fish fillet should take only a few minutes to cook. It should still be juicy and firm, not totally dried out and flaky. Follow this recipe for sauteed fish and I'm sure you will love the results.

Sautéed Fish*

1 whole fillet of flounder or sole
flour for dredging
salt

1 tablespoon of parsley, chopped
juice of ½ lemon
3-4 tablespoons of butter

Melt the butter in a frying pan. Cut the fillet in half lengthwise. Salt and dredge the fillet in flour. Saute for a few minutes on each side. Remove the fish from the pan and place on a serving dish.

Add the chopped parsley and lemon juice to the remaining butter in the pan. Swirl and pour over the fish.

Sauteed Scallops

6-8 ounces sea scallops
lemon juice
chopped parsley

butter
salt, pepper

Heat a few spoons of butter. Saute the scallops for just a few minutes in the hot butter, tossing. While they are cooking, season them with the salt and pepper. Add the lemon juice and the chopped parsley and serve immediately. Serves one or two.

Baked Fish With Vegetables*

1 fillet of fish (flounder, sole, etc.)
1 carrot, peeled and sliced in julienne
1 stalk of celery cut in julienne
1 small onion, cut in julienne
½ cup sliced mushrooms

juice of one lemon
1 tablespoon butter
flour for dredging fish
salt and pepper

Heat the butter in a small saute pan. Dredge the fish in the flour and place in the pan. Season and saute for approximately one minute on each side, then remove from the pan and keep on a plate. Saute all the other vegetables in the remaining butter for about 4-5 minutes. Place on an ovenproof pan, place the fish on top and bake at 375 degrees for about 8 minutes or until done.
   Good Appetite!

Baked Stuffed Fish

1 whole fish, about 3 pound, striped
   bass, red snapper or sea trout
1 cup white wine
½ cup heavy cream

salt, pepper
1 cup fish stock or water
2 tablespoons chopped parsley

Stuffing:
½ pound mushrooms, sliced
1 cup breadcrumbs
1-2 cloves garlic, crushed
salt, pepper
dash Pernod

½ cup butter
2 tablespoons chopped parsley
juice of ½ lemon
1 egg

First make the stuffing. Saute the mushrooms and garlic in a little of the butter. Cool a little. Mix in the breadcrumbs, egg, lemon juice, the rest of the butter, parsley, salt, pepper and Pernod. Reserve. Clean and bone the fish. Sprinkle the cavity with salt and pepper. Stuff with the mushroom filling. Place in a baking pan. Pour in the white wine and the fish stock. Bake in a 375⁰ oven until fish is done, about 30 minutes.
   Remove the fish from the baking pan to a serving platter and keep warm. Pour the liquid from the baking pan into a small saucepan. Add the heavy cream and reduce the sauce. Add the chopped parsley, pour over the fish and serve hot. Serves 6 to 8.

Fish Timbale

6 ounces fillet of fish (flounder, fluke or sole)
2 egg whites
4 tablespoons clarified butter
2 slices of white bread, soaked in water and firmly squeezed dry
salt and pepper to taste
few pistachio nuts (optional)

Put the fish fillet in the food processor and run it until the fish seems like a paste or puree. Add the egg whites, bread, clarified butter and salt and pepper. Mix for a few more seconds and then remove from the machine. Add pistachio nuts if desired.

Grease some timbale molds and put the mousse in the molds. Poach in a water bath or bain marie in the oven at 325 degrees for approximately 35 minutes or until done. Serves 4 to 6.

Fish - Nouvelle Cuisine

6 slices sole or fluke
2-3 tablespoons chopped shallots
1 cup white wine
½ cup heavy cream
2 tablespoons butter
2 tablespoons chopped parsley

1 recipe fish mousse (follows)
whites of 2 leeks
2 carrots
2 stalks celery
salt, pepper

Julienne the leeks, carrots and celery finely. Blanch them in boiling salted water until barely tender. Refresh and reserve.

Make the fish mousse. Spread a little of the mousse on top of each fillet.

Butter a saute pan. Sprinkle with the shallots. Place the fish, mousse side up, in the pan. Add the white wine. Poach on top of the stove until just barely cooked, about 8 to 10 minutes, depending on the thickness of the fillets. Drain the liquid from the pan off into a small saucepan. Reduce the liquid by half its volume. Add the heavy cream and again reduce by half. Season to taste.

In a separate pan saute the julienned vegetables in the 2 tablespoons of butter until they are hot and crisp. Place on a serving plate. Arrange the fish fillets over the julienned vegetables. Pour the sauce over the fish, sprinkle with the parsley and serve immediately. Serves 6.

Fish Mousse

6 ounces fluke or flounder
2 egg whites
salt, pepper

2 ounces butter
½ cup heavy cream, lightly whipped

Place the fish in a food processor or blender and grind. With the motor on, add the egg whites and the butter. Season to taste. Remove from the machine and chill. When cold, fold in the lightly beaten cream.

Cold Fish Dishes

Here are some interesting cold fish dishes. First a fish salad to help you use up those leftovers. It makes a great lunch or even a nice light dinner in the summertime.

Then I'll give you a few new ways to give some variety to tuna fish.

Cold Fish Salad

1 pound cooked fish in chunks
1 green pepper, diced
1 stalk celery, diced
½ cup mayonnaise
lemon juice

¼ cup chopped onion
¼ cup diced pimento
1 small carrot, grated
salt, pepper

Any firm fleshed white meat fish can be used.

Finely chop all the vegetables. Grate the carrot. Combine all the vegetables with the mayonnaise. Add the fish and mix carefully. Season to taste with the salt, pepper and lemon juice.

Chill and serve on a lettuce leaf garnished with chopped parsley and a tomato slice or wedge.

Vegetables can be chopped in a food processor. Mix fish in by hand.

Cold Crabmeat Salad

1 can crabmeat
dill cocktail sauce, page 77.
lettuce

4-5 water chestnuts
dill sprigs, garnish

Make the dill cocktail sauce. Slice the water chestnuts thinly. Shred the lettuce to form a bedding for the salad.

Place the lettuce on the bottom of serving plates or glasses. Mix the crabmeat, the water chestnuts and the dressing gently. Spoon over the lettuce. Top with a dill sprig and serve chilled. Serves 4 to 6.

Herring Salad

1 cup apple, chopped
1 cup onions, chopped
½ cup red beets, diced
¼ cup salad oil

1 large pickle, chopped
1 cup herring fillets, diced
¼ cup red wine vinegar

Chop and mix the salad ingredients. Toss with the oil and vinegar. Serve cold. Serves 6 to 8.

Tuna Salad

1 7-ounce can of tuna
½ cup chopped onion
½ cup sliced cucumbers
½ cup sliced tomato

¼ cup sliced radishes
ketchup to taste
salt and pepper

Mix together all the ingredients, adding ketchup, salt and pepper to taste. Eat well chilled and enjoy!

Tuna Spread

1 7-ounce can tuna fish
½ cup chopped onion
1 teaspoon of paprika
salt and white pepper

1-2 tablespoons of mayonnaise
½ cup chopped celery
few pimentos

Mix all the ingredients together to make this tuna spread.

Tips:

How to Buy Meat

Cutting and Tenderizing Meat

Trussing Meat

Roasting Meat

Temperature charts for pork

Resting Meat

Pork chart

Veal chart

Temperature charts for veal

Boning a Breast of Veal

Cutting a Pocket in a Breast of Veal

Lamb chart

Temperature charts for lamb

Beef chart

Temperature charts for beef

Marinating Meats

Shish-Kabobs

Meat Loaf

Beef Tartare

Chapter 9
Meat

Recipes:

Cold Pork with Prunes and Apples

Hot Pork with Prunes

Pork Robert

Roast Pork Shoulder

Sautéed Pork Budapest

Schweinepfeffer

Stuffed Boned Breast of Veal
    with Bread Stuffing

Assiette Diplomat*

Ragout Fin au gratin

Roast Veal Shank

Ossobuco

Swiss Veal Assiette

Veal Birds

Veal Piccata

Veal Pojarski with Brown
    Cream Sauce

Lamb and Lima Beans*

Lamb Stew

Scotch Lamb

Stuffed Lamb Shoulder

Beef Esterhazy

Beef Rouladen

Beef Stroganoff

Braised Beef*

Brisket with Potatoes

Peppered Beef

Sauerbraten

Shish-Kabobs

Meat Loaf

Stuffed Eggplant

Stuffed Cabbage Leaves

Stuffed Peppers

Meat Pate or Spread

Beef Salad

Cold Meat Plate

Rolled Sandwiches

Cold Ham Salad

Ham Rolls with Horseradish
    Cream

Beef Tartare

*Indicates Dinner for One

How To Buy Meat

Beef

Good beef should be bright red in color with some marblization or fat layers present on the inside of the meat. The outside fat layer, if there is one, should be white to a very light yellow in color.

There are many different grades of meat; prime, choice, good, etc. The lower the grade of meat, the less marblization it has. Prime meat contains the most fat, therefore it is the most tender when cooked and of course, the most expensive to buy. Illustration 31. However, it's not always the healthiest cut of meat to eat.

Choice meat contains a little less marblization and is a little tougher, but it has more flavor and is better for you. And it costs less, too.

Lamb

Lamb is a dark meat. Fresh lamb should be dark red in color. The outside fat layer should be very white. Lamb does not have much marblization even though it is graded prime, choice and good.

Pork

Fresh pork meat should have a pinkish color and the fat layer should be very white. The meat should have a fresh smell. When you buy pork loin or pork roast, make sure the outside skin is removed. Sometimes up to one-third of a loin roast can be fat. This is too much, so before you cook it, either you or your butcher should remove some of the fat.

Veal

Good veal is difficult to buy in this country. Milk-fed veal is the whitest in color, the most tender, and the best quality you can buy. Veal should be light pink in color, have very little fat, and no skin at all. Each muscle of the veal has a different degree of tenderness and should be cooked differently. So make sure, before you buy your meat, you know what part of the animal it comes from.

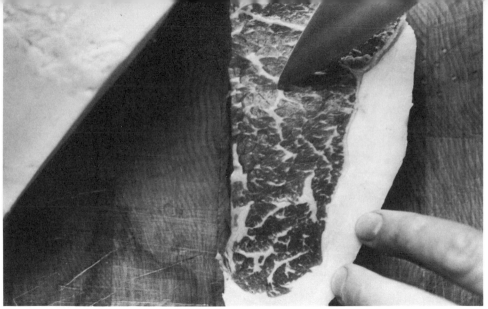

Illustration 31.

Cutting And Tenderizing Meat

All raw meat should be cut against the grain. I like to tenderize meat that I saute by pounding it a little before cooking. Don't hammer away like a mad butcher and try to double the size of your meat. Just pound it enough to break down some of the cell structure. This will make the meat more tender to eat.
Illustration 32.

When your meat is cut against the grain and then cooked, you eat it with the grain. This makes it much easier to both cut and chew.

Also, pound the meat right before cooking. If you pound the meat and let it sit around for a few hours, it will loose too much moisture.

Dredge your meat in a little flour only right before you saute it, for if you flour your meat and then let it sit around, your meat will be soggy.

Illustration 32.

Trussing Meat

If you want to roast a piece of meat that has a very uneven shape, truss or tie it first. The more even in width the roast is, the more evenly it will cook. Trussing a roast keeps it from expanding and losing its shape. Sometimes I tie an evenly shaped piece of meat just to make sure it stays that way. Just remember to remove the strings before you serve the roast, they're difficult to chew.

It's always hard to guess how much string you will need, somehow I usually get too much or too little. If, when you tie your meat, you find that you don't have enough string, don't remove what you have done and start again. Simply knot on an extra piece and continue. No one will see or know about the extra knot unless you tell them.

Starting at one end of the meat, loop the string around and tie a knot, leaving a few inches of one end of the string free. Then at intervals of approximately two inches, form circular loops of string around the meat and hold it in place by using a slip knot.

To tie a slip knot, just bring the string under and around the meat. Hold the top straight part of the string in your left hand. Illustration 33. With your right hand, form a knot by looping the other end of the string over, around and through this straight piece. Illustration 34. Pull the knot tight with your right hand while holding the string steady with your left hand. Illustration 35. You want to tighten the loop so that it holds firmly around the meat. Continue to repeat this process until you reach the end of the meat, then turn it upside down. Pull the string under and around each circular loop so that it forms a straight line across the center of the meat. Illustration 36. When you reach the end where you started, tie a knot, using the free end of the string you left previously. Illustration 37. Trussing the meat this way will hold it evenly while it cooks.

Illustration 33.

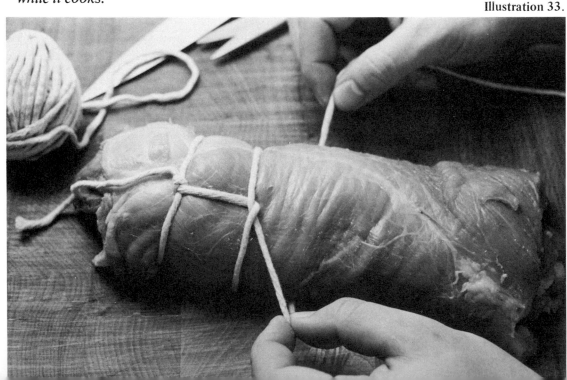

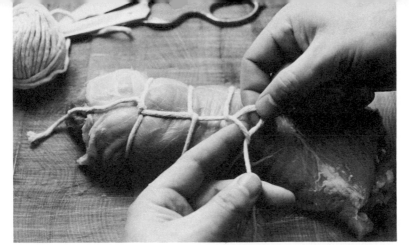

Illustration 34.

Illustration 35.

Illustration 36.

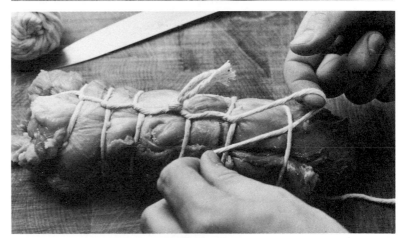

Illustration 37.

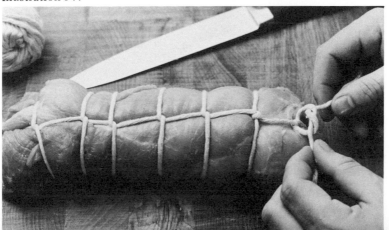

125

Roasting Meat

The biggest mistake people make with a roast is to put it directly into a hot oven. It should always be seared first on the top of the stove. Heat a little oil in a large roasting pan and then brown your roast for a few minutes on each side. Then put it into the oven to cook. Cooking it this way will keep more juice inside of your roast and it will taste much better.

There are a few exceptions to this rule. Don't try to turn a 30 pound turkey around in a roasting pan, just put it in the oven. Also a standing rib roast does not have to be browned first. There is a fat layer on one side of the meat and a bone layer on the other side to seal and protect the meat. But do put it into a hot oven for 30 minutes, then turn the heat down to finish cooking your roast.

TEMPERATURE CHARTS FOR PORK

Timetable for roasting pork

Cut of meat [1]	Approximate ready-to-cook weight	Approximate roasting time at 325 ° F.		Internal temperature of meat when done
		Fresh or thawed [2]	Frozen	
	Pounds	*Hours*	*Hours*	*° F*
Fresh:				
Ham.................................	12 to 16........	5½ to 6................................		170
Ham, half........................	5 to 7..		5 to 5½.......	170
Ham, boneless, rolled......	10 to 14........	4 2/3 to 5½.............................		170
Loin, center cut..............	3 to 5.............	2 to 3 1/3.............	3 to 4..........	170
Shoulder, picnic..............	5 to 8.............	3 to 4.................	4 to 5..........	170
Shoulder, picnic, bone-boneless, rolled.	3 to 5.............	2 to 3.................................		170
Shoulder, Boston butt....	4 to 6.............	3 to 4.................................		170
Shoulder, Boston butt, boneless, rolled.	3 to 5.............	2¼ to 3¼.................................		170
Spareribs........................	3 to 4.............	2.....................................		
Cured, cook-before-eating:				
Canadian bacon..............	2 to 4.............	1 1/3 to 2 1/3............................		160
Ham...............................	5 to 7.............	2 to 2½.....................................		160
Ham...............................	10 to 14........	3½ to 4¼...................................		160
Shoulder, picnic, boneless	5 to 8.............	3 to 4 2/3..................................		170
Shoulder, Boston butt, boneless.	2 to 4.............	1½ to 2 1/3..............................		170
Cured, fully cooked:				
Ham...............................	5 to 7.............	2...................................		140
Ham...............................	12 to 16........	3½ to 4..................................		140
Canned ham, boneless...	6 to 10..........	1½ to 2½.................................		140

[1] All cuts of meat listed in the table contain bone unless specified otherwise.
[2] Meat at refrigerator temperature at start of roasting.

Resting Meat

You should always let meat or fowl stand, or rest, for 10 to 15 minutes after cooking, before carving. There is a reason for this. You give the juices time to settle back into the meat. If you cut a roast as soon as you take it out of the oven, the juice will run all over your carving board. Your board will be beautifully juicy but your meat will be dry. The term "resting meat" applies to any kind of meat or fowl that you roast.

You can keep your meat warm while it's resting, if necessary, by covering it lightly with a piece of foil or a lid. If you have no room on your countertop, you can let the meat rest back in your oven. Just make sure you turn off the heat. Then place your meat back inside and leave the oven door at least part way open.

Timetable for broiling pork

Cut of meat	Approximate thickness	Approximate total cooking time [1]
	Inches	Minutes
Bacon slices		4 or 5
Canadian bacon	¼	6 to 8
	½	8 to 10
Chops, rib or loin	½ to ¾	30 to 35
Ham slices, cook-before-eating	¾	13 or 14
	1	18 to 20
Ham slices, fully cooked	1	10

[1] Meat at refrigerator temperature at start of broiling.

Timetable for braising pork

Cut of meat	Approximate weight or thickness	Approximate braising time [1]
		Hours
Chops, rib or loin	¾ to 1½ inches	¾ to 1
Spareribs	2 to 3 pounds	1½
Steaks, shoulder	¾ inch	¾ to 1
Cubes	1 to 1¼ inches	¾ to 1

[1] Meat at refrigerator temperature at start of braising.

RETAIL CUTS OF PORK

WHERE THEY COME FROM AND HOW TO COOK THEM

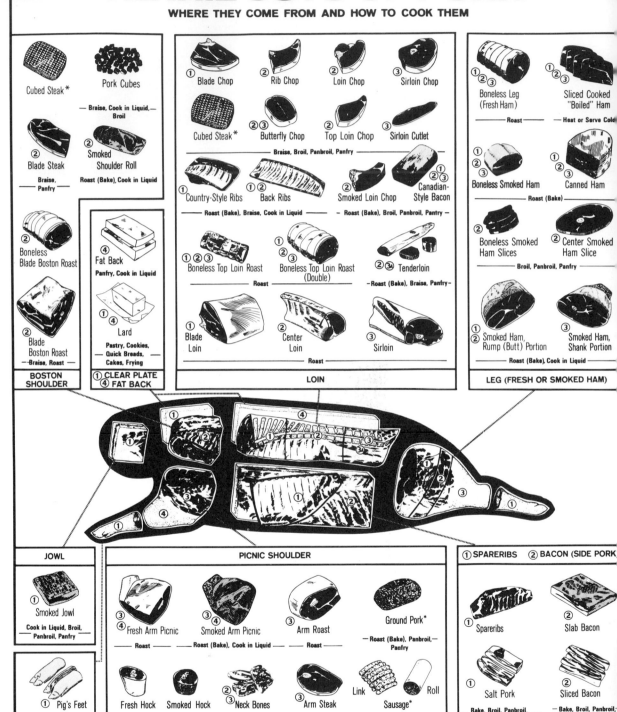

BOSTON SHOULDER

Cubed Steak*

Pork Cubes
— Braise, Cook in Liquid, — Broil

② Blade Steak
— Braise, Panfry —

② Smoked Shoulder Roll
Roast (Bake), Cook in Liquid

② Boneless Blade Boston Roast

② Blade Boston Roast
— Braise, Roast —

① CLEAR PLATE ④ FAT BACK

④ Fat Back
Panfry, Cook in Liquid

①④ Lard
Pastry, Cookies, Quick Breads, Cakes, Frying

LOIN

① Blade Chop   ② Rib Chop   ② Loin Chop   ③ Sirloin Chop

Cubed Steak*   ②③ Butterfly Chop   ② Top Loin Chop   ③ Sirloin Cutlet
— Braise, Broil, Panbroil, Panfry —

①②③ Country-Style Ribs   ①②③ Back Ribs   Smoked Loin Chop   ①②③ Canadian-Style Bacon
— Roast (Bake), Braise, Cook in Liquid —   — Roast (Bake), Broil, Panbroil, Panfry —

①②③ Boneless Top Loin Roast   ① Boneless Top Loin Roast (Double)   ②③④ Tenderloin
— Roast —   — Roast (Bake), Braise, Panfry —

① Blade Loin   ① Center Loin   ③ Sirloin
— Roast —

LEG (FRESH OR SMOKED HAM)

①②③ Boneless Leg (Fresh Ham)   ①②③ Sliced Cooked "Boiled" Ham
— Roast —   Heat or Serve Cold

①②③ Boneless Smoked Ham   ①②③ Canned Ham
— Roast (Bake) —

② Boneless Smoked Ham Slices   ② Center Smoked Ham Slice
— Broil, Panbroil, Panfry —

②③ Smoked Ham, Rump (Butt) Portion   ③ Smoked Ham, Shank Portion
— Roast (Bake), Cook in Liquid —

JOWL

① Smoked Jowl
Cook in Liquid, Broil, Panbroil, Panfry

① Pig's Feet
— Cook in Liquid, Braise —

PICNIC SHOULDER

③④ Fresh Arm Picnic   ③④ Smoked Arm Picnic   ③ Arm Roast   Ground Pork*
— Roast —   — Roast (Bake), Cook in Liquid —   — Roast —   — Roast (Bake), Panbroil, — Panfry

Fresh Hock   Smoked Hock   ②③ Neck Bones   ③ Arm Steak   Link Sausage* Roll
— Braise, Cook in Liquid —   — Cook in Liquid —   — Braise, Panfry —   — Panfry, Braise, Bake —

① SPARERIBS   ② BACON (SIDE PORK)

① Spareribs   ② Slab Bacon

① Salt Pork   ② Sliced Bacon
— Bake, Broil, Panbroil, — Panfry, Cook in Liquid   — Bake, Broil, Panbroil, — Panfry

*May be made from Boston Shoulder, Picnic Shoulder, Loin or Leg.

This chart approved by
National Live Stock and Meat Board

© National Live Stock and Meat Board

Pork

This is a Swedish recipe for stuffing a pork roast with prunes. Prunes may be funny looking but they also taste very good. It's delicous hot and even better cold. Once you try it , I'm sure you will love this recipe.

Cold Pork With Prunes And Apples

2-3 pounds boneless loin roast of pork
1 carrot, chopped
1 onion, chopped
1 stalk celery, chopped

pitted prunes for stuffing
1 recipe poached apple rings, page 180
oil, few spoons
pitted prunes, soaked in port or
    Armagnac for garnish

    With a sharp knife, make a hole horizontally through the center of the roast. **Illustration 38**. Enlarge the hole with the back end of a wooden spoon. **Illustration 39**. Fill the cavity with the pitted prunes.

    Brown all sides of the meat in a little oil. Add the chopped vegetables and a little water to the pan. Roast the meat in a moderate oven (375°) for about 1 hour, or until done.

    Let cool completely and slice.

    Place the meat on a platter. Decorate with poaced apple rings filled with the macerated prunes.

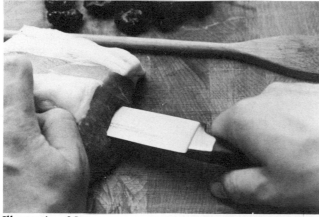

Illustration 38.

Illustration 39.

Danish Salad, page 46, plus
Carrot Salad, page 33,
Austrian Cabbage Salad, page 31,
and Green Bean Salad, page 39

Assorted Potatoes

Hot Pork With Prunes

2 pound boneless loin roast
1 carrot
1 onion

pitted prunes
1 stalk celery
1 cup meat stock

With a sharp knife, make a hole through horizontally through the center of the roast. Enlarge the hole with the back of a wooden spoon. Fill the cavity with the pitted dried prunes.
Roast 30 minutes in a medium oven. Add the carrot, celery and onion which have been chopped. Continue roasting meat for another 20 to 25 minutes, adding water a little at a time as needed to deglaze the pan.

Remove the meat and let stand for about 10 minutes before carving. Continue to deglaze the pan on the top of the stove with stock. Pour the sauce over roast and serve. Serves 6 to 8.

Pork Robert

6 slices boneless pork loin
1 tablespoon dry english mustard
1 cup stock
2 tablespoons chopped parsley
salt, pepper
3 tablespoons oil
1 package egg noodles

2 tablespoons chopped shallots
¼ cup white wine
½ cup heavy cream
¼ cup chopped kosher dill pickles
flour for dredging
3 tablespoons butter

Dissolve the dry mustard powder in the white wine.

Pound the pork slices. Salt and pepper them and dredge them in the flour. Saute the pork in the hot oil for a few minutes only, do not overcook. Remove the pork to a serving plate and keep warm. Add the shallots to the frying pan. Than add the pickle and the mustard.

Deglaze the pan with the stock, add the heavy cream and reduce the sauce for a few minutes.

Pour the sauce over the pork slices, garnish with the chopped parsley. Serve with buttered noodles. Serves 4 to 6.

Roast Pork Shoulder

whole pork shoulder, with skin
salt, pepper
beer

1 large onion, chopped
1 teaspoon caraway seeds

Score pork skin diagonally about ½ inch deep. Salt and pepper meat. Place in a roasting pan, skin side down. Place chopped onion and caraway seeds around the pork. Fill the pan with ½ inch of water. Roast in a moderate oven for one hour.

Remove the pork and the broth from the roasting pan. Place the pork back in the oven skin side up. Brush often with the beer for 1½ to 2 hours.

Reduce and deglaze the pan often, using the reserved broth and water, if necessary. Strain the sauce.

When the roast is finished, remove the skin and cut it into pieces. Slice the meat and put 2 pieces of skin on each serving. Serve with the sauce.

Sautéed Pork Budapest

4 slices of boneless loin of pork   1 green pepper
1 red pepper   1 onion, chopped
2 ounces cooked ham, sliced   6 strips of bacon, diced
salt, pepper, paprika   flour, for dredging
¼ cup heavy cream   2 tablespoons oil

Slice the green pepper and the red pepper into julienne strips. Slice the ham into julienne also. Dice the bacon.

Pound the pork slices and salt and pepper them. Dredge them in flour. Heat the oil in a frying pan. Saute the pork in the hot oil until browned, about five minutes on each side. Remove the pork and keep warm.

Cook the bacon in the frying pan. Drain the fat. Add the onion, red pepper, green pepper and the ham. Saute for a few minutes. Add the paprika and immediately, the cream. Bring to a boil and correct the seasonings. Pour over the meat and serve. Serves 4.

Schweinepfeffer*

4 ounces thinly sliced pork   ¼ cup sliced mushrooms
2 tablespoons chopped onions   salt, cracked black peppercorns
1 tablespoon oil   ½ cup white wine
¼ cup heavy cream   chopped parsley

Salt and pepper the pork slices. Heat the oil and saute the meat for a minute or two. Add the chopped onions and the mushrooms and continue to saute for a few minutes longer.

Remove the pork, mushrooms and onions to a warm serving plate.

Deglaze the pan with the wine and reduce the liquid by half. Add the cream and heat well. Reduce the liquid again.

Pour the sauce over the meat and sprinkle with the chopped parsley. Serve immediately. Serves one.

Alternate: This recipe can also be made with veal.

Stuffed Egg Platter, pages 94 and 95

Beef Tartare, page 164

RETAIL CUTS OF VEAL

WHERE THEY COME FROM AND HOW TO COOK THEM

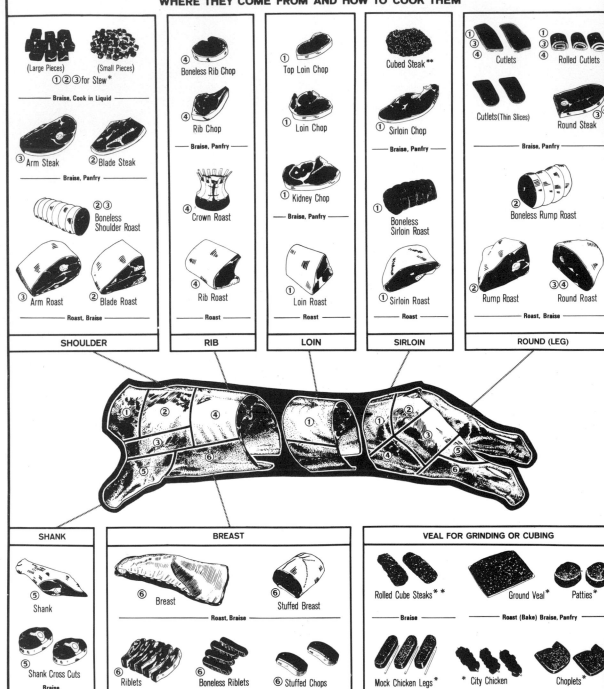

SHOULDER

(Large Pieces)   (Small Pieces)
①②③ for Stew *

— Braise, Cook in Liquid —

③ Arm Steak   ② Blade Steak

— Braise, Panfry —

②③ Boneless Shoulder Roast

③ Arm Roast   ② Blade Roast

— Roast, Braise —

RIB

④ Boneless Rib Chop

④ Rib Chop

— Braise, Panfry —

④ Crown Roast

④ Rib Roast

— Roast —

LOIN

① Top Loin Chop

① Loin Chop

— Braise, Panfry —

① Kidney Chop

— Braise, Panfry —

① Loin Roast

— Roast —

SIRLOIN

Cubed Steak **

① Sirloin Chop

— Braise, Panfry —

① Boneless Sirloin Roast

① Sirloin Roast

— Roast —

ROUND (LEG)

① ③ ④ Cutlets   ① ③ ④ Rolled Cutlets

Cutlets (Thin Slices)   ③ ④ Round Steak

— Braise, Panfry —

② Boneless Rump Roast

② Rump Roast   ③ ④ Round Roast

— Roast, Braise —

SHANK

⑤ Shank

⑤ Shank Cross Cuts

— Braise, Cook in Liquid —

BREAST

⑥ Breast   ⑥ Stuffed Breast

— Roast, Braise —

⑥ Riblets   ⑥ Boneless Riblets   ⑥ Stuffed Chops

— Braise, Cook in Liquid —   — Braise, Panfry —

VEAL FOR GRINDING OR CUBING

Rolled Cube Steaks **   Ground Veal *   Patties *

— Braise —   — Roast (Bake) Braise, Panfry —

Mock Chicken Legs *   * City Chicken   Choplets *

— Braise, Panfry —

*Veal for stew or grinding may be made from any cut.

**Cube steaks may be made from any thick solid piece of boneless veal.

This chart approved by
National Live Stock and Meat Board

© National Live Stock and Meat Board

TEMPERATURE CHARTS FOR VEAL

Timetable for roasting veal

Cut of meat	Approximate ready-to-cook weight	Approximate roasting time at 325° F.[1]	Internal temperature of meat when done
	Pounds	*Hours*	*° F.*
Veal			
Leg................................	5 to 8	3 to 3 1/3	170
Loin................................	4 to 6	2 1/3 to 3	170
Rib(rack)........................	3 to 5	2 to 3	170
Shoulder, rolled..............	3 to 5	2¼ to 3½	170

[1] Meat at refrigerator temperature at start of roasting.

Timetable for broiling veal

Cut of meat	Approximate thickness	Degree of doneness	Approximate total cooking time[1]
	Inches		*Minutes*
Veal			
Patties [2].............................	¾	Well done	15

[1] Meat is at refrigerator temperature at start of broiling.
[2] Broiling is not recommended for other cuts of veal.

Timetable for braising veal

Cut of Meat	Approximate ready-to-cook weight or thickness	Approximate total cooking time
		Hours
Veal		
Chops.. ½ to ¾ inch		¾ to 1
Pieces for stew (shoulder)......................1-inch cubes		1½ to 2
Shoulder, rolled......................................3 to 5 pounds		2 to 2½
Steaks (cutlets)..½ to ¾ inch		¾ to 1

Selecting Fresh Fish

Chicken Curry Dinner, page 62 with Fried Bananas, page 180

Black Forest Cake, page 197

Boning A Breast Of Veal

*The easiest way to bone a breast of veal is to have your butcher do it for you. In case he won't, here is a good way to bone it yourself, if necessary. Place the veal on a chopping board, with the ribs facing you. With a sharp knife, cut a small flap on the top of each rib bone. **Illustration 40**. Cut down firmly to free the top edge of the bone. **Illustration 41**. Then, using the point of your knife, make a slit down the center of each bone to loosen the cartilage covering. **Illustration 42**. Lift the breast, and pressing down against the meat at an angle, break free the tops of the bones. Grasp each rib bone by the top and pull out. **Illustration 43**. You should be able to remove them easily. Use the bones around your roast for extra flavor.*

Illustration 40.

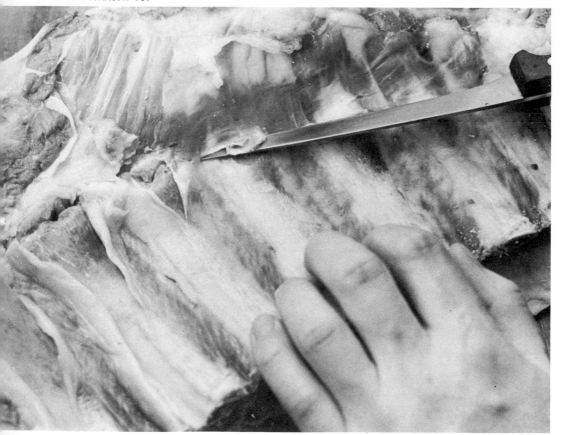

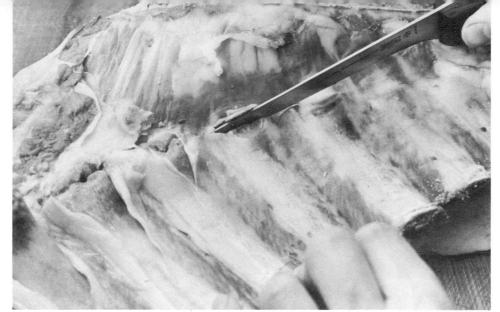

Illustration 41.

Illustration 42.
Illustration 43.

Kiwi Tart, page 222

Buche de Noël, page 199

Strawberry Torte, page 204

Cutting A Pocket

*Place the veal breast, bone side down, with the widest end facing you. With a sharp knife, separate the meat where it naturally forms two layers. Use your hand to both free the meat and feel where you are going. **Illustration 44.** Just be careful to leave the sides and bottom attached and you will have a nice large pocket for stuffing.*

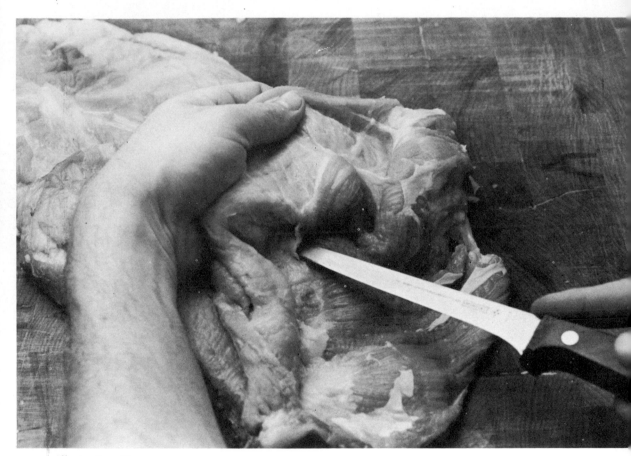

Illustration 44.

Stuffed Boned Breast Of Veal

1 veal breast	butter
1 onion	1 carrot
1 stalk celery	salt and pepper
1-2 tablespoons cornstarch	

Bone the veal breast and make a pocket in the meat. Reserve the bones. Stuff the veal pocket with bread stuffing. Brush the roast with butter and season with salt and pepper. Roast in a moderate oven for one hour.

Add the reserved veal bones which have been coarsely chopped. Add the onion, carrot and celery which have also been chopped. Add enough water to deglaze the pan as needed. Continue roasting in a moderate oven one more hour.

Remove the roast. Degrease and strain the sauce.

Thicken with a little cornstarch mixed to a paste with cold water, if necessary. Serve sauce hot over the roast. Serves 8 to 12.

Bread Stuffing

10 stale french rolls (or 1 large loaf), thinly sliced
1 cup milk, or more
4 strips bacon

salt, pepper, nutmeg
1 onion
½ cup chopped parsley
4-5 eggs

Heat the milk and pour it over the bread. Weight down with a plate. Saute the bacon and chopped onion together.

Add the onion mixture to the bread. Add the parsley and the eggs. Mix well. Season to taste and stuff the veal pocket.

Assiette Diplomat*

4 ounces thinly sliced veal
2 tablespoons chopped onion
1 tablespoon oil
¼ cup heavy cream

1 ounce sliced mushrooms
salt and pepper
½ cup white wine
chopped parsley

Salt and pepper the veal slices. Saute in oil a few minutes. Add the onion and mushrooms and continue to saute a few minutes longer. Remove the veal, mushrooms and onion from the pan to a serving plate. Deglaze the pan with the wine, reduce by half.

Add the cream, heat. Pour the sauce over the veal, Garnish with chopped parsley, and serve. Serves one.

This dish can also be made with pork instead of veal.

Ragout Fin Au Gratin

8 ounces veal, in one piece
1 stalk celery, chopped
4 cups water
salt, pepper
juice of ½ lemon
8 ounces mushrooms, sliced
1 egg yolk
Hollandaise sauce or grated
   parmesan cheese

1 carrot, chopped
few slices onion
bay leaf, thyme
2 ounces butter, plus 1 tablespoon
2 ounces flour
few drops Worchestershire sauce
½ cup heavy cream

Place the carrot, onion, celery, bay leaf, thyme and the water into a stock-pot. Add salt and pepper. Bring to a boil and simmer for ten minutes. Add the veal and continue to simmer until the veal is tender. Remove the meat, let cool a little and dice. Reserve two cups of the cooking stock.

Saute the mushrooms in one tablespoon of butter, covered, for a few minutes. Reserve.Make a roux with the two ounces of butter and the flour and cook a little. Remove from the heat and cool. Heat the two cups of reserved stock from the veal. When boiling, add the hot stock to the cooled roux, stirring. Cook for fifteen to twenty minutes.

Add the meat, mushrooms, lemon juice and seasonings. This dish may be prepared ahead of time to this point and refrigerated. At serving time, mix the egg yolk and cream to make a liason. Heat the Ragout Fin and add the liason to the hot sauce, stirring. Do not boil after adding the liason.

Spoon into individual gratin dishes or timbales. Top with a little of the hollandaise sauce or sprinkle with a little grated cheese and place under the broiler until browned. Serve immediately. Serves 4 to 6.

Roast Veal Shank

A veal shank comes from the front upper thigh of a calf. It's a very tasty piece of meat if cooked properly and is inexpensive.

1 veal shank
2 carrots, chopped
2-3 tablespoons of oil
water

1 onion, chopped
2 stalks celery, chopped
salt, pepper

Cut both ends off the shank, or better yet, ask your butcher to do this for you. Turn the meat so that the bone is visible. Slice the meat once, lengthwise, close to the bone. Salt and pepper the roast.

Heat the oil in a pan and brown the veal on all sides. Add a little water to the bottom of the pan and place the roast in a 375° oven. After 45 minutes, add the chopped vegetables to the pan. Add water as needed, scraping loose the glaze formed on the bottom of the pan each time.

Continue to roast until brown and tender. This should take about 2 hours, total roasting time.

Remove the veal and let it rest in a warm place. Deglaze the pan and strain the sauce. Slice the roast and serve with the strained pan juices.

Ossobuco

2 whole veal shanks	2 stalks celery, chopped
1 carrot, chopped	white of 1 leek, chopped
1 onion, chopped	3 or 4 tablespoons tomato puree
2 tomatoes, chopped	½ cup white wine
2 cups veal or chicken stock	bay leaf, thyme
1 or 2 cloves garlic, crushed	salt, pepper
2 or 3 tablespoons oil	water, as needed

Have your butcher saw the veal shanks into one to one and one-half inch thick slices. Salt and pepper the veal. Heat the oil in a large pan. Saute the veal in the oil to brown on all sides.

Add the chopped onion, carrot, celery, leeks, and garlic to the pan and continue to saute for a few more minutes. Deglaze the pan well with one cup of water.

Place the veal in a 375⁰ oven and roast for one hour. Add the tomatoes and the tomato puree to the pan. Continue to roast for another thirty minutes, or until the veal is tender. Add more water to the pan as needed to keep the meat from sticking.

Remove from the oven and deglaze the pan a few more times on the top of the stove with water. The last time deglaze with the white wine. Add the stock and cook for another fifteen to twenty minutes. Remove the veal shanks to a serving platter. Strain the sauce and serve over the veal. Serve with noodles or rice. Serves 8.

Swiss Veal Assiette

8 ounces veal, cut into slivers	¼ cup chopped onion
½ cup chopped mushrooms	½ cup diced swiss cheese
salt, pepper	oil
¼ cup heavy cream	½ cup white wine
lemon juice to taste	chopped parsley

Salt and pepper the veal. Saute in oil for a few minutes. Add the onions and the mushrooms to the pan and continue to saute a few minutes longer. Add the diced cheese and stir well.

Deglaze the pan with the wine and the cream. Add lemon juice to taste and correct the seasonings. Serve garnished with the chopped parsley. Serves two.

Veal Birds

8 thin slices of veal
2 ounces butter
salt, pepper
½ cup dry marsala wine

8 thin slices of cooked ham
8 hard boiled eggs
flour
½ cup veal stock

Pound the veal slices. Season with salt and pepper. Place a slice of ham on each piece of veal. Place a hard boiled egg in the center and roll up the veal. Close with a toothpick. **Illustration 45**. Dredge veal in flour.

Melt butter and saute veal, turning until brown. Pour in wine and stock. Bake, covered in a moderate oven for about 30 minutes, or until veal is tender.

To serve, remove toothpicks. They are very hard to chew. Slice each piece of veal in half, and present egg side up on serving platter. Pour some sauce over veal, serve the rest on the side. Serves 4 to 8.

Illustration 45.

Veal Piccata

6 veal scallops
juice 1 lemon
½ cup dry vermouth
2 tablespoons minced parsley
2-3 tablespoons oil

flour to coat
thin sliced lemon
salt, pepper
2 tablespoons butter

Pound the veal until thin and even. Season with salt and pepper and dredge in the flour, lightly.

Heat the oil and saute the veal briefly, until it is browned. Remove from the pan and keep warm.

Deglaze the pan with the vermouth. Add the lemon juice and butter and cook for a minute or two.

Pour over the meat and garnish with with chopped parsley and the lemon slices. Serves 4 to 6.

Veal Pojarski

1 pound ground veal
1 small onion, chopped
3 tablespoons chopped parsley
dash nutmeg
2-3 tablespoons butter
6 pieces penne (noodles)

5-6 ounces bread, soaked in water
    and squeezed dry
salt, pepper
2 eggs
oil

Soak and squeeze dry the bread. Saute the onion in the butter. Mix the meat, bread, onions, seasonings and eggs together. Shape the farce, or meat mixture, to look like pork chops. Insert a piece of uncooked penne where the bone should be.

Saute the chops in hot oil to brown on both sides. Remove from the frying pan. Save the drippings from the pan to make your sauce. Place the chops in a 400° oven for about 30 minutes or until done. Serve with the brown cream sauce on the side. Serves 6.

Brown Cream Sauce

1 small onion, chopped
1 cup stock
2 tablespoons chopped parsley
salt, pepper

½ cup white wine
½ cup heavy cream
juice of ½ lemon
buerre manie, if needed

Saute the onion in the remains left in the veal frying pan until soft. Deglaze the pan with the wine. Add the stock, seasonings and the lemon juice. Cook for a minute or two. Add the cream and the parsley. Thicken the sauce with a beurre manie, if needed. Serve hot with the veal.

LAMB CHART

RETAIL CUTS OF LAMB — WHERE THEY COME FROM AND HOW TO COOK THEM

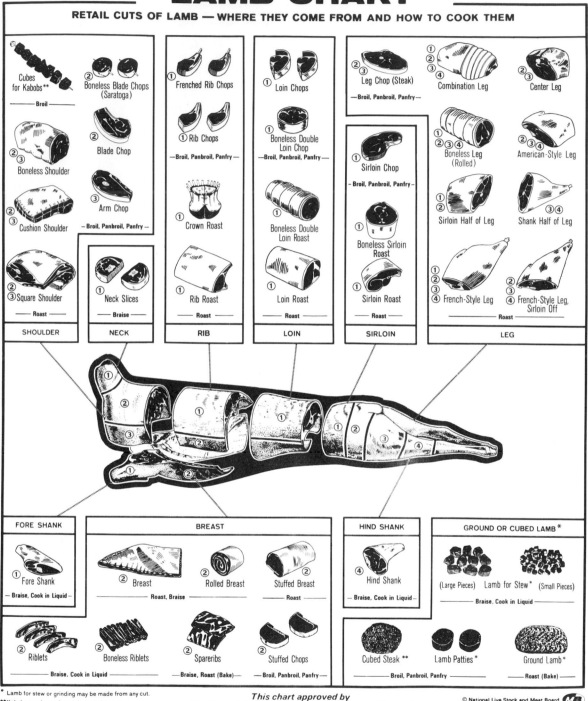

SHOULDER

Cubes for Kabobs**

② Boneless Blade Chops (Saratoga)

② Blade Chop

③ Arm Chop

— Broil, Panbroil, Panfry —

②③ Boneless Shoulder

②③ Cushion Shoulder

②③ Square Shoulder

— Roast —

NECK

Neck Slices

— Braise —

RIB

① Frenched Rib Chops

① Rib Chops

— Broil, Panbroil, Panfry —

① Crown Roast

① Rib Roast

— Roast —

LOIN

① Loin Chops

① Boneless Double Loin Chop

— Broil, Panbroil, Panfry —

① Boneless Double Loin Roast

① Loin Roast

— Roast —

SIRLOIN

②③ Leg Chop (Steak)

— Broil, Panbroil, Panfry —

① Sirloin Chop

— Broil, Panbroil, Panfry —

① Boneless Sirloin Roast

① Sirloin Roast

— Roast —

LEG

②③④ Combination Leg

②③ Center Leg

①②③④ Boneless Leg (Rolled)

②③④ American-Style Leg

①② Sirloin Half of Leg

③④ Shank Half of Leg

①②③④ French-Style Leg

①②③④ French-Style Leg, Sirloin Off

— Roast —

— Broil —

FORE SHANK

① Fore Shank

— Braise, Cook in Liquid —

① Riblets

— Braise, Cook in Liquid —

BREAST

② Breast

② Rolled Breast

Stuffed Breast

— Roast, Braise —

— Roast —

Boneless Riblets

② Spareribs

② Stuffed Chops

— Braise, Roast (Bake) —

— Broil, Panbroil, Panfry —

HIND SHANK

④ Hind Shank

— Braise, Cook in Liquid —

Cubed Steak **

— Broil, Panbroil, Panfry —

GROUND OR CUBED LAMB*

(Large Pieces) Lamb for Stew* (Small Pieces)

— Braise, Cook in Liquid —

Lamb Patties*

Ground Lamb*

— Roast (Bake) —

* Lamb for stew or grinding may be made from any cut.

**Kabobs or cube steaks may be made from any thick solid piece of boneless Lamb.

This chart approved by
National Live Stock and Meat Board

© National Live Stock and Meat Board

TEMPERATURE CHARTS FOR LAMB

Timetable for roasting lamb

Cut of meat	Approximate ready-to-cook weight	Approximate roasting time at 325º F. [1]
	Pounds	*Hours*
Leg..............................	5 to 8	3 to 4
Leg, boneless, rolled..................	3 to 5	2 to 3
Rib (rack)................................	4 to 5	3 to 3 1/3
Shoulder...................................	4 to 6	2 1/3 to 3
Shoulder, cushion-style..............	3 to 5	1¾ to 2½
Shoulder, boneless, rolled.........	3 to 5	2¼ to 3 1/3

[1] Meat at refrigerator temperature at start of roasting.

Timetable for broiling lamb

Cut of meat	Approximate thickness	Approximate total cooking time [1]
	Inches	*Minutes*
Chops, loin, rib, or shoulder.........	1	12 (medium)
		14 (well done)
	1½	18 (medium)
		22 (well done)
Patties.....................................	1	15 to 18 (medium)
		20 (well done)
Steaks, leg...................................	1	12 to 14 (medium)
		16 to 18 (well done)

[1] Meat is at refrigerator temperature at start of broiling.

Timetable for braising lamb

Cut of meat	Approximate ready-to-cook weight or thickness	Approximate total cooking time [1]
		Hours
Breast, boneless, rolled........	1½ to 2 pounds..........................	1½ to 2
Breast, stuffed.....................	2 to 3 pounds............................	1½ to 2
Neck slices..........................	¾ inch......................................	1
Riblets.................................	....	1½ to 2
Shanks.................................	¾ to 1 pound each....................	1½ to 2
Shoulder chops....................	¾ to 1 inch...............................	¾ to 1
Pieces for stew.....................	1½ inches..................................	1½ to 2

[1] Cooking time is for meat braised at simmering temperature.

Lamb And Lima Beans*

½ chopped onion
1 tablespoon oil
8 ounces frozen lima beans
½ cup chicken stock

garlic
salt and pepper
1 peeled, diced potato
5-6 ounces shoulder or leg of lamb
(sliced ¼ inch)

Heat a small pot then saute onion in oil until golden brown. Add lima beans and chicken broth, some garlic, salt and pepper to taste. Add potato.

In another pot, saute lamb. Then add lamb to first pot and cover. Place in oven for approximately 35-40 minutes till done. Serve immediately. Serves one.

Lamb Stew

2 pounds boned lamb shoulder, cubed
1 cup chopped onion
½ cup white wine
¼ cup tomato puree
2 pounds potatoes
bay leaf, pinch thyme

2 tablespoons oil
1-2 cloves garlic, chopped
1 cup water, or more as needed
salt, pepper
1-2 tablespoons chopped parsley

Heat the oil in a frying pan. Sprinkle the lamb cubes with salt and pepper. Brown the meat in the hot oil on all sides. Pour off some of the extra fat from the pan. Add the chopped onions and cook for 5 minutes. Add the garlic and the herbs. Deglaze the pan with the white wine. Add the tomato puree and one cup of water. Cover and simmer for one hour. Add more water, if needed, to keep the lamb from sticking.

Peel and dice the potatoes. Add them to the lamb and continue to simmer until both the lamb and the potatoes are tender, about 30 minutes. Add more water as needed while cooking.

Remove the bay leaf and correct the seasonings. Serve hot. Serves 6.

Scotch Lamb

1 leg of lamb
2 carrots
2 stalks celery
2 turnips
2-3 cloves garlic
1-2 cups water or stock

Mirepoix: 1 onion, chopped
1 carrot, chopped
1 stalk celery, chopped
2-3 tablespoons oil
salt, pepper

Bone the leg of lamb without cutting the meat open.

Cut the carrots, celery and turnips into small strips. Sliver the garlic. With a sharp knife, make a hole in the lamb and insert one of the vegetable strips. Continue until all of the vegetables and the garlic have been used. Season with salt and pepper.

Brown the lamb in the oil and place in the oven. After 45 minutes, add the chopped mirepoix vegetables. Continue roasting until the lamb is done. This should take another 45 minutes. Remove the meat and keep warm.

Add some of the water or stock and deglaze the pan a few times to make a sauce.

Slice the lamb onto a serving plate. Pour on some of the sauce and serve hot. Serves 8.

Stuffed Lamb Shoulder

1 lamb shoulder
1 onion, chopped
few spoons chopped parsley
2-3 eggs
Mirepoix: 1 onion, chopped
         1 carrot, chopped
         1 stalk celery, chopped

1 pound ground lamb
1 clove garlic, chopped
3-4 ounces bread, soaked and
    squeezed dry
salt, pepper
butter or oil
few spoons tomato puree
1-2 tablespoons cornstarch diluted
    in cold water

Make the stuffing: Saute the onion in the butter until soft. Add the garlic and the ground lamb. Brown, stirring. Mix in the bread which has been soaked in water and squeezed dry. Add the eggs and seasoning and mix well.

Bone the shoulder of lamb. Butterfly the meat and pat the stuffing onto the shoulder. Roll it up and tie.

Salt and pepper the meat. Brown the roast on all sides in a little oil. Place in a pan with the removed bone and a little water. Bake in a moderate oven until the meat is about half cooked.

Add the mirepoix to the pan and return to the oven until the meat is tender.

Remove the roast and set it aside to rest in a warm place.

To make the sauce, glaze the pan down several times with water. Add in the tomato puree.

Strain the sauce and thicken with the cornstarch mixture, if needed. Serve the sauce with the roast lamb shoulder.

RETAIL CUTS OF BEEF

WHERE THEY COME FROM AND HOW TO COOK THEM

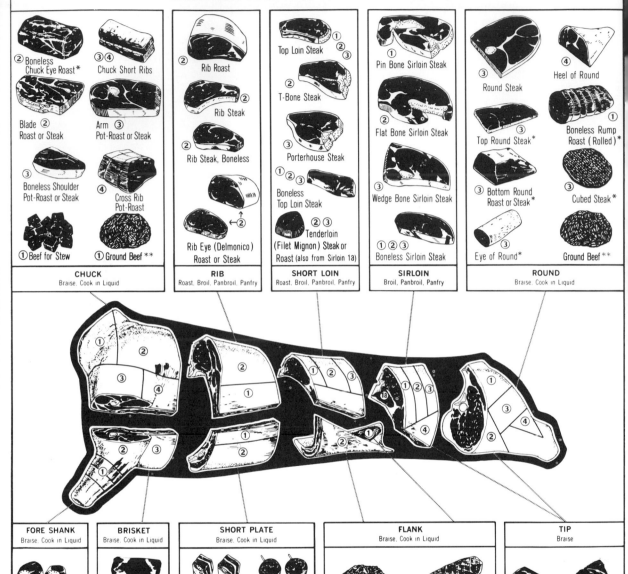

② Boneless Chuck Eye Roast*

③④ Chuck Short Ribs

Blade ② Roast or Steak

Arm ③ Pot-Roast or Steak

③ Boneless Shoulder Pot-Roast or Steak

④ Cross Rib Pot-Roast

① Beef for Stew

① Ground Beef**

CHUCK
Braise, Cook in Liquid

② Rib Roast

② Rib Steak ②

② Rib Steak, Boneless

②←①

Rib Eye (Delmonico) Roast or Steak

RIB
Roast, Broil, Panbroil, Panfry

① Top Loin Steak ②③

② T-Bone Steak

Porterhouse Steak

①②③ Boneless Top Loin Steak

②③ Tenderloin (Filet Mignon) Steak or Roast (also from Sirloin 1a)

SHORT LOIN
Roast, Broil, Panbroil, Panfry

① Pin Bone Sirloin Steak ②③

② Flat Bone Sirloin Steak

Wedge Bone Sirloin Steak

①②③ Boneless Sirloin Steak

SIRLOIN
Broil, Panbroil, Panfry

③ Round Steak

④ Heel of Round

③ Top Round Steak*

① Boneless Rump Roast (Rolled)*

③ Bottom Round Roast or Steak*

Cubed Steak*

③ Eye of Round*

Ground Beef**

ROUND
Braise, Cook in Liquid

FORE SHANK
Braise, Cook in Liquid

① Shank Cross Cuts

② Beef for Stew (also from other cuts)

BRISKET
Braise, Cook in Liquid

③ Fresh Brisket

③ Corned Brisket

SHORT PLATE
Braise, Cook in Liquid

① Short Ribs

①② Skirt Steak Rolls*

①② Beef for Stew (also from other cuts)

Ground Beef**

FLANK
Braise, Cook in Liquid

Ground Beef**

① Flank Steak*

① Beef Patties**

① Flank Steak Rolls*

TIP
Braise

④② Tip Steak*

④② Tip Roast*

④② Tip Kabobs*

*May be Roasted, Broiled, Panbroiled or Panfried from high quality beef.
**May be Roasted, (Baked), Broiled, Panbroiled or Panfried.

This chart approved by
National Live Stock and Meat Board

TEMPERATURE CHARTS FOR BEEF

Timetable for roasting beef

Cut of meat	Approximate ready-to-cook weight	Approximate roasting time at 325° F. [1]	Internal temperature of meat when done
	Pounds	*Hours*	*° F.*
Beef			
Standing ribs [2]			
Rare....................................	4 to 6	2¼ to 2½	140
Medium...............................	4 to 6	2½ to 3 1/3	160
Well done...........................	4 to 6	2¾ to 4	170
Rare....................................	6 to 8	2½ to 3	140
Medium...............................	6 to 8	3 to 3½	160
Well done...........................	6 to 8	3½ to 4¼	170
Rolled rib			
Rare....................................	5 to 7	2 2/3 to 3¾	140
Medium...............................	5 to 7	3¼ to 4½	160
Well done...........................	5 to 7	4 to 5 2/3	170
Rolled rump			
(choice grade)....................	4 to 6	2 to 2½	150 to 170
Sirloin tip			
(choice grade)....................	3½ to 4	2 1/3	140 to 170
	6 to 8	3½ to 4	140 to 170

[1] Meat at refrigerator temperature at start of roasting.
[2] Eight-inch cut. For l0-inch ribs allow about 30 minutes less time.

Timetable for broiling beef

Cut of meat	Approximate thickness	Degree of doneness	Approximate total cooking time [1]
	Inches		*Minutes*
Beef			
Steaks (club, porterhouse,	1	Rare	15 to 20
rib, sirloin, T-bone,	1	Medium	20 to 25
tenderloin)	1	Well done	25 to 30
	1½	Rare	25 to 30
	1½	Medium	30 to 35
	1½	Well done	35 to 40
	2	Rare	35 to 40
	2	Medium	40 to 45
	2	Well done	45 to 55
Patties..	¾	Rare	8
	¾	Medium	12
	¾	Well done	14

[1] Meat is at refrigerator temperature at start of broiling.

Timetable for braising beef

Cut of meat	Approximate ready-to-cook weight or thickness	Approximate total cooking time
		Hours
Beef		
Pot roast, such as chuck or round.....................3 to 5 pounds		3 to 4
Steak, such as chuck or round..........................¾ to 1 inch		1 to 1½
Flank steak... ½ inch		1½ to 2
Short ribs... 2 by 2 by 4 inches		1½ to 2½
Pieces for stew.. 1½-inch cubes		1½ to 2½

Beef Esterhazy

1½ inch slice top round
1 tablespoon sugar
½ cup red wine
1 carrot, diced
1 stalk celery, diced
2 tablespoons butter or oil
Garnish: 1 leek, white part only
        1 carrot
        1 stalk celery
        1 small onion

1 onion, diced
2 tablespoons tomato puree
½ cup either beef or chicken stock,
      or demi-glace or water
salt, pepper

Pound the meat. Sprinkle it with salt and pepper. Heat the oil in a frying pan and saute the meat, turning, until it is seared. Remove the meat and set it aside.

To the same frying pan, add the onion and the sugar. Saute for a few minutes until the onion becomes glazed. Add the diced carrots and celery, the tomato puree, red wine and stock.

Put the steak back into the pan and braise in a moderate (375⁰) oven until the meat is tender, about 1 to 1½ hours. Add more water, if needed, as the meat braises.

Meanwhile, prepare the garnish. Julienne finely all of the vegetables. Blanch them in boiling salted water for a few minutes only. Refresh under cold water, drain and reserve the garnish.

When the meat is done, remove the meat to a serving plate. Strain the sauce through a sieve. Pour the sauce over the steak.

Garnish with the julienned vegetables and serve. Serves 4 to 6.

Beef Rouladen

6 slices top round of beef
1 onion, chopped
2 tablespoons pickles, diced
butter or oil

1-2 tablespoons Dijon mustard
½ slice raw bacon, diced
salt and pepper

Sauce

1 carrot, chopped
1 stalk celery, chopped
2 cups stock
1-2 tablespoons cornstarch, diluted
    in cold water

1 onion, chopped
bacon rind
1 cup red wine

To prepare rouladen, saute the onion in butter until golden.

Pound the meat and sprinkle with salt and pepper. Paint each slice with the mustard. Fill with a mixture of sauteed onion, pickles, and raw bacon.

Roll and close with a toothpick.

Saute the beef on all sides in hot fat until browned. Add the chopped vegetables for the sauce and the bacon rind. Stir and brown a little. Add red wine and stock and braise until the meat is tender. Remove the meat and strain the sauce. Thicken with the cornstarch mixture.

Serve the meat with the sauce and mashed potatoes. Serves 6.
Optional fillings: Ground meat or bread stuffing.

Beef Stroganoff

12 slices tenderloin
2 tablespoons butter
2 tablespoons flour
2 tablespoons powdered English
    mustard
few spoons white wine
½ cup sour cream
salt, pepper

2 cups beef stock
½ cup sliced mushrooms
1 cup sliced tomatoes
1 cup sliced onion
½ cup sliced pickles
2 tablespoons tomato ketchup
butter or oil, few spoons

Make a roux with the 2 tablespoons butter and the flour. Let cool a little. Heat the beef stock and add this to the cooled roux, cook for about 20 minutes. Reserve thickened beef stock to use later.

Dissolve the mustard powder in the white wine and set aside.

Season the meat with salt and pepper and saute in a little butter or oil. When lightly cooked, remove and place in a chafing dish.

Saute the onion in the same pan until golden.

Add the mushrooms, tomatoes and the pickles. Saute a few minutes. Add the thickened beef stock and the sour cream, ketchup and mustard. Cook a minute or two and pour over the beef slices.

This dish will keep warm well in a chafing dish for a few hours. Serves 12.

Braised Beef*

6-8 ounces Beef (top round or
   bottom round)
½ cup chopped carrot
½ cup chopped onion
½ cup chopped celery

½ cup red wine
½ cup water
2 tablespoons tomato puree

In a heavy casserole, brown the beef on both sides. Remove from the pan and gently saute the carrot, onion and celery. Return the beef to the pan and add the red wine and water. Cook in the oven (375°) for 45 minutes to one hour. Enjoy!

Brisket With Potatoes

1 brisket
1 stalk celery, chopped
bay leaf, salt, pepper, parsley stems
1 potato recipe (follows)

2 pounds extra beef bones
1 carrot, chopped
1 onion, sliced
water to cover
Horseradish sauce, page 74.

Place the brisket and any extra beef bones, if you have them, in a deep pot. Add the vegetables, season, cover with water and bring to a boil. Skim the pot as foam forms on the surface. Simmer for about one and a half hours, or until the meat is tender. Remove the meat from the pot. Place the beef in a roasting pan and brown in a 400° oven until the meat takes on a little color and browns. Slice the beef and serve with the potatoes and the horseradish sauce. Serves 8 or more.

Potatoes

4 or 5 potatoes
2 carrots, chopped
1 onion, chopped
salt, pepper

1 or 2 leeks, chopped
2 stalks celery, chopped
2 to 3 tablespoons oil or butter
1 or 2 cloves garlic, crushed
broth from cooking the brisket

Peel and dice the potatoes. Heat the butter or oil in a casserole. Add the chopped leeks, onion, carrots and celery. Saute for a few minutes and then add the potatoes and the garlic. Season. Pour on some of the beef broth left from cooking the brisket. Place in a 400° oven and cook until the potatoes are done. Add more beef liquid, if needed as the potatoes cook. They should not get too dry. Serve with the sliced brisket.

Peppered Beef

4 eight ounce slices beef tenderloin,
    well trimmed
2-3 tablespoons oil
½ cup finely chopped onion
¼ cup canned green peppercorns

salt, pepper
¼ cup brandy
¼ cup stock or demi-glace
½ cup heavy cream

Pound the beef. Salt and pepper the slices.

Heat the oil and saute the beef 2 to 3 minutes on each side, depending on rareness desired. Remove the meat from the pan and keep warm.

Add the onions to the drippings remaining in the pan and saute for a few minutes until golden brown.

Deglaze the pan with the brandy, stock or demi-glace and cream. Add the green peppercorns and cook, stirring constantly, until the liquid is reduced by half.

Pour the sauce over the meat and serve immediately. Serves 4.

Marinating Meats

The purpose of marination is to tenderize meat. The chemical reaction of the acid present in the marinade, whether it be lemon juice or vinegar, is to break down some of the cell structure of the meat. It will thereby make a lower grade of meat, which is normally tougher, more tender and easier to chew.

Americans love to marinate flank steak or London broil. Germans have their sauerbraten. Here is my favorite recipe for this dish.

Sauerbraten

6 pounds beef eye roast
1 cup tomato puree
½ to 1 cup sour cream

oil
flour
½ to 1 cup heavy cream

Marinade:
1 cup red wine vinegar
1 onion, chopped
2 stalks celery, chopped
1 clove garlic
salt and pepper

2 cups red wine
1 carrot, chopped
4 bay leaves
2 whole cloves
water to cover

Mix together ingredients for marinade. Place meat in the container and cover with the marinade for 4 days to 1 week (refrigerated).

Remove meat. Dry well. Salt and pepper outside and brown in oil on all sides.

Strain the liquid from the marinade. Add the remaining vegetables to the roast.

Boil the liquid from the marinade separately. Remove any foam or scum that rises to the surface.

Add 1 cup tomato puree to the roast and deglaze the pan several times with some of the marinade liquid.

Dust the roast with flour. Fill the pan with stock and bake in a moderate oven for 2 to 3 hours.

When done, remove the meat and reserve.

Strain the sauce. Add sour cream and heavy cream.

Correct seasonings to taste.

Slice the meat and serve with the sauce. Serves 12 or more.

Shish-Kabobs

I always marinate meat for kabobs after it is threaded onto skewers. A marinade will make the meat slippery and hard to handle. You have a much better chance of poking a hole in your hand if the meat is wet. It is just much easier to put on the skewers when it is dry.

When you go to cook your kabobs, just lift them out of the marinade and they're all ready for the grill. Very simple, very easy this way.

Shish kabobs are usually made with one kind of meat. But it's even nicer when you use two or three different kinds. It makes a much more interesting meal to have several flavors and textures at the same time.

Shish-Kabobs

1 pound boned lamb
1 pound boned veal
1 pound boned pork

2 onions, peeled and cut into quarters
1 large green pepper

Marinade:
    2 cloves garlic, crushed
    1 teaspoon oregano
    ½ cup oil

juice of 2 lemons
bay leaf
salt, pepper

Cut all the meat into evenly shaped cubes. Pound to tenderize. Cut the green pepper into squares, about the same size as the onion slices.

On skewers, thread the meats alternately with the onion and the green pepper.

Lay the skewers flat in a large pan.

Combine all the ingredients for the marinade and mix well. Pour the marinade over the kabobs, turning them in the liquid to coat them evenly. Cover well and refrigerate for several hours or overnight, turning them every few hours.

To cook, drain the kabobs and broil them over a barbeque, turning often for about 12 to 15 minutes. Skewers may also be broiled under a grill, about 4 inches from the heat. They may also be sauted in a little hot oil in a frying pan, turning often. Makes 6 to 8 skewers.

Meat Loaf

If you used just pork to make a meatloaf, it would taste very fatty. Veal alone would be too expensive. And meat loaf made of beef only would be very dry. If you combine and use all three of these meats at the same time, you will get a meat loaf that has a nice flavor, an interesting texture, and isn't too fatty.

2/3 pound ground pork
2/3 pound ground veal
2/3 pound ground beef
5 slices white bread, soaked in
    water and squeezed dry
1 medium onion, chopped
1/2 cup parsley, chopped
3 eggs plus 2 hard boiled eggs for filling
salt, pepper, nutmeg
crushed garlic, optional

Combine all the ingredients (except the hard boiled eggs) in a large mixing bowl. You can stretch the volume by adding more bread. Form into a large loaf shape and place onto a baking pan. Make an indentation with your hand along one side of the loaf. Place the hard boiled eggs into this trench and reshape the meat loaf around them, back into a loaf shape. Bake at 350⁰ for 1½ hours.

Serve your family the meat loaf from the side with the hard boiled egg in it for one meal. Serve the other half for a different meal. They will never know it's the same meat loaf!

Good either hot or cold, I hope you enjoy this recipe.

Stuffed Eggplant

1 eggplant
salt, pepper
3 cups meatloaf mixture (see recipe)
1/2 cup water

Cut the eggplant in half, level off the bottom. Do not peel. Hollow out the eggplant halves, salt and pepper them. Fill each half with the meatloaf mixture. Score the top of the meatloaf in a decorative pattern.

Place in a casserole, pour the water onto the bottom of the pan, cover and bake in a 375⁰ oven for about 35 minutes or until done. Serves 2.

Stuffed Cabbage Leaves

Filling:

1 large head cabbage
2 pounds ground meat (or meat loaf mixture)
1 medium onion, chopped
½ cup of parsley, chopped
5 slices of white bread, soaked in water, then squeezed.
3 whole eggs
salt, pepper, nutmeg and garlic to taste

Sauce:

4 slices of bacon, diced   1 can tomato sauce (8 ounce)
1 can tomatoes (16 ounce)   ¼ cup chopped onion

Cut and core out the cabbage and remove 8 outer leaves. Set to one side and chop the remaining cabbage (about 6 cups). Place in a baking dish and sprinkle with a little salt. Take the 8 outer leaves and chop out about 2 inches of the thick center vein. Boil for 3 minutes or until the leaves are limp. Set aside. Combine all the other ingredients in a large mixing bowl. Place about ½ cup of meat mixture in the center of each cabbage leaf. Fold in the sides and roll the ends over the meat. Then place the roll with the seam side down on top of the chopped cabbage.

Saute the onion and bacon until crisp. Add the tomatoes (undrained), tomato sauce and the bay leaf. Simmer for 5 minutes. Pour over the cabbage rolls and bake at 350 degrees for 1-1½ hours.

Serve hot and enjoy! Serves 8.

Stuffed Peppers

6 green peppers   ½ pound ground beef
1 cup cooked rice   ½ pound ground veal
1 onion, chopped   ½ pound ground pork
3-4 ounces bread   3 tablespoons chopped parsley
2 eggs   salt, pepper
2 tablespoons butter or oil   1 small can pimentos, diced (optional)
2 cups stock

Soak the bread in water. Squeeze dry.
Saute the chopped onion in the butter until golden.
Mix the meats, the bread, onion, eggs, rice, parsley and pimentoes together. Season to taste with salt and pepper.
Cut the green peppers in half. Remove the seeds. Fill with the meatloaf mixture.
Place the stuffed peppers in a baking pan. Pour the stock over the peppers. Bake in a moderate (375°) oven for about 1 hour or until tender. Serve either hot or cool.
If cool, slice the peppers and arrange them decoratively on a platter. Serves 6.

Cold Meat Salads

I'd like to give you a few recipes for some very interesting meat salads. They can be used as an appetizer or for lunch or even as part of a buffet table. I wouldn't serve them all at the same time, but do try them, one at a time.

Cold meat salad makes a good lunchbox item instead of the usual sandwich. One note of caution, don't let meat salad sit around too long without refrigeration. If it spoils, it can make you sick.

Meat Paté Or Spread

1 cup cooked meat, diced	½ onion, chopped
4 ounces butter	juice of ½ lemon
salt, pepper	1-2 tablespoons brandy

Place all the ingredients into a food processor and blend well. Serve on toast or crackers.

Beef Salad

2 cups sliced cooked beef	1 onion, finely sliced
½ tomato, finely sliced	½ green pepper, finely sliced
2 small dill pickles, finely sliced	2 tablespoons tomato ketchup
salt, pepper	

Combine all of the above ingredients. Let rest a few hours in the refrigerator to develop flavor. If salad needs to be tarter, add a little juice from the dill pickles and mix in.

Any cooked meat can be used, just don't call it beef salad, if you don't use beef. Serves 4.

Cold Meat Plate

Use all kinds of assorted cold cuts.

Using a silver plate or glass tray, arrange a layer of assorted meats. Then make rolls out of the remaining meat and place on top. Garnish with hard-boiled eggs and parsley and tomato wedges.

Rolled Sandwiches

Cut the crusts from sliced sandwich bread. Roll flat with a rolling pin to get a very thin and large piece of bread.

Cold Ham Salad

Use leftover ham cut into very small pieces.

chopped celery	chopped pickles
mayonaise	salt and pepper

Mix above ingredients together. Spread over flat bread then roll up to a wheel. I'm sure your children will enjoy these sandwiches.

Ham Rolls With Horseradish Cream

6 slices cooked ham	1 cup heavy cream
3 tablespoons horseradish, drained	¼ cup water
juice ½ lemon	1 tablespoons gelatin

Soften the gelatin in the lemon juice and water, heat to dissolve. Cool a little.

Whip the cream lightly. Stir in the horseradish and the dissolved gelatin.

Spread out the ham slices. Pour the cream mixture over the slices, smoothing with a palette knife. Refrigerate to let the mixture thicken a little. Roll the ham slices and let set.

Slice into rounds and place on a serving plate or onto canape bases. Serves 8 to 10.

Beef Tartare

Beef tartare is a raw hamburger dish. People sometimes get turned off if you tell them this, but once they taste it, they usually love it. One important thing, the beef you use for tartare must be absolutely fat free. Call it a European meat dish instead of raw meat and try serving it once. I have it on my restaurant menu and it's a very popular item.

Beef Tartare

1 pound ground top round	3-4 tablespoons finely chopped onion
1 teaspoon capers	1 anchovy fillet, mashed
½ teaspoon dijon mustard	½ teaspoon paprika
salt, pepper	1 egg yolk

Mix all the above ingredients together. Season to taste.

Mound on a plate and garnish with onion rings, parsley sprigs, hard boiled eggs and anchovy fillets. Serves 4.

Chapter 10

Poultry

Tips:
Roasting guide
Cutting a Chicken
Trussing a Chicken
Duck
Carving a Turkey

Recipes:
Chicken and Rice*
Chicken Legs Stuffed with Sauerkraut
Chicken breasts with Almonds
Chicken with Tomatoes*
Coq au Vin
Stuffed Chicken Breasts
Tarragon Chicken
Chicken Salad Hawaiian
Cornish Hens with Chestnuts and Brandy
Cornish Hens with Cabbage
Roast Duck ''My Way''
Roast Goose
Roast Turkey
Turkey Florentine
Turkey Salad Valencia

*Indicates Dinner for One

ROASTING GUIDE

Kind of poultry	Ready-to-cook weight[1]	Approximate roasting time at 325° F. for stuffed poultry[2]	Internal temperature of poultry when done
	Pounds	*Hours*	*° F.*
Chickens....................................	1½ to 2½........	1 to 2.............	
(Broilers, fryers, or roasters)	2½ to 4½........	2 to 3½..........	
Ducks..	4 to 6..........	2 to 3.............	
Geese..	6 to 8..........	3 to 3½..........	
	8 to 12........	3½ to 4½..........	
Turkeys....................................	6 to 8..........	3 to 3½..........	
	8 to 12........	3½ to 4½..........	180 to 185 in center of inner thigh muscle
	12 to 16........	4½ to 5½..........	
	16 to 20........	5½ to 6½..........	
	20 to 24........	6½ to 7.............	

1 Weight of giblets and neck included.

2 Unstuffed poultry may take slightly less time than stuffed poultry. Cooking time is based on chilled poultry or poultry that has just been thawed—temperature not above 40° F. Frozen unstuffed poultry will take longer. Do not use this roasting guide for frozen commercially stuffed poultry; follow package directions.

Cutting A Chicken

Visiting a factory where they cut up poultry is much like visiting an assembly line anywhere. One person cuts the wings off the chicken, another the legs, a third the breasts, and so on down the line. At the end of the line, someone else assembles the chicken parts into packages. What this means to you, the consumer, is that even though you are buying only one cut-up chicken in a package, you could actually be getting parts from four or five different chickens. If you cook these parts for the same amount of time, some of the pieces could be overcooked and some undercooked.

I would suggest that you buy a whole chicken, use a sharp German knife, and cut it up yourself. You will save money, because it's cheaper to buy poultry whole. And this way you can be sure that you are cooking chicken parts that all come from the same chicken. Here is how to cut up a chicken yourself:

*Place the chicken on its side on your cutting board with the backbone facing towards you. Place your knife at the tail edge on one side of the backbone. Cut the whole way down on one side of the backbone. Tilt the chicken back and hold onto the tail. Cut along the other side of the backbone, from tail to neck, the same way you made the first cut. **Illustration 46**. You can then re-move the whole backbone in one piece.*

*Then place the chicken, breast side down, on your board. With your fingers, break out the center breastbone, **Illustration 47**. removing it and any attached* *cartilage. Then cut the chicken in half, through the center of the breast. Turn your chicken halves over and cut each piece through mid-way between the breast and the leg. **Illustration 48**. You should now have four pieces of chicken plus the backbone. Feel for the joint connecting the drumstick to the thigh. Cut the legs in half right at this joint. **Illustration 49**. Cut the wings off the breasts. **Illustration 50**.*

You now have eight nice even pieces of chicken plus the backbone. You can even save up the giblets and the backbones to make a nice pot of chicken stock.

Illustration 46.

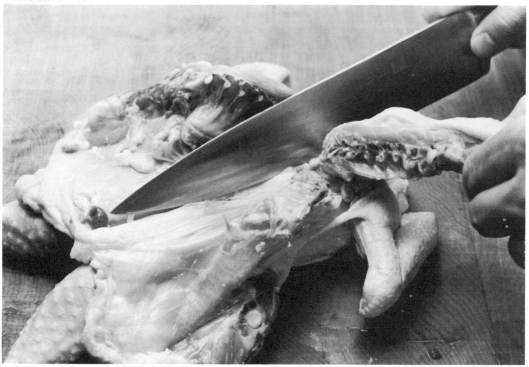

Illustration 47.

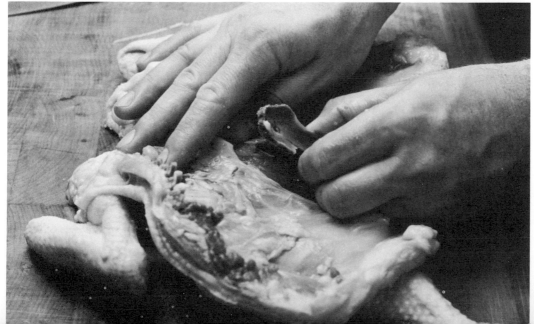

Illustration 48.

Illustration 49.   Illustration 50.

Trussing A Chicken

You don't need a trussing needle or any complicated equipment to truss a chicken. All you really need is a chicken and some string. Cut off about three or four feet of string, depending on the size of your chicken.

*Most books on trussing fowl begin by telling you to cut off the wing tips. Don't do this, your chicken needed them and so do you. Just turn the wing tips back underneath the chicken. They will push the breast up and hold the wings in place. **Illustration 51**.*

*Next, leaving about six inches of string free, loop the string around the end of one drumstick. Carry it outside and loop it around the other drumstick. **Illustration 52**.*

*Tuck the loose neck skin under the chicken. Then bring the string up and around, circling the chicken, between the wings and around the neck. **Illustration 53**. Bring up the free end of the string and, pulling tightly, tie the two ends together between the breast and the legs. **Illustration 54**.*

*Trussing your chicken this way pulls up the breast and the legs and keeps the chicken plump. You can actually see the difference. **Illustration 55**.*

I only truss chickens, never turkeys, If you try to truss a large turkey, you would probably need 30 feet of string. It's great for the string business, but silly to do.

Illustration 51.

Illustration 52.

Illustration 53.

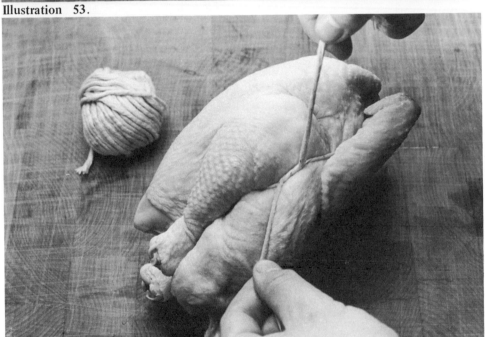

Illustration 54.   Illustration 55.

Chicken And Rice*

1 whole chicken breast, 6 ounces
1 cup chicken stock
2 tablespoons chopped onion
flour for dredging
1-2 tablespoons oil

½ cup rice
4 mushrooms, cut into halves
salt, pepper
2 tablespoons butter

Skin and bone the chicken breasts. Salt and pepper them and dredge them in the flour.

Saute the chicken in the hot oil for a minute of two on each side. Heat the 2 tablespoons of butter in a separate frying pan. Add the onion and cook until transparent. Add the rice and the mushrooms, and stir until all the grains of rice are coated by the butter. Add the stock and then the chicken breasts.

Cover the pan with a lid and put it in a 375° oven for 18 to 20 minutes. Eat immediately and enjoy! Serves one.

Chicken Legs Stuffed With Sauerkraut

4 whole chicken legs
2 tablespoons oil or butter
flour for dredging
1 red pepper
1 cup chicken stock

1 small can sauerkraut
salt, pepper
1 green pepper
1 teaspoon paprika

Bone the whole legs of the chicken. Spread out the meat and pound to even the meat. Sprinkle with salt and pepper.

Blanch the sauerkraut in boiling water, rinse and drain well.

Dice the green and red peppers. Mix them with the sauerkraut and season to taste.

Stuff the chicken legs with a layer of the sauerkraut stuffing. Roll and fasten each leg with a toothpick. Dredge the legs in flour. Heat the butter or oil in a pan and brown the meat on all sides. Add the paprika to the pan, and then the chicken stock.

Place in a 375° oven for 45 minutes or until done. Remove the chicken and keep warm. Reduce the sauce, correct the seasonings and serve with a starch such as noodles, rice or potatoes.
Serves 4.

Chicken Breasts With Almonds

chicken breasts
2 eggs, plus water
butter

flour to dredge
sliced almonds

Partially crush the almonds and mix with a little flour. Skin and bone the chicken breasts. Flatten. Season with salt and pepper. Dredge in flour. Dip in the egg wash made by beating the eggs with a little water. Coat the chicken with the almond mixture. Saute the breasts in hot butter until browned, turning once. Serve at once.

Chicken With Tomatoes*

1 tablespoon butter
1 chicken breast
2 tomatoes (peeled and diced)

flour to dredge
a few sliced mushrooms
garlic (if desired)
½ cup white wine (if desired)

Heat up a little saute pan, add some butter, then saute the chicken breast which was pounded and dredged in flour. Brown on both sides then add some sliced mushrooms, tomatoes, garlic and white wine. Bake in oven for approximately 15-20 minutes. Serve over noodles. Serves 1.

Coq Au Vin

1 chicken
2-3 carrots, turned
1 cup white wine
2 tablespoons flour
salt, pepper

1 onion, chopped
10 mushroom caps, cut in half
1 cup chicken stock
4 tablespoons butter

Cut the chicken into quarters and remove some of the bones. Season with the salt and pepper and saute in the butter until lightly browned. Remove the chicken pieces.

Add the vegetables to the pan and saute them for a few minutes. Sprinkle with the flour and mix it in well. Add the white wine and then the stock. Bring to a boil and season. Add the chicken pieces back to the pot, cover with a lid and place in a moderate oven for 45 minutes to one hour or until the chicken is tender. Serve with noodles with shallot butter. Serves 4 to 6, depends on size of chicken.

p. 56

Stuffed Chicken Breasts

2 whole chicken breasts
8 ounces mushrooms, sliced thin
2 ounces ham, julienned
1 small onion, chopped fine

6 tablespoons butter
salt, pepper
1 tablespoon chopped parsley
flour for dredging

Saute the chopped onions in 2 tablespoons of the butter until they are soft. Add the sliced mushrooms and continue to cook, stirring, for 3 or 4 minutes. Add the julienned ham, and season with salt, pepper, add the chopped parsley. Cook and stir until the mixture is fairly dry.

Cut the 2 whole chicken breasts into halves. Pound a little to tenderize. Sprinkle with salt and pepper. Place one quarter of the filling on one end of each breast. Fold in half and pat well to seal. Dredge the breasts in the flour. Saute them in the remaining butter (or oil) until done, turning once. They should take about 4 to 5 minutes on each side. Serve hot. Serves 4.

Tarragon Chicken

2 whole chicken breasts, cut in half
2 tablespoons chopped shallots
1-2 tablespoons chopped fresh
    tarragon
3 tablespoons butter or oil

½ cup white wine
½ cup cream
salt, pepper
beurre manie, if needed

Salt and pepper the chicken breasts. Saute them in the hot butter or oil, turning. Remove when done and keep warm on a heated platter. Add the chopped shallots to the pan and saute for a few minutes.

Deglaze the pan with the white wine. Add the heavy cream and the chopped tarragon. Thicken the sauce with the beurre manie if needed. Pour the sauce over the chicken and serve. Serves 4.

Chicken Salad Hawaiian

1 to 2 cups diced cooked chicken
1 peach half, diced
few drops lemon juice
2 tablespoons whipped cream

1 pineapple ring, diced
1-2 lettuce leaves
2 tablespoons mayonnaise
garnish: parsley, pineapple,
            tomato wedge

Cut the chicken, pineapple and peach into the same size pieces. Finely shred or julienne the lettuce leaves.

Mix the above ingredients in a bowl. Add the mayonnaise, whipped cream and lemon juice and stir together.

Serve garnished with parsley sprigs, a pineapple ring and a tomato wedge, if desired. Serves 2 to 4.

Cornish Hens With Chestnuts And Brandy

6 cornish hens
1 can chestnuts
brandy
1 onion, chopped
½ cup white wine
3 eggs

livers from the birds
sage, thyme, salt and pepper
2-3 tablespoons butter
2 cups breadcrumbs
1 cup chicken stock

Saute the onion in the butter. When soft, add the livers from the birds, and saute until they turn brown. Season. Let cool and dice.

Mix the onions, livers, breadcrumbs, eggs, seasonings and drained chestnuts well. Mix in some brandy, if desired.

Sprinkle the cavities of the birds with salt and pepper and a little brandy. Stuff the birds.

Brown the hens on all sides in a little butter or oil. Extra bones and giblets can be added to the pan.

Place in a 425⁰ oven and roast for about 45 minutes or until done. Remove the birds and set aside to keep warm.

Pour off the fat from the roasting pan. Deglaze the pan with a little brandy, the white wine and the stock. Correct the seasonings, strain the sauce and serve with the hens. Serves 6.

Cornish Hens With Cabbage

1 onion, chopped
1 large head cabbage, shredded
4 tablespoons butter
⅔ cup white wine
2 tablespoons oil
4 cornish hens

1 carrot, finely chopped
1 apple, peeled and diced
few juniper berries, crushed
few spoons Cognac
juice ½ lemon
salt, pepper

Saute the onion, carrot and apple in the butter for a few minutes. Add the cabbage and cook, stirring, until wilted. Add the white wine and the lemon juice, crushed juniper berries and mix in. Place in the bottom of a greased casserole.

Meanwhile, salt and pepper the hens. Brown them for a few minutes on each side in the hot oil.

Place the hens on the bed of cabbage. Deglaze the pan in which you browned the hens with the cognac. Pour over the hens.

Roast, uncovered, in a moderate (375⁰) oven for 40 minutes, or until nicely browned and done, basting occasionaly.

Garnish with the chopped parsley and serve directly from the casserole.

Duck

If you cook duck "My Way", it will always be crisp on the outside, juicy on the inside and contain no fat layer. People like duck, but they don't know how to cook it so that it comes out greasless.

When you roast the duck breast side down in water, as the recipe will tell you, the boiling water removes the heavy fat layer that is present between the breast meat and the skin. The final roasting, breast side up, will then crisp the skin.

If your duck is frozen, as most are, be sure to remove the plastic bag by making a cut with your knife along the back of the duck. If your knife slips and you cut the duck by accident, it won't matter as much if the cut is on the back of the bird than if it were on the breast.

Try roasting duck my way. It will always be crispy, moist, tender and absolutely fatless.

Roast Duck "My Way"

1 duck	1 onion, chopped
1 apple, sliced	salt and pepper
1 cup or more water	

Remove the giblets from the duck and salt and pepper the cavity. Salt the outside of the duck. Place the duck, breast side down in a roasting pan. Place the apple, onion and giblets (not the liver) around the duck. Fill the pan with the water **Illustration 56**. Roast in a 375⁰ oven for one and one-half hours. Remove the pan and drain off the liquid. Turn the duck breast side up. **Illustration 57**. Roast an additional one to one and a half hours, or until done.

One duck serves two people.

If you wish to make a sauce for your duck, here is a very simple one that will taste good.

Remove most of the grease from the roasting pan. Deglaze the pan several times using water or stock. The bottom of the pan will carmelize from the natural sugar present in the apple and the onion and give your sauce a nice brown color. Degrease the sauce, strain and serve with the duck. Serves 2.

stration 56.

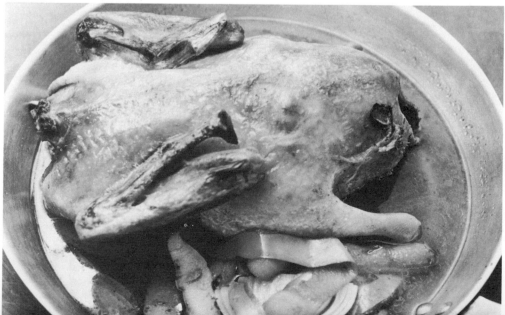

Illustration 57.

Roast Goose

1 goose
salt and pepper
thyme

1 apple
1 onion
water or stock

Salt and pepper cavity and outside of goose. Sprinkle thyme inside cavity. Place the goose breast side down in a roasting pan. Slice the apple and onion and place in pan around goose. Fill the pan with about one inch of water. Roast 2 to 2½ hours in a moderate oven. Drain off most of the liquid. Turn goose breast side up and put back in oven to brown. Cook until done.

Remove most of the greese from the pan. Deglaze the roasting pan several times using water or stock. The bottom of the pan will carmelize.

Degrease the sauce, strain, correct seasonings and serve with the carved goose. Serves 4 to 6.

Carving A Turkey

There is a ritual at holiday time in this country, the sole purpose of which seems to be embarassing father while everyone watches. Carving an unfamiliar bird in front of family and friends is usually a disaster. Father gets nervous and the rest of the food gets ice cold.

Do it my way. Carve your turkey ahead of time in the kitchen and present it as a beautiful and finished platter. Father keeps his cool and the mess stays in the kitchen. There is no turkey all over the dining room table. And best of all, all the food stays hot because it is still on the stove. You don't serve all the vegetables until the turkey platter is ready.

Now here is how to carve that turkey; First of all, let the bird rest for 10 to 20 minutes, depending on it's size. Then you cut each side of the breast off in one whole piece. With your knife, cut down on one side of the breastbone, *Illustration 58, 59*. then continue cutting up to the wishbone and down to the wing. Remove the whole breast in one piece. Do the same on the other side. Slice the breast meat at an angle *Illustration 60*. and arrange the slices either back on the carcass or on a platter. I like to put the meat on a platter, it is easier to serve and looks better. Cut off the wings and the thighs. Then cut the drumsticks off and slice some of the dark meat from the thighs. Arrange all of your meat on a platter. And now you can serve all the trimmings which have remained hot in the kitchen. Try it my way this year and you will never carve a turkey at the table again.

Illustration 58.

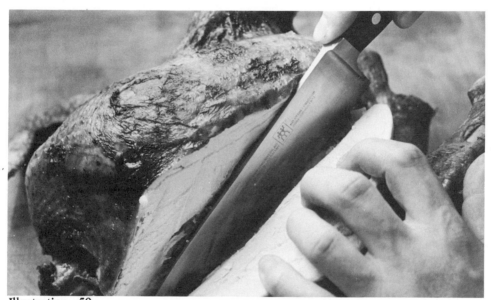

Illustration 59.
Illustration 60.

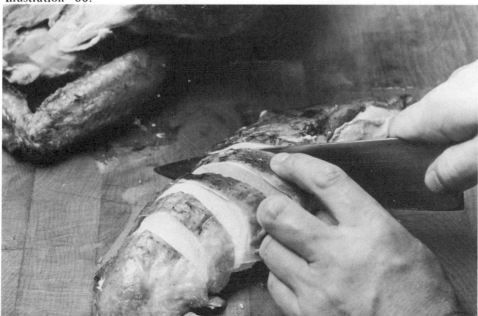

Roast Turkey

turkey	1 onion
salt and pepper	parsley sprigs
butter	

Place onion and parsley inside cavity. Salt and pepper bird. Place turkey in a pan with a little water in the bottom. Roast uncovered until dark, in a moderate oven.

When dark, cover, but baste occasionally.

Roasting time will depend on the size of the bird, about 20 minutes per pound. Baste the bird with butter during the last 10 minutes of cooking time. Remove from oven and let rest before carving.

Carve and arrange as described.

I never stuff my bird. It's a mess to spoon the stuffing out at serving time. Stuffing is much better baked in a loaf pan for you can slice it down much easier. And it has a crunchier taste because the top has browned nicely.
See stuffing recipes, chapter three.

Turkey Florentine

2 cups sliced cooked turkey	1 ten ounce package frozen spinach
½ cup breadcrumbs	2 tablespoons chopped parsley
4 tablespoons melted butter	salt, pepper

Blanch the spinach in boiling salted water. Refresh and drain well. Chop.

Butter a casserole dish. Place the turkey in a layer on the bottom. Smooth the spinach over the turkey. Sprinkle with the breadcrumbs and the chopped parsley. Drizzle the top well with the melted butter. Bake the casserole in a 350⁰ oven for 15 to 20 minutes, or until hot. Serves 2 to 4.

Turkey Salad Valencia

2 cups diced cooked turkey	1 orange
1 pineapple ring, diced	¼ cup mayonnaise
2 tablespoons heavy cream	salt

Peel the orange and cut it into segments. Mix all the ingredients together. Serve on a lettuce leaf garnished with chopped toasted almonds.

Chapter 11
Garnishes

Tips:
Oranges

Garnishes:
Poached Apple Rings
Fried Bananas
Lemon Twist Garnish
Cranberry Orange Relish
Jelly Oranges
Orange Stars
Chocolate Dipped Strawberries

Poached Apple rings

apples	½ cup sugar
½ cup white wine	water
1 prune per apple ring, soaked in port	
or armagnac	

Peel and core the apples. Slice into rings.

Place in a baking dish. Dust with the sugar. Pour the white wine and a little water into the pan.

Poach in the oven until barely tender. Cool.

Drain well and fill the cavity with the drained soaked prunes. Serve cold with pork roast.

Poached apple rings are also good with roast chicken or duck.

Fried Bananas

½ banana per person	flour
1 or 2 eggs	dried breadcrumbs
butter	

Peel and slice bananas in half, lengthwise.

Beat the egg(s) just a little.

Dip the bananas first is the flour, then in the egg and last in the dried breadcrumbs.

Saute in hot butter until golden brown, turning. Serve immediately.

Serve with any curry dish, such as the chicken curry or lamb curry.

Lemon Twist Garnish

Here is how to make a quick and attractive lemon garnish. Cut your lemon into one-eighth inch slices. Take a slice in your hand and with a small sharp knife, cut two-thirds of the way around the slice between the rind and the segments.

*Place the slice on a flat surface and form a loop with the cut peel. Pull the end of the peel through the loop. If you pull it tight it will stand up like a twisted knot and look very pretty. **Illustration 61**. A sprig of parsley can be placed in the center of the slice, if desired.*

Illustration 61.

Oranges

There is a way to get the orange flavor out of the orange rind without actually using the rind in your recipe. Use a cube of sugar and rub it against the skin of the fruit. The cube will turn orange in color and will absorb the flavor and the etheric oils present in the rind. Then use this sugar cube in your recipe. The flavor it gives will be worth the work.

Some recipes do call for the grated orange rind. Be careful when you grate the rind, you only want the orange part of the skin, not the white pith that is underneath.

If you need to julienne orange rind, make sure you use a sharp knife. Cut the peel off in very thin layers. The white part of the orange skin is very bitter and you want as little of it as possible attached to the rind.

All of the things I have said about oranges applies equally as well to other citrus fruits such as lemons, limes and grapefruits.

Cranberry-Orange Relish

2 cups cranberries
½ cup sugar
1-2 tablespoons Kirsch

2 oranges
¼ cup toasted sliced almonds

Remove the rind and the pith from the oranges, cut them into quarters, and remove the seeds. Place the oranges and the berries in a food processor or blender. Grind until the mixture is coarsely chopped. Remove and mix in the rest of the ingredients. Chill.

Jelly Oranges

4 oranges
few drops red food coloring
½ to 1 cup of sugar

2-3 tablespoons gelatin
orange juice

Slice the oranges in half. Remove the insides carefully so as not to puncture the shells. The easiest way to do this is to use a teaspoon to separate the flesh of the orange form the skin. *Illustration 62.* Be careful not to pull out the white stem in the center or you will make a hole in the bottom of the orange. Just pinch it off near the bottom. Place the shells into an empty muffin tin.

Squeeze the juice from the pulp and add enough additional orange juice to measure three cups. Soften the gelatin in a little of the juice. Heat the rest of the juice with the sugar. Add the softened gelatin and cook and stir until the mixture boils and all the gelatin is well dissolved. Add the red food coloring until the mixture is a deep color. Place a little of the mixture into a saucer and place it in the refrigerator for a few minutes as a test. The consistancy should be very firm. If it is not firm enough, reboil and add additional gelatin. Test again. Fill the orange halves and place the muffin tin into the refrigerator. Chill until very firm. Slice and use as a garnish.

Illustration 62.

Orange Stars

    Orange stars are very impressive garnishes and are very easy to make. You need a sharp knife and an orange. Place the orange on its side and with your knife, make zig-zag cuts penetrating half way through the center all the way around the orange. Your knife cuts should touch one another, alternating in direction. **Illustration 63.** *The orange should come right apart to form 2 halves or "stars". You can do the same thing with a lemon, only don't call it an orange star, call it a lemon star.*

    These orange stars look beautiful as a garnish on cold meat platters. They can also be hollowed out, following the method used to make jelly oranges, and filled with fresh fruit salad as a dessert.

Illustration 63.

Chocolate Dipped Strawberries

Chocolate dipped strawberries make a beautiful garnish on a dessert plate. They look good and taste even better. All you need is some good dipping chocolate (I prefer semi-sweet), and some nice firm strawberries with the stems attached. Melt your chocolate using a double boiler, see page 14. Do not add any water to the chocolate, simply stir until it is melted and smooth.

Make sure your strawberries are absolutely dry and free from blemishes. Hold the strawberries by the stem and dip them, three-quarters of the way, into the melted chocolate. Let the excess chocolate drip off over the bowl and place them on parchment or waxed paper to set. *Illustration 64.*

When all your strawberries are dipped, refrigerate them in order to allow the chocolate coating to harden. These are best when eaten on the same day that they are dipped. Keep them refrigerated until serving time.

Illustration 64.

Chapter 12
Desserts

Tips and Basics:

Apricot Glaze

Baking Cakes

Coronets

How to fill a Pastry Bag

Pre-portioning a Cake

Cake Decorating

Genoise

Vanilla Beans

Recipes:

Genoise

Rum Syrup

Mocha Buttercream

Chocolate Buttercream

Pastry Cream I

Pastry Cream II

Pâte a Choux

Royal Icing

Cakes and Tortes:

Tips:

Hazelnut Decorations

Strawberries

Mexicain Decoration

Recipes:

Black Forest Cake, Chocolate Spongecake

Blueberry Yogurt Cake, 1-2-3 Dough

Buche de Noël

Frozen Sacher Torte

German Applecake

German Chocolate Cake

Nut Cream Filling

Hazelnut Torte

Strawberry Torte

Walnut Torte Mexicain, Chocolate Ganache

Cream Puff Desserts:

Apricot Alsacienne

Dessert Swans

Eclairs, Chocolate Glaze

Profiteroles en Glace

Crepe Desserts:

Tips:

Crepes

Recipes:

Swiss Dessert Crepes

Other Fillings:

      Pear Filling

      Preserves

      Pastry Cream and Sauce or Fruit

      Ice Cream or Sherbet

      Whipped cream, Fruit and Sauce

      Fruit Filling with Vanilla Sauce

      Chocolate Mousse and Whipped Cream

      Lemon Mousse and Strawberries

Fruit Desserts:

Apple Beignets

Black Forest Apples

Swedish Apples

Frozen Banana Soufflé

Frozen Lingenberry Soufflé

Fresh Fruit Salad with Kirsch

Strawberry Cream

Ice Cream Desserts:

Flambéed Apples with Honey

Banana Flambé

Hot Blueberry Dessert

Cherries Jubilee

Coupe Chestnut Hill

Meringue Easter eggs, Praline Powder

Peach Melba

Brandied Peaches

My Favorite

Pôire Belle Hélène

Strawberries Romanoff

Wish of a King

Mousses and Molds:

Chocolate Mouse

Lemon Mousse

Mocha Charlotte Russe

Orange Cream Mold

Zabaglionne

Frozen Zabaglionne

Wine Jelly

Tarts:

Tips:

Kiwi Fruit

Recipes:

Apple Tart

Blueberry Tart, Shortcrust Pastry

Kiwi Tart or Strawberry Tart

Pear Tart

Swiss Apple Tart

Candies:

Candies with Dried Fruit

Peanut Brittle

Cookies:

Meringue Mushrooms

Pinwheel Cookies

Drinks:

Egg Nog

Lemon Syllabub

Tips And Basics

Apricot Glaze

Apricot glaze is used in most European bakeries and pastry shops. We often use it to cover fruits on pies and tarts. The glaze will make the fruit shine as well as keeping it from drying out. A layer of apricot glaze can be used also to hold chopped nuts on a cake or tart.

Sometimes a cake recipe will instruct you to paint the top of your cake with apricot glaze before you spread it with a fondant or chocolate glaze. There is a reason for this. If the cake is very porous and you poured a hot glaze over the top, a lot of it would be absorbed into the cake itself. The apricot glaze acts as a seal and allows you to spread the hot glaze over the cake. It will look much better and be easier to handle this way.

Apricot glaze can be made with apricot preserves and water. Just heat some preserves in a little saucepan with some water until it becomes liquid enough to handle. You can either use it like it is or strain it to remove any large pieces of apricot. Use a pastry brush for spreading the glaze. Any leftover glaze can be stored in the refrigerator and reheated when needed.

Baking Cakes

If you notice that all my cake recipes call for nine inch springform pans, it is not a coincidence. It is much easier to remove a cake from a pan with sides that slide off. This way, all the cakes we bake in the restaurant are the same size and we can easily put different layers together for a variey of color, texture and taste. People are always impressed by multilayered cakes. You can do the same thing at home, too.

Instead of baking one cake, bake two different cakes at the same time. It's not much more effort as long as all your ingredients are out and your oven is hot. When the cakes are cool, cut each of them into three layers. Let's say you have made a chocolate cake and a walnut cake. Use two chocolate layers and put one walnut layer in the center. Wrap up the extra layers and refrigerate them for a few days or put them in the freezer. Use them the next time you need a cake, only alternate the layers the other way, walnut on top and bottom and chocolate in the middle. If you use a different frosting, your family will never believe it's the same cake. Very simple, very easy and very impressive.

Before you put your cake in the oven to bake, you should always place the pan on a flat baking sheet or cookie sheet. You do this for two reasons. First, it distributes the heat of the oven better and you cake will bake more evenly. And, in case you pan leaks, it's much easier to clean a cookie sheet than it is to clean an oven.

Get into the habit of checking your cake when half the baking time is up. If one side is getting done more quickly than the other, turn it around to finish baking. The heat in most ovens is uneven and turning the cake during baking usually keeps it from developing burnt spots.

There is one way to test if a cake is done without having to poke holes all over the place. Use two fingers and press down lightly on the center of the cake. If it is done, the cake will spring back and you won't be able to see any marks where you pressed. If your fingerprints remain indented, then the cake is not done. It is much faster and easier to test a cake this way. Your cake won't look like swiss cheese and you won't have to wash a cake tester.

Also, in my restaurant, we always invert our cakes onto a rack as soon as we take them out of the oven. Wait a minute or two and then with a towel, loosen the sides of the springform pan. As soon as you can handle it (but while still hot), remove the pan itself. The top of the cake will flatten out this way. Your cake will not look like a mountain and will be much easier to ice.

Coronets

Coronets or paper cones are wonderful to use when you want to decorate with a Royal icing or for writing words on a cake. You should use parchment paper to make a coronet. You can find this paper in almost any gourmet food store, cheese shop or pot store.

Cut a long triangle out of the paper. Then, holding the long edge of the paper in your left hand, grip the bottom corner of the paper in your right fingers. Fold the paper over into a cone shape, placing the turned edge into the center of the triangle. Hold the top of the cone together with your right fingers and with your left hand, roll the rest of the paper around the center cone. Illustration 65.

Hold the center seam at the top of the cone with both hands and adjust the coronet to make it very tight and pointed at the bottom end. Fold the top edge of the coronet inside to secure the seam or use a staple to fasten it together. Illustration 66.

Fill the coronet and fold down the top edges a few times to secure the filling inside the bag. Cut a small piece off the end of the tip with a scissors or knife. Squeeze from the top of the bag with your right hand and guide with your left just as you would with a pastry bag. Illustration 67. The nice part about coronets is that you throw them away when you are finished with them, there is no messy pastry bag to wash.

Illustration 65.

Illustration 66.

Illustration 67.

How To Fill A Pastry Bag

Lots of people are afraid to use a pastry bag because they don't know how to fill one or use one without making a mess. Here is an easy way to fill a bag, guaranteed to keep the icing inside the bag and not all over your hands.

*Overlap or fold down the edge of the bag one-third of the way from the top. Grip the bag in your left hand, between the folds, using your thumb and forefinger to support the bag. Then with your right hand, using a scraper, fill the bag. Use the thumb and forefinger that are between the folds to help scrape off the icing or whatever it is that your are using. **Illustration 68.** Remember to never fill the bag more than two-thirds of the way full. Then turn up the part of the pastry bag that you had overlapped. Fold the edges together and twist them around a few times so that you have the bag secured at the top.*

You need two hands to use a pastry bag. With your right hand, you apply pressure and squeeze from the top of the bag, not the middle. The forefinger of your left hand acts as a guide for the tube. Squeeze with your right hand and guide with your left. Of course, if you are left-handed, reverse the whole procedure.

If you are not used to working with a pastry bag and you would like some practice, here's a good tip. Go out and buy yourself a large jar of mayonnaise. This is one time when the store bought kind is just fine. Use it to practice with, the consistancy is great. You can scrape it up and refill your bag as often as you like. The more you practice using a pastry bag the easier it becomes.

Illustration 68.

Pre-Portioning A Cake

This is a technique we use in restaurants when we serve cakes. They are always pre-marked in single serving portions in the kitchen when they are made. Try doing this at home, too. This way when you go to slice the cake, the family doesn't fight over whose piece is bigger, they are all exactly the same.

Ice your cake completely, but don't put any decorations on top. Then, with the edge of a large flat knife, or palette knife, lightly press down on the cake from top to bottom, directly in the center. Then mark the cake the same way in the other direction, from side to side. You should now have the cake evenly divided into four quarters. Most cakes are usually scored into twelve portions. With your knife going the whole way across the cake, divide a one-quarter portion of the cake into three pieces. If you pressed with your knife the whole way across the cake, you will have marked two one-quarter portions at the same time. Do the same thing on the other side. You should now have twelve even portions marked on your cake. Illustration 69. This technique works equally well if you want to divide your cake into ten portions or sixteen portions or whatever you need.

When your cake is all marked, then decorate the top any way you like. Knowing where each piece will be cut enables you to decorate them separately and evenly. Everyone gets a rosette or a nut or a cherry on their portion. The decorations will look nicer when you cut the cake and all the kids will get the same size piece and not fight over who gets the cherry.

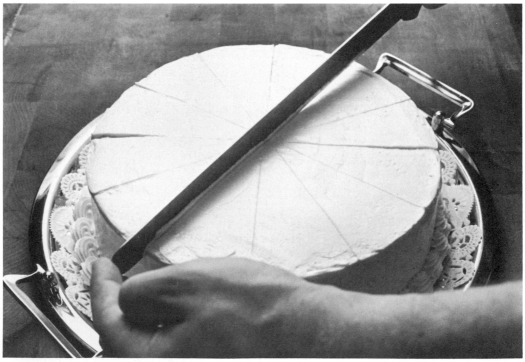

Illustration 69.

Cake Decorating

There are lots of different ways to decorate a cake using a pastry tube. Try out different tips and see the effect they give. The illustrations show several examples of techniques you can use. Just remember to use only one of them on each cake. **Illustrations 70, 71 and 72.**

Illustration   70.

Illustration   71.

Illustration   72.

Genoise

Genoise is a very fancy sounding word for a very easy, very delicious French spongecake. Many European cakes and tortes use a genoise base. There are many, many things you can do with this cake. It keeps very well wrapped tightly in your refrigerator for up to a week. It even freezes beautifully.

Genoise

6 eggs	¼ cup butter, melted and cooled
1 cup sugar	1 cup flour

Butter and flour a 9 inch springform pan.

Beat the eggs and sugar over a double boiler for a few minutes, until warm. Mix on a high speed in a mixer until the mixture is very light in color and high in volume.

Fold in the flour, then the butter.

Pour at once into the prepared pan.

Bake the cake in a 350⁰ oven for about 30 minutes or until done. Turn out onto a rack to cool.

This cake will keep well for several days if wrapped tightly and refrigerated. Cake also freezes well.

Chocolate Genoise:
Substitute half of the flour for sifted cocoa powder.

Cake may also be baked in a greased, floured and lined jelly-roll pan, 11 x 16'' for about 25 minutes.

In Europe, most cake layers are sprinkled generously with brandy or liqueur before they are iced. This serves two purposes. One, it keeps your cake moister for a much longer period of time. It will never have that dried out taste, unless, of course, it stands around for two weeks. Two, it adds more flavor to your cake. So try it my way and always douse your cake this way. The kids will love it, they'll go to sleep right after the party.

If you don't want to use liqueur straight to pour on your cake, here is a nice rum syrup that is a little milder in flavor. It can be stored in a covered jar in the refrigerator for a week or two.

Rum Syrup

¼ cup water	2 tablespoons sugar
2 tablespoons dark rum	

Bring the sugar and the water to a boil. Cook for a few minutes. Remove the syrup from the heat and cool. Add the rum.

Enough for one 9 inch torte or cake.

Any liqueur can be substituted for the rum, if desired.

Buttercream Frostings

Mocha Buttercream

1 cup milk	2 egg yolks
1 ounce cornstarch	2 ounces sugar

Heat ¾ cup of the milk. Mix the egg yolks with the sugar, cornstarch and the rest of the milk. Whisk the egg mixture into the hot milk. Cook and stir until thick. Turn out onto a plate and sprinkle with sugar to keep a skin from forming. Cool.

1 pound butter	½ cup sugar
1 heaping tablespoon instant coffee	3 tablespoons brandy

Whip the butter and the sugar until light and fluffy. Blend in the above pastry cream base. Dissolve the coffee powder in the brandy and mix into the cream. Enough to ice one nine inch torte.

Chocolate Buttercream

Substitute 3 ounces melted chocolate for the coffee powder in the above recipe. Cool chocolate and add. Then add in brandy.

Pastry Cream #1.

2 egg yolks	1 cup heavy cream, whipped
1 ounce cornstarch	3 ounces sugar
1 cup milk	1 teaspoon vanilla extract or vanilla bean

Mix the sugar, cornstarch and the egg yolks with a little bit of the milk in a bowl. Heat the remaining milk. If using a vanilla bean, split it lengthwise, scrape out the vanilla and heat it with the milk.

Add the egg yolk mixture to the hot milk, and stir, over heat until thickened. Sprinkle with a little sugar to prevent a skin from forming. Cool.

Stir in the whipped cream, and if using, the vanilla extract.

If you have trouble with your pastry cream base and it lumps on you, there is an easy way to save the day. Just run it through a food processor or blender for a minute or two and your lumps will be gone.

Here is another version of a pastry cream. This one in a little thicker, as it leaves out the whipped cream. It is good for tarts where you would prefer a thicker cream.

Pastry Cream #2.

2 tablespoons flour or cornstarch
¾ cup sugar
4 egg yolks

1 teaspoon vanilla
1 cup of light cream or milk

Combine all the ingredients in a saucepan, stirring until the mixture is boiling. When thoroughly mixed remove from the heat and cool quickly.

Pâte 'A Choux

1 cup flour
4 ounces butter
salt

1 cup water
4 eggs
1 ounce sugar

Melt the butter in the water. When boiling, add the flour, salt and sugar all at once. Cook, stirring, until mixture forms a ball and is dry. Remove from the heat and let cool a minute. Add in the eggs, one at a time, beating well after each addition to thoroughly incorporate the egg. Fill a pastry bag and pipe onto a baking sheet as your recipe describes. Bake in a hot oven for about 30 minutes or until browned, puffed and dry.
Remove and cool before filling.

This is a decorating icing used to make patterns, such as the Mexicain decoration, or for writing on cakes.

Royal Icing

½ egg white
1 cup or more confectioners sugar

few drops lemon juice

Mix the egg white with the lemon juice and ⅔ of the sugar until smooth and thick. Gradually beat in the rest of the sugar until the icing is stiff enough to pipe. Use for decorating cakes.
The best way to make this icing is in a small bowl using a wooden spoon. It is too small a quantity to do in a mixer.

Vanilla Beans

I like the flavor of real vanilla beans and, where possible, use them instead of vanilla extract. Vanilla beans should be stored in a glass jar filled with sugar. The sugar keeps the beans dry and also will take on a delightful vanilla flavor. You can use this vanilla sugar as well as the vanilla beans.

To use a vanilla bean, split it in half lengthwise, with a knife. You will see tiny black specks down the center of the bean. Scrape these out with your knife and use them. Don't try to strain out the tiny black specks from your sauce, for that is the real vanilla flavor.

The vanilla bean or pod can also be added to your sauce for additional flavor when cooking. Try to remember to remove them afterwards, as they are hard to chew. Vanilla beans can even be re-used. Remove them from your sauce. Wash and dry them off and add them back to the jar with the sugar.

Cakes And Tortes

Black Forest Cake

1 recipe chocolate spongecake	Kirshwasser
1 fifteen ounce can pitted black cherries	½ cup plus 3 tablespoons sugar
1 tablespoon gelatin powder	2 tablespoons cornstarch
1 quart heavy cream	shaved dark chocolate

Bake spongecake and cool. Slice into 3 or 4 layers.

Drain the cherries, reserving juice. Save 12 cherries.

Heat the juice with ½ cup sugar. When boiling, add the cornstarch which has been mixed with a few spoons of cold water. Cook until mixture thickens and clears. Add cherries to sauce.

Place bottom layer of cake on cake dish. Arrange the hot cherry mixture over this layer.

Dissolve the gelatin in about ¼ cup Kirschwasser, heat and cool. Whip the cream and sugar until stiff. Fold the gelatin mixture into the cream.
Top the cherry layer with a layer of whipped cream.

Place the second cake layer on top. Sprinkle generously with Kirsh. Top with more whipped cream. Repeat until all layers are used up.

Frost top and sides of cake with cream, reserving a little for decoration. Shave some dark chocolate over the top of the cake.

Top with 12 rosettes of whipped cream and place a cherry on each rosette.

Chocolate Spongecake

6 eggs
4 ounces flour
2½ ounces cocoa powder

½ pound sugar
2 ounces cornstarch
2 ounces melted butter, cooled

Beat eggs with sugar until very light in color and doubled in volume. Sift the dry ingredients together. Fold into the egg mixture. Blend in the melted butter. Pour into a greased and floured 9'' springform pan. Bake at 350⁰ for 35 minutes or until cake tests done.

Turn upside down on a pan dusted with sugar or flour or place on a rack to cool.

Blueberry Yogurt Cake

1-2-3 dough
3 ounces marzipan or almond paste
1 eight ounce container plain yogurt
2 eggs

1 cup dried breadcrumbs or stale
    cake crumbs
3 ounces sugar = 3/8 cup (rounded 1/3)
8 ounces sour cream
2 pints blueberries

Topping:
1 egg plus 1 egg white
1 tablespoon flour

3 tablespoons sugar

Butter and flour a 9 inch springform pan. Pat out and press a layer of 1-2-3 dough on the bottom and about ¾ way up the sides of the pan. Sprinkle with a thick layer of crumbs.

Place the marzipan and the eggs in the bowl of a mixer. Whip with the flat beater until smooth. Add in the sugar, yogurt and sour cream and mix again. Fold in the blueberries. Pour into the prepared crust. Bake in a 375⁰ oven for 1 hour, or until almost done.

Prepare topping. Mix together the egg, egg white and the sugar. Mix in the flour. Pour over the cake and continue to bake for another 15 to 20 minutes, or until the topping is set and lightly browned. Serves 10 to 12.

Option: If you prefer a more tart cake, the sour cream can be eliminated and 16 ounces of plain yogurt used.

1-2-3 Dough

1 cup sugar   2 cups butter
3 cups flour   1 egg

Mix all ingredients together until well blended. Chill. Dough can be stored for a week or two in the refrigerator or it can be frozen. This amount of dough is enough to make two cakes. If you need only enough for 1 crust, halve the ingredients and eliminate the egg.

Buche De Noël

1 recipe genoise baked in a jelly roll pan. See page 194
1 recipe chocolate buttercream, reserve 3 or 4 tablespoons of the cream
        before adding the chocolate. See page 195
1 recipe pastry cream #2. See page 196
meringue mushrooms. See page 225
1 recipe rum syrup. See page 194
cocoa powder, confectioners sugar
Holly sprigs, cranberries

Bake the genoise layer. Turn out onto a towel and remove the paper liner. Cool for a minute and roll up in a towel. Wrap well and refrigerate until ready to use.

Prepare the rum syrup, chocolate buttercream and pastry cream.

Unroll the cake and sprinkle it with the rum syrup. Spread the layer evenly with the pastry cream. Roll up and carefully place on a serving platter. Cut off one edge of the cake, diagonally, and place it on top of the cake roll to form a tree stump.

Spread the reserved white buttercream on the ends and the top stump of the log.

Spread the chocolate buttercream on top of the log and around the stump. Mark ridges with a fork to form the bark.

Fill a small coronet with some of the chocolate buttercream (or use some plain melted chocolate). Mark rings on the white buttercream. Decorate the log and the platter with the meringue mushrooms.

Sprinkle with the confectioners sugar for snow.

Decorate with holly leaves and cranberries (holly berries are not edible) and cocoa powder as desired. Have fun!

Frozen Sacher Torte

½ of a chocolate cake layer   5 egg yolks
3 ounces sugar   2 whole eggs
6 ounces chocolate, melted   brandy
2 cups cream, whipped   raspberry or apricot jam for coating

(handwritten marginal notes: 6 Tblspns; 16 oz)

Place the chocolate cake layer in the bottom of a springform pan. Sprinkle with lots of brandy. This keeps the cake from freezing too hard. Brush with a layer of jam.

Mix the eggs, egg yolks and sugar together in a metal bowl. Place the bowl over a pot of boiling water and beat until it becomes very thick and increases in volume. Remove the bowl from the heat and continue beating until the mixture is cool to the touch.

Add the melted chocolate and brandy to taste. Fold in the whipped cream. Pour the chocolate parfait over the cake layer and freeze overnight. To serve, remove the rim of the springform pan and slice as you would a cake. Serves at least 12.

Any chocolate cake can be used. You can use the chocolate genoise, chocolate sponge or German chocolate cake recipe.

Illustration 73.

German Applecake

This is my grandmother's recipe for her applecake. It's a very moist delicious cake that uses apples with a sour cream egg-custard filling. The crust is also excellent and very easy to make. It is a great cookie dough and can even be used as a crust for fruit tarts.

When I came to this country I had no idea that everyone would love this cake so much. It has been one of the most popular recipes both on television and in my restaurant.

German Applecake

Crust: 1-2-3 Dough

1 cup sugar	2 cups butter or margarine
3 cups flour	1 egg

Combine ingredients quickly to a pastry consistency - do not overwork the dough. Let rest in refrigerator for a while.

Grease and flour a 9'' springform pan. Press dough into pan, covering bottom and reaching about halfway up the sides.

Recipe makes enough dough for 2 cakes.

Filling:

4-5 large baking apples	1 cup sour cream
½ cup heavy cream	½ cup sugar, or less, depends on apples
juice of 1 lemon	few drops vanilla
2 eggs	breadcrumbs
1 tablespoon cornstarch	
apricot glaze	

Peel apples, core and cut in half. Cut small strips crosswise on top of the apples to score them. *Illustration 73.*

Sprinkle the bottom of the crust with the breadcrumbs to form a thin even layer. Place the apples in the pan, rounded side up. Fill in spaces with pieces of apples.

Mix the rest of the ingredients together and pour over the apples. Bake in a preheated 375° oven for one hour to 1½ hours, or until the apples are tender and the filling set.

Cool slightly and paint the top of the cake with melted apricot glaze.

German Chocolate Cake

5 ½ ounces butter   10 ½ ounces sugar
4 eggs   3 ounces cocoa powder
dash salt   1 tablespoon brandy, or more
1 teaspoon baking powder   6 ounces sour cream
⅓ teaspoon baking soda   1 teaspoon vanilla
nut cream filling   9 ounces flour
chocolate buttercream frosting, page 195

Cream the butter and the sugar well. Beat in the eggs, one at a time. Sift together the flour, cocoa, salt and baking powder. Mix the sour cream with the baking soda.

Add the flour mixture, alternately with the sour cream, to the butter mixture. Stir in the vanilla and the brandy.

Pour into a greased and floured nine inch springform pan. Bake in a 375^0 oven for about 40 minutes, or until done. Invert to cool.

When cool, split in half. Sprinkle with a little brandy and spread the nut cream filling on the bottom of the cake. Place the other half on top. Frost with the chocolate buttercream and decorate as desired.

Nut Cream Filling

1 cup sugar   ¼ cup flour
1 cup heavy cream   ¼ cup butter
dash salt   piece of vanilla bean or 1 teaspoon
1 cup chopped almonds   vanilla extract

Place the sugar, salt and flour into a saucepan. Stir in the cream. Add the butter, salt and vanilla. Cook on a low flame, stirring occasionally, until the mixture comes to a boil. Simmer for an additional few minutes. Cool a little and stir in the nuts. Refrigerate to let harden before using. May be made a day ahead.

Any nuts, such as pecans, walnuts, etc. may be substituted for the almonds.

Hazelnut Decorations

Many European cakes and tortes are made with hazelnuts or filberts. They have an unusual and lovely flavor. The dark skins are bitter and should be removed before you use the nuts. Place the hazelnuts on a baking sheet and put them into a 350° oven for about 15 minutes. Remove the pan and let the the nuts cool down a little. Then it is very simple to rub the skins off. Not all of the skin has to be removed so don't worry if it still remains on a few of the nuts, use them anyway.

Many pastry chefs have a trick of tossing the nuts into the air from a large bowl outdoors. The skins are supposed to blow right off if you do this properly. But be careful of the wind direction, or you can end up with a face full of nut skins.

*Here is a beautiful decoration you can make using skinned hazelnuts and a little bit of melted chocolate. Pick out twelve of your nicest nuts. Melt an ounce of chocolate and let it cool a little. If it becomes too thick, stir in a little bit of cream. Then dip one end of the nut into the chocolate and place it on your cake, chocolate side down. **Illustration 74**. It looks good and tastes good, too.*

Illustration   74.

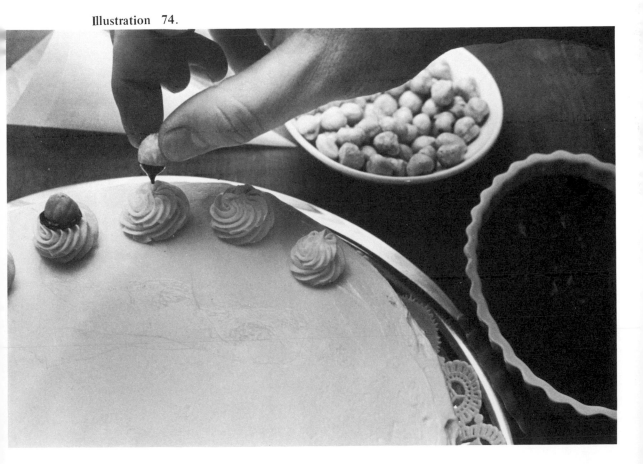

Hazelnut Torte

2 cups ground hazelnuts
1 teaspoon baking powder
pinch salt
1 tablespoon brandy
chocolate hazelnut decorations

½ cup sugar
¼ cup cornstarch
6 eggs, separated
1 recipe mocha buttercream, page 195

Butter and flour a nine inch springform pan. Toast the hazelnuts and remove the skins. Cool and grind. Mix the cornstarch and the baking powder with the ground nuts.

Beat the egg yolks with the sugar until light and fluffy.

Beat the egg whites with the salt until stiff.

Fold, alternately, the nut mixture and the egg whites into the yolk mixture. Stir in the brandy.

Pour the batter into the prepared pan.

Bake in a 350⁰ oven for 40 to 45 minutes or until the cake tests done. Invert to cool.

When cool, split the cake in half. Sprinkle the layers with a little brandy, if desired. Frost with mocha buttercream. Decorate the top of the cake with swirls of mocha buttercream and the chocolate hazelnuts.

Strawberries

If you leave strawberries, or almost any berry, in its original container with the plastic wrap over the top, as they usually come, they will rot quickly. Condensation builds up between the box and the plastic wrap. This extra moisture will spoil your berries. Remove the strawberries and store them in a flat container in your refrigerator. It would be even better if you lined the container with a towel to absorb the extra moisture in the berries.

Don't wash strawberries when you buy them. Wait until you are ready to serve or use them. Also make sure you wash your berries with the stems still attached, don't remove them first. The berries will be less waterlogged this way and be firmer. So wash your berries right before you use them and then hull them last.

Strawberry Torte

1 nine-inch layer of 1-2-3 dough
      page 201.
½ nine inch genoise cake layer
Kirschwasser
1 envelope Doctor Oetkers glaze
1 cup sliced almonds, toasted

1½ cups pastry cream#1, page 195
one pint strawberries
few drops red food coloring (optional)
apple juice

Butter the bottom round of a nine inch springform pan. Roll out the 1-2-3 dough to cover the round. Prick well and bake in a 400° oven until browned, about 15 minutes. Remove and let cool.

When ready to assemble, wash and hull the strawberries and cut them in half lengthwise.

Spread a little of the pastry cream on the baked shell. This will hold your cake layer in place. Place the genoise layer on top of the cream and sprinkle it very generously with Kirschwasser. Cover the top of the cake with about one cup of the pastry cream. Place the strawberries on the torte, pointed sides in, in concentric circles around the cake, starting from the outside edge. Place the sides of the springform pan around the cake so that your glaze will not run all over the place.

Make the glaze, following the directions on the packet, using apple juice for the liquid. Color with a few drops of red food coloring, if desired. Pour the glaze over the tart while it is still warm. The glaze sets very quickly, so don't wait too long to do this.

Let the cake sit until it is set, about 10 minutes. Remove the springform pan carefully. Spread the remaining pastry cream on the sides of the torte. Press the toasted almond slices onto the sides. Refrigerate. Cake should be served the same day it is made.

Mexicain Decorations

*Here is a very impressive way to decorate a cake. Pour the chocolate glaze over the top of the cake and let it harden a little. Fill a paper coronet with a little Royal icing. Start at the right side of the cake and pipe lines, from top to bottom, at three-quarter to one inch intervals. Cover the top of the cake with these lines. **Illustration 75.***

*Turn the cake so that the lines are horizontal. With a long, thin bladed knife barely touching the cake "pull" the lines toward you about every inch and a half. **Illustration 76.** Turn the cake upside down, so that the lines are still horizontal, but what was the top is now the bottom. Repeat this dragging action with your knife, marking the cake between the one and one-half inch intervals you made before. Refrigerate your cake to let the decorations harden. You'll hate to cut the cake because it will look so gorgeous.*

Alternately, this type of decoration can be reversed be using melted chocolate in a coronet to mark the lines on a backround of any firm light icing, as shown in the illustration.

Illustration 75.

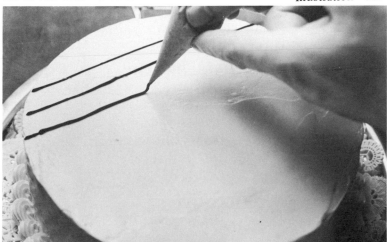

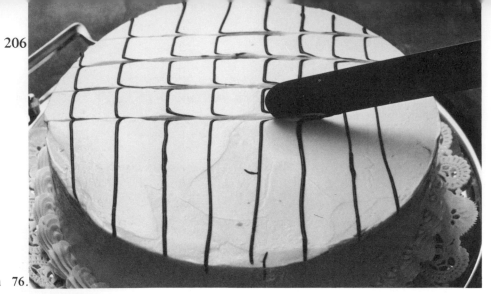

Illustration 76.

This is a version of the hazelnut torte done in a completely different way.

Walnut Torte Mexicain

2 cups (7½ ounces) ground walnuts
¼ cup (2 ounces) cornstarch
½ cup (4 ounces) sugar
1 tablespoon Cognac or brandy
1 recipe chocolate ganache
apricot glaze

one teaspoon baking powder
6 eggs, separated
1 tablespoon lemon juice
pinch salt
1 recipe Royal icing, page 196

Toast the walnuts in a 350⁰ oven for ten to fifteen minutes. Cool and grind. Mix the nuts with the cornstarch and the baking powder.

Beat the egg yolks with the sugar until thick and light.

Beat the egg whites with a pinch of salt until stiff.

Fold, alternately, the nuts and the egg whites into the yolk mixture.

Stir in the lemon juice and the Cognac.

Pour into a 9 inch greased and floured spring form pan.

Bake in a 350⁰ oven for about 40 minutes or until done.

Invert to cool. Set the cake on a rack which has been placed over a pan or tray. Sprinkle the cake with Cognac, if desired.

Coat the cake with the melted apricot glaze. Let sit for a few minutes until dry. Pour the warm ganache over the cake, smoothing carefully with a palette knife. Let sit for a few minutes.

Pipe the royal icing in parallel lines on top of the cake. Decorate with the Mexicain design, following instructions given. Refrigerate until firm. Lift the cake carefully off the rack onto a serving dish. Serves 12.

Chocolate Ganache

6 ounces chocolate (semi-sweet)
1 teaspoon instant coffee powder

6 ounces heavy cream

Melt all the ingredients together in a saucepan, stirring. When chocolate is melted, remove from the heat and cool a little. Pour over the cake.

Cream Puff Desserts

Apricot Alsacienne

1 recipe pate a choux, page 196   1 recipe pastry cream #2, page 196
canned or poached apricot halves   confectioners sugar

Pipe the pate a choux into round balls, or cream puff shapes on your baking sheet. Bake and let cool.

Split the cream puffs in half. Fill with the pastry cream. Top with an apricot half and dust with confectioners sugar. Do not let sit for more than an hour or two before serving as cream puffs will get soggy.

Dessert Swans

1 recipe pate a choux, page 196   2 cups heavy cream
½ cup sugar

Pipe the pate a choux into bodies and necks of swans as described in the recipe for cheese swans, page 106. Bake and let cool.

Whip the cream and sugar together until stiff. Pipe into the bodies of the swans. Assemble with the wings and the necks. This is a spectacular and easy dessert.

Eclairs

1 recipe pate a choux, page 196   pastry cream #1 or #2, pages 195 or 196.
chocolate glaze

Pipe the pate a choux into oblong shapes on your baking sheet. Bake and let cool. Split in half lengthwise and fill with the pastry cream. Place the top halves of the eclairs onto the bottoms. Spoon the chocolate glaze over the tops. Do not assemble more than two hours before serving time.

Chocolate Glaze

3½ ounces semi-sweet chocolate   2½ tablespoons butter
2 tablespoons cold water   ½ cup sifted confectioners sugar

Heat the chocolate until melted. Add the sugar and the butter, cut into pieces. Stir until smooth. Remove from heat and add the water, one tablespoon at a time. Use when lukewarm to frost the tops of the eclairs. Makes about ¾ cup glaze.

Profiteroles En Glace

1 recipe pate a choux, page 196
hot chocolate sauce, page 78

small ice cream balls, chocolate or
    vanilla
sweetened whipped cream

Pipe the pate a choux into small cream puff shapes. Bake and let cool. When cool, split in half. Fill each cream puff with a small ball of ice cream, place the tops on and press to close. Put the cream puffs into the freezer immediately.

At serving time, place three or four of the filled cream puffs into a dessert dish. Pour on the sauce, pipe some whipped cream rosettes into the dish and serve immediately. Cream puffs may be filled the day before and frozen.

Alternates:

1. Fill the cream puffs with vanilla ice cream and serve with a caramel sauce.

2. Fill with vanilla ice cream or raspberry sherbet and serve with a raspberry sauce.

3. Or go really wild. Fill and serve with any combination of more than one sauce and filling at the same time.

Crepes

When I make crepes, I always add some club soda to my batter at the last minute. The carbonation in the soda will make your crepes very light. I know it sounds strange, but if you try it once I'm sure you'll like the results.

You can make your batter up at least one-half hour before you are ready to prepare your crepes. But don't add the soda until the last minute or you will lose the results that the carbonation produces.

*To make crepes, pour a little butter or oil into a hot frying pan. Pour some crepe batter into the pan **Illustration 77** and let it cover the bottom by tilting the pan back and forth. **Illustration 78**. The amount of batter you need will depend on the size of the pan. You would normally use one ounce of batter for a small crepe.*

*When the edges begin to brown, turn the crepe over. The easiest way to do this is to use a palette knife. Cook for just a minute or two on the bottom side, then turn the crepe out of the pan. **Illustration 79**.*

Illustration 77.

Illustration 78.

Illustration 79.

Crepes

¾ cup flour   2 eggs
1 tablespoon sugar   pinch salt
milk, about 1 cup   butter or oil
optional: club soda

    Mix the eggs with the flour, sugar and salt. Add the milk until the mixture is of the right consistency. Add a dash of club soda, if desired, to produce a lighter crepe.

    Heat a few spoons of oil or butter in a crepe pan. Pour in some batter and tilt to coat the pan with a thin layer of the batter. Cook until done on the bottom side. Turn and cook on the other side.

Swiss Dessert Crepes

2 crepes
1 apple, peeled and chopped
¼ cup raisins

1-2 tablespoons butter
Kirsch, optional
confectioners sugar

Saute the apple and the raisins in the butter. When cooked, place half of the mixture on each crepe. Sprinkle the filling with a little Kirsch if you like. Roll the crepe and sprinkle the outside with a little confectioners sugar. Serve warm garnished with an apple wedge.

Filled crepes make a lovely dessert after a light meal. There are many kinds of crepe fillings and here are some other suggestions for you to try.

Pear Filling

Make the apple filling, but substitute pears for apples.

Preserves

Spread the crepes with a thin layer of your favorite jam or preserves. Roll them up like you would a jelly roll. Sprinkle the tops with confectioners sugar and serve warm.

Pastry Cream And Sauce Or Fruit

Fill each crepe with two tablespoons of vanilla pastry cream and fold up the crepe. Serve with chocolate sauce or a hot fruit sauce or sliced strawberries with a dusting of confectioners sugar.

Ice Cream Or Sherbet

Fill the crepes with a scoop of your favorite ice cream, roll and serve immediately. Or you can use sherbet instead of the ice cream.

Whipped Cream, Fruit And Sauce

Fill the crepes with sweetened whipped cream and fold over. Serve with fresh fruit or a hot fruit sauce or even a chocolate sauce with some chopped nuts.

Fruit Filling With Vanilla Sauce

Fill with the apple or pear filling and roll up. Serve with a warm vanilla sauce.

Chocolate Mousse And Whipped Cream

Fill each crepe with two tablespoons of chocolate mousse and fold. Serve with a chocolate sauce and sweetened whipped creeam.

Lemon Mousse And Strawberries

Fill each crepe with two tablespoons of lemon mousse and fold over. Serve with sweetened whipped cream and sliced strawberries.

Fruit Desserts

Apple Beignets

4 apples, peeled, cored and sliced
Batter:

2 cups flour
2 tablespoons sugar
2 tablespoons oil
2½ cups beer

oil for frying at 350⁰

4 egg yolks
4 egg whites, beaten
dash salt

Combine the ingredients for the batter, mix well. fold in the egg whites last. Dip apple rings in the batter.

Place the rings in the hot oil and fry until golden brown.

Drain.

Sprinkle with cinnamon-sugar or serve with a vanilla sauce, page 78.
Serves 4 to 8.

Black Forest Apples

4 apples
4 tablespoons honey
4 tablespoons Kirschwasser

4 tablespoons raisins
4 tablespoons almonds

Cut off a lid from the top of each apple and reserve for cap. Peel the apple one-third of the way down. Core out the center with a melon ball corer. Be careful not to cut through the bottom of the apple.

Fill each apple with one tablespoon of the raisins and the nuts. Pour one tablespoon of honey into each apple and sprinkle with the Kirshwasser. Place the lids back on the apples.

Put them into an ovenproof pan with a little water, just enough to cover the bottom.

Bake in a 350⁰ oven for about 25 minutes, or until done.

Swedish Apples

3 apples
1 cup white wine

4 tablespoons sugar
6 teaspoons lingonberries

Cut apples in half. Peel about 1 inch off top edge of each apple half. Scoop out the center with a melon ball cutter. (Be careful not to cut through bottom of the apple)

Put a teaspoon of lingonberries in the center of each half. Place in a baking pan. Sprinkle the sugar on top of apples. Pour the wine over the apples. (You may substitute part water for the wine or use just water with a little lemon juice.)

Bake in a 375 oven for 15 minutes or until apples are fairly tender. Remove, pour sauce formed in the bottom of the pan over apples and serve.

Frozen Banana Soufflé

2⅓ cups mashed bananas
1-2 tablespoons rum
½ cup plus 2 tablespoons sugar
pinch nutmeg

¼ cup water
1 teaspoon lemon juice
5 eggs, separated
1 cup heavy cream

optional garnish:
    chocolate sauce

toasted sliced almonds
sweetened whipped cream

Dissolve the gelatin in the water.

Put the egg yolk, ½ cup sugar and the water in a large bowl. Place the bowl over a pot of boiling water. Beat with a whisk until thick and light in color. Remove from the heat and continue to beat until the mixture cools down a little.

Whip one cup of the cream and set aside.

Puree the bananas with the rum and lemon juice. Add this puree to cooled egg yolk mixture.

Beat the egg whites until foamy. Add the remaining 2 tablespoons of sugar and beat until stiff.

Fold the egg whites and the whipped cream into the banana mixture. Pour into a large souffle dish or a 9 inch springform pan.

Freeze for at least 6 hours.

Serve with whipped cream. Toasted nuts or chocolate suace may be used if desired. Serves 12

Frozen Lingonberry Soufflé

10 egg yolks
1 pound sugar
1 quart whipped cream

10 whole eggs
1 jar (8 ounces) lingonberries
Kirshwasser

Beat the whole eggs, the egg yolks and the sugar over heat (the top of a double boiler or a bowl placed over a pan of water). Beat until they have doubled in volume and have reached the consistency of mayonnaise. Remove from the heat and beat until cool.

Strain the lingonberries. Add the fruit and some of the juice to the egg mixture. Add Kirsh and fold in the whipped cream.

Freeze in a souffle dish, overnight. Serves 12.

Fresh Fruit Salad With Kirsch

1 chopped pear
1 chopped apple
1 chopped banana
5-10 strawberries
10-15 grapes

1 orange
¼ cup of toasted almonds
1 ounce of Kirsch
1-2 tablespoons of sugar or more

Mix together all the ingredients and chill well before serving.
I hope you enjoy this dessert!

Strawberry Cream

1 cup pureed strawberries
3-4 tablespoons sugar
juice of ½ lemon

1 cup sour cream
1 cup heavy cream

Puree enough strawberries to make one cup of pulp. Mix the strawberries with the sour cream, the sugar and the lemon juice.
Whip the heavy cream until stiff. Fold into the strawberry mixture.
Serve garnished with some whipped cream and a whole strawberry on top.

Ice Cream Desserts

Flambeed Apples With Honey

2 apples, peeled and sliced
juice of 1 lemon
a little butter

2 tablespoons of honey
splash of Kirschwasser

Melt the butter in a saute pan and add the sliced apples. Saute gently for a few minutes, then add the honey and stir in the lemon juice. When everything is mixed together well add the Kirschwasser and ignite.
Serve hot over ice cream, cheesecake or your favourite cold dessert.

Banana Flambé

2 tablespoons butter
2 bananas
½ cup sugar

juice of ½ orange
juice of ½ lemon
1 ounce Grand Marnier

Peel bananas and cut lengthwise. Saute in butter for a short time. Remove bananas from pan. Add sugar and juices to butter with Grand Marnier. Bring to boil. (Make sure sugar is dissolved). Put bananas back in pan and simmer. Optional, serve over vanilla ice cream. Sprinkle with toasted, sliced almonds.

Hot Blueberry Dessert

½ cup water
2 cups blueberries
1 teaspoon cornstarch, dissolved in
    ¼ cup cold water

½ cup sugar
1-2 tablespoons Kirsch
ice cream

Heat the water, sugar and blueberries. Bring the mixture to a boil and add the kirsch.
Dissolve the cornstarch in the water and add, stirring, to the hot blueberry mixture.
Simmer for a few minutes, until the sauce thickens.
Serve hot over vanilla ice cream.

Cherries Jubilee

2 tablespoons butter
¼ cup sugar
¼ cup orange juice
a few drops of lemon juice

½ cup cherry juice
1 cup cherries (canned bing)
½ tablespoon cornstarch
2-3 tablespoons Kirsch

Heat up a little pan. Brown the butter with sugar. Add all the juices and bring to boil. Thicken with cornstarch (dissolved with a few drops of water). Add cherries and let simmer. Add kirschwasser. Simmer for a few more minutes.
You can flambe this dish if you like, but I prefer not to as it destroys the taste of the Kirsch.
Pour over vanilla ice cream. Optional - garnish with fresh whipped cream and toasted, sliced almonds. Serves 4.

Coupe Chestnut Hill

double chocolate ice cream
hot chocolate sauce, page 78
sweetened whipped cream

Cognac
candied chestnuts in vanilla syrup

Place a few scoops of chocolate ice cream into a serving dish. Place two tablespoons or more of drained chestnuts on top of the ice cream. Sprinkle with a little Cognac. Pour on the hot chocolate sauce. Garnish with rosettes of sweetened whipped cream and serve immediately. A chocolate lover's delight!

Meringue Easter Eggs

1 recipe genoise, baked in a flat pan
1 recipe praline powder
6 egg whites
1½ cups sugar

1 quart vanilla ice cream, softened
1 cup chopped pecans
brandy

Cut the genoise into eight oval shaped pieces.

Mix the praline powder into the softened vanilla ice cream. Mix in the pecans and the brandy.

Form the ice cream into oval shapes and mound on top of each cake slice. Place on a tray or pan and put them into the freezer until they become very firm. May be left in the freezer overnight.

Make the meringue by beating the egg whites until they are thick. Add the sugar, gradually, while beating and continue to beat until the mixture is very firm and shiny. Fill a pastry bag with the meringue and pipe decoratively over the ovals so that they resemble fancy Easter eggs. Return to the freezer. Serve frozen.

The eggs may be dusted with a little cocoa powder so it looks like the meringues have been cooked, if desired.

Praline Powder

1 cup sugar   ½ cup almonds

Heat the sugar in a heavy frying pan until it melts and turns a light golden color. Stir occasionally so that the sugar does not burn. Stir in the almonds. Pour out onto a sheet of aluminum foil placed on a baking sheet. Let cool. When cold, break into pieces and powder in a blender or food processor.

Be very careful when you handle the carmelized sugar, it can give you a very nasty burn. Never stick your finger in the pot to taste, you could lose any skin that comes in contact with the melted sugar.

Peach Melba

1 canned or poached peach half,
     per person
toasted almond slices

Melba or raspberry sauce
vanilla ice cream
sweetened whipped cream

Place a peach half in the bottom of a serving dish. Scoop some vanilla ice cream on top. Pour on melba or raspberry sauce. Garnish with rosettes of sweetened whipped cream and toasted almond slices. Serve immediately.

Brandied Peaches

4 cups water	1 cinnamon stick
1 cup sugar	8-10 washed, whole peaches
½ orange peel	3 ounces brandy
½ lemon peel	3 ounces Grand Marnier

Bring water, sugar and cinnamon to boil, add orange and lemon peel. Add peaches and poach for approximately 6-8 minuites. (Depends on ripeness of the peaches). Let mixture cool for a while then remove the peaches and peel them. Once peeled, the peaches can be placed in a jar or bowl.

Bring the sugar water back to a boil and add the brandy and Grand Marnier. Pour this liquid over the peaches through a strainer. Make sure that the peaches are completely covered. Let brandied peaches sit in the refrigerator for a few days then serve plain or with ice cream.

My Favorite

1 package frozen raspberries in syrup, thawed	1 tablespoon cornstarch, dissolved in a little water
¼ cup sugar	Framboise
vanilla ice cream	sweetened whipped cream

Drain the thawed raspberries. Heat the juice with the sugar in a small sauce-pan until the liquid boils. Add the dissolved cornstarch mixture to the boiling raspberry liquid, stirring. Cook for a few minutes. The mixture will thicken and clear. Add the raspberries and a tablespoon or two of Framboise.

Scoop some vanilla ice cream into three serving dishes. Pour the hot raspberry mixture over the ice cream. Garnish with rosettes of sweetened whipped cream and serve immediately. Serves 3.

Pôire Belle Hélène

Pears, ½ per person	vanilla ice cream
chocolate sauce	toasted almond slices
sweetened whipped cream	

Peel, cut in half, and core the pears. Poach them until they are tender in water with some sugar, lemon juice and a piece of cinnamon stick. Cool the pears in the liquid until ready to serve.

For each serving, place one pear half in a dish. On top place one or two scoops of vanilla ice cream. Pour hot chocolate sauce over the top. Sprinkle with some toasted almond slices. Top with sweetened whipped cream.

Strawberries Romanoff

3 cups strawberries
⅓ cup Grand Marnier
vanilla ice cream

sugar, to taste
½ cup orange juice
sweetened whipped cream

Wash, then hull the strawberries. Put them in a bowl with the sugar, Grand Marnier and orange juice. Toss well and let sit, for an hour or two, refrigerated, to develop flavor.

At serving time, place a scoop of vanilla ice cream in a dessert dish, top with some of the strawberry mixture and pipe whipped cream rosettes around the sides.

This should be enough for 8 or 9 servings.

Wish Of A King

1 genoise, baked in a flat pan
chocolate ice cream
chocolate sauce, page 78

½ pear per person, poached
sweetened whipped cream
toasted almond slices

Peel, halve and core the pears. Poach in a syrup of sugar, water and lemon juice until tender. Let the pears cool in the liquid.

Cut out a round of genoise for each portion. Place on dessert plates. Drain the pears, and place, core side up, on top of each cake round. Fill the hollows with a scoop of chocolate ice cream.

Pour chocolate sauce over the pears, top with rosettes of sweetened whipped cream. Sprinkle with the toasted almonds and serve immediately.

Mousses And Molds

Chocolate Mousse

5 ounces chocolate
4 egg whites (beaten)

½ cup whipped cream
brandy
Kahlua

Melt the chocolate in a double boiler and when cooled fold in the whipped cream and beaten egg whites. Add brandy and Kahlua to taste. Serve well chilled. Serves 4 to 6.

Lemon Mousse

½ cup of lemon juice
½ cup of sugar
4 egg yolks, beaten

2 teaspoons lemon rind
2 cups of whipped cream

Heat the sugar, lemon juice, lemon rind and egg yolks in a saucepan. Stir until thickened. Cool and fold in the whipped cream. Chill well before serving.
Serve plain, with sweetened whipped cream or with sliced strawberries. Serves 6 to 8.

Mocha Charlotte Russe

1-2 packages lady fingers
½ cup water
¾ cup sugar
dash vanilla
2 cups milk

2 tablespoons gelatin
6 egg yolks
2 tablespoons instant coffee powder
2 tablespoons brandy
2 cups whipped cream

Decoration:
      1 cup heavy cream whipped with ¼ cup sugar
      reserved lady fingers

Line a buttered 9 inch springform pan around the sides with the lady fingers. Reserve the remaining ones for decoration.
Soften the gelatin in the water.
Heat the milk with the instant coffee powder and the gelatin mixture. Place the egg yolks and sugar in a saucepan. When the milk mixture is hot, whisk it carefully into the yolks. Continue to cook, stirring constantly, until the custard will coat a spoon.
Remove from the heat and chill just until the custard begins to thicken. Fold in the whipped cream and the brandy.
Pour the mixture carefully into the prepared spring form pan. Chill until set. Unmold.
Decorate with the reserved lady fingers and the whipped cream. Serves 12.

Orange Cream Mold

1 tablespoon gelatin
3 eggs
1 teaspoon grated orange peel
1 tablespoon lemon juice

¼ cup fresh orange juice
¾ cup sugar
1 cup heavy cream

Mix gelatin with orange juice and the lemon juice in small saucepan. Let stand a few minutes, then dissolve over heat.

Beat eggs with the sugar. When doubled in volume, beat in the gelatin mixture and the orange rind. Whip heavy cream until stiff and blend in to the orange mixture. Place in mold and chill at least 3 hours. Unmold and serve with orange segments or fresh strawberries. Serves 6 to 8.

Zabaglione

1 cup white wine
1 cup sugar
dash lemon juice

1 cup Marsala
4 egg yolks
2 whole eggs
strawberries

Place all the ingredients except the strawberries into a large bowl. Place the bowl over boiling water and beat constantly until the sauce thickens and reaches the consistency of mayonnaise.

Place the strawberries in wine glasses. Pour on the hot zabaglione and serve immediately.

Sauce can also be served cold. Cool down and mix with a little whipped cream. Pour over strawberries at serving time. Serves 6 to 8.

Frozen Zabaglione

5 egg yolks
½ cup dry Marsala
2 cups heavy cream

5 tablespoons sugar
¼ cup white Rum
¼ cup confectioners sugar

Place the egg yolks and granulated sugar in a bowl. Mix. Stir in the marsala and rum and place over a pot of boiling water. Whip until very thick. Remove from the heat, place the bowl onto a cold towel, and continue to stir until the mixture cools.

Beat the cream with the confectioners sugar until stiff. Fold into the cooled egg yolk base.

Pour into individual timbale molds or a ring mold and place in freezer until firm.

Unmold and serve with fruit, if desired. Serves 8 to 10.

Wine Jelly

2 cups white wine
2 tablespoons plain gelatin

2 tablespoons sugar
Fruit of your choice

In a saucepan bring the white wine, sugar and gelatin to a boil. Remove from the heat and allow to cool. Place the fruit in a wine glass, use bananas, strawberries, grapes, sliced apples, etc. Pour in the cooled liquid. Refrigerate and serve with whipped cream.

I wish you success with this recipe!

Tarts

Apple Tart

Crust:
1 stick butter or margerine
pinch salt
3 tablespoons ice water

1½ cups flour
1 tablespoon sugar

Mix butter into dry ingredients until finely crumbled. Add enough ice water to form into a ball. Let dough rest in refrigerator for a little while.

Filling:

8-9 large apples
1 teaspoon cinnamon
sugar to taste

juice of ½ lemon
1-2 tablespoons apple brandy
apricot glaze

Peel, core and coarsely dice 6 of the apples. Cook them in a pan with just a few spoons of water, stirring often until the apples form a reasonably dry sauce. Add the lemon juice, sugar to taste and the cinnamon. Mix in the apple brandy. Sauce should be tart. Cool.

Roll out the dough and place in a buttered tart shell or a low-sided quiche pan with a removable bottom.

Bake the dough blind in a preheated 400° oven for about 10 minutes. Cool a little.

Spread a thin layer of applesauce on the bottom of the tart. Peel and core and thinly slice the remaining apples. Place in a decorative ring on top of the apple filling. Sprinkle with a little additional cinnamon and sugar.

Bake in a preheated 400° oven until the crust is brown and the apples are tender, about 35-40 minutes. Remove from oven and glaze the top of the tart with apricot glaze.

Serve warm with sweetened whipped cream. Serves 10.

Blueberry Tart

This is a very unusual blueberry tart. Half of the blueberries are cooked in the filling and the other half are then folded in raw. The cooked blueberry filling makes a tart and juicy base for the fresh taste that the raw blueberries give this tart.

You can also use the 1-2-3 dough to make your crust. It will taste even better.

Blueberry Tart

1 recipe shortcrust pastry
⅔ cup sugar
1 tablespoon current jelly
½ cup water

4 cups blueberries
grated rind and juice of 1 lemon
3 ounces flour
sweetened whipped cream

Line a buttered 9 inch tart shell with the pastry. Bake blind in a 375⁰ oven for 10 minutes. Remove foil and weights and continue to bake until done, about 20 more minutes. Cool a little.

Place 2 cups of the blueberries in a saucepan along with the sugar, lemon rind and juice, current jelly, the flour and the water. Cook the mixture over moderate heat, stirring often until it comes to a boil. Continue to cook and stir for ten additional minutes ... It will become almost jam-like in consistency.

Add the remaining blueberries and stir them into the mixture. Pour the mixture into the baked crust, leveling off the top.

Serve warm or chilled with sweetened whipped cream. Serves 10.

Shortcrust Pastry

1 ¼ cup flour
3 ounces butter (6 tablespoons)
2-3 teaspoons milk

1 tablespoon sugar
½ egg, beaten

Combine the dry ingredients. Cut in the butter until the mixture resembles fine meal. Add the beaten egg and enough milk to form a dough. Chill well.

Crust will benefit from a second chilling, after it has been rolled and placed in the tart shell.

Kiwi Fruit

*The kiwi, or Chinese gooseberry is a most unusual and delicious egg-shaped fruit. It has a fuzzy brown skin on the outside which must be peeled off before it can be eaten. **Illustration 80** The inside of the fruit, which is completely edible, is green in color. Kiwis are very high in vitamin C.*

A kiwi is ripe when the flesh will give a little when you gently press with your hand. If is feels rock hard, let your kiwis ripen at room temperature for a few days before you use them.

Illustration 80.

Kiwi Tart

½ recipe 1-2-3 dough, page 199
1 ounce cornstarch or flour
1 cup milk
½ cup sugar
1 piece vanilla bean

2 egg yolks
6 kiwis
1 cup heavy cream
1-2 tablespoons Kirsh
apricot glaze

Butter and flour a 9 inch tart shell with a removable bottom. Pat the 1-2-3 dough into the shell. Prick well with a fork and bake in a 400° oven for about 20 minutes or until browned and done. Let cool.

Heat ¾ cup of the milk with the vanilla bean.

Mix the egg yolks with the cornstarch, sugar and the remaining milk. Add the egg mixture to the hot milk, stir and cook until thick. Spread on a plate and sprinkle with sugar to cool.

Whip the cream. Stir the Kirsch into the cooled pastry cream base. Fold in the whipped cream. Spread the cream filling into the baked and cooled crust.

Peel the kiwis and slice them thinly. Arrange decoratively on the cream. Brush the apricot glaze on top of the tart. Tart is best served the same day it is made. Serves 10.

Strawberry Tart

If kiwis are unavailable, you can use strawberries instead. Only don't call it a kiwi tart, call it a strawberry tart.

Pear Tart

Crust:
1 cup sugar   3 cups flour
2 cups butter or margarine   1 egg

Pastry Cream:
2 tablespoons flour or cornstarch   ¾ cup sugar
1 cup light cream or milk   4 egg yolks
1 teaspoon vanilla

2 poached pears, or more
apricot preserve
blanched almonds

To make the crust, combine all the ingredients quickly to a pastry consistency. Do not overwork the dough, let rest in the refrigerator for a while. To make the pastry cream, combine all the ingredients in a saucepan and bring to a boil, stirring all the time. Cool quickly.

Line a tart pan with the dough and bake in a hot oven until golden brown. When cooled, fill with pastry cream and arrange sliced pears over it. Top with apricot preserves and almonds.

Swiss Apple Tart

Crust:

½ cup sugar   1 cup butter
1½ cups flour

Work together the flour, sugar and butter to form a dough. Chill. Pat the dough into a buttered and floured 10" tart shell. Prick well. Bake in a 375⁰ oven until browned, about 15 to 20 minutes. Remove from oven.

Filling:

3 apples   juice of ½ lemon
dash cinnamon and ginger   ¼ cup sugar
1 cup light cream   2 eggs
1 tablespoon flour   grated rind of ½ lemon

Mix together the flour, spices, lemon rind and sugar.
Stir the cream into the eggs and whisk in the flour mixture. Stir until smooth.
Peel, core and grate or julienne finely the apples. Sprinkle with the lemon juice. Drain well. Place the drained apples into the bottom of the crust. Pour the filling over the apples.
Bake in a 375⁰ oven until browned and set, about 40 minutes. Serves 10.

Candies

Candies With Dried Fruit

1 cup figs
1 cup dates
½ cup raisins

½ cup almonds (or walnuts or pecans)
½ cup dried prunes
½ cup dried apricots (or other fruits)

Chop all above ingredients to a fine consistency. Roll a little bit in the palm of your hands into a ball shape. Then roll ball into coconut flakes or ground nuts. Keep refrigerated until you are ready to eat them. Don't tell your children that these candies are good for them or they might not eat them!

Peanut Brittle

2 cups sugar

1½ cups peanuts

Heat the sugar in a saucepan and cook until brown and syrupy. Add the peanuts and mix together well. Remove from the pan and spread the mixture on a baking tray. When set cut into large pieces. Enjoy!

Cookies

1-2-3 Dough And Cookie Recipe

1 cup sugar
2 cups butter or margerine

3 cups flour
1 egg

Combine ingredients quickly to a pastry consistency. Do not overwork the dough. Let rest in refrigerator for a while.

Pinwheel Cookies

Divide dough in half. Add 2 tablespoons cocoa powder to half and work in. Roll out each half into a square and place one on top of the other. Roll up (jelly roll style) and chill for 30 minutes. Cut into ¼ inch slices *Illustration 81* and place on a greased and floured cookie sheet. Bake 375° for 15-20 minutes.

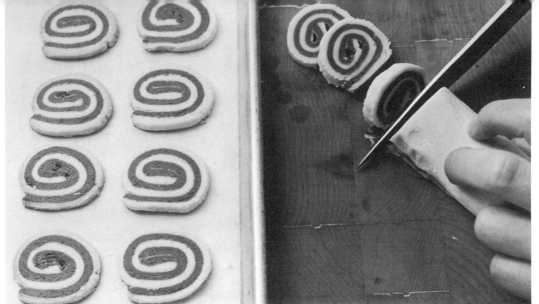

Illustration 81.

Meringue Mushrooms

Meringue mushrooms are cookies that are usually used for decoration on a Buche-Noel or Christmas-log cake. They look very pretty and can be used anytime you need a fancy cookie, not just for the holidays.

Meringues are very hard to make on a day when the humidity is high. They will get soggy very quickly. Make sure you dry them out well in the oven. Baking meringues should really be considered a long slow drying process.

Meringue Mushrooms

5 ounces egg whites (approximately 3)   10 ounces sugar

Beat egg whites until foamy. Begin adding the sugar very gradually while beating. Add two-thirds of the sugar only. Continue to beat until the mixture is very firm and shiny. Fold in rest of sugar quickly.

Place most of mixture in a pastry bag with a small plain tube. On a lined baking sheet, squeeze out stems and mushroom caps.

Bake in a 250⁰ oven for 30 minutes with the door propped open a little. Turn off oven and leave meringues in the oven for several hours to dry out.

Cover and store the remaining meringue mixture.

Cut openings in the bottom of the dried mushroom caps with a small knife. Spread a little of the reserved uncooked meringue into the openings and insert the pointed end of the stem. *Illustration 82*.

Options: Sprinkle the mushrooms with cocoa powder to resemble soil.

You can use melted chocolate on the bottom of the caps instead of meringue to imitate gills.

Store meringues in an airtight covered container in a cool dry place. Don't put them in your refrigerator.

Illustration   82.

Drinks

Egg Nog

6 eggs, separated   ¼ cup Rum
⅓ cup sugar plus 1 tablespoon sugar   ⅓ cup Bourbon
1-2 cups heavy cream, whipped   nutmeg

Beat egg yolks with the ⅓ cup sugar. Beat eggs whites with 1 tablespoon sugar. Fold all ingredients together and sprinkle with some nutmeg. Drive carefully after drinking!

Lemon Syllabub

peel of 1 lemon   4 cups heavy cream
1 cup cream Sherry   ⅓ cup lemon juice
1 cup Madeira   1 cup sugar
nutmeg

Soak the lemon peel in the wines for at least one hour. Remove the peel. Whip the cream softly. Beat in the wines, the lemon juice and the sugar. Pour into parfait or wine glasses, sprinkle with the nutmeg and serve immediately, with a spoon. Serves 8.

Chapter 13
Wine

FOOD & WINE AFFINITIES

FOOD	WINE	TEMP.
Caviar	Brut Champagne; iced Vodka	Iced
Smoked salmon, canapes, crudites, nuts, smoked oysters & clams, etc.	Brut Champagne; dry Sherry, Montilla or Manzanilla; dry Madeira; dry Vermouth on the rocks	Chilled
Raw oysters & clams, seviche	Chablis; Chardonnay; Muscadet; Alsatian Riesling	Chilled
Consomme, turtle soup	Medium dry Sherry or Madeira, or no wine	Room temperature
Bisques and cream soups	No wine, or any white wine left over from preceding courses	Chilled
Heavy vegetable or meat soups	No wine, or whatever red wine is to follow unless the soup is the main course, then a light red wine such as Beaujolais, Zinfandel, regional Bordeaux (e.g. Medoc)	Cool room temperature
Cold buffet meals	Light, semi-dry white wine (American Chablis, Vouvray, Chenin Blanc, French Colombard, German Qualitatswein such as Zeller Schwarze Katz or Liebfraumilch); any Rose wine; Beaujolais	Chilled
Barbecues - Chicken & Pork	Same as cold buffet wines, rose wines, Beaujolais, light Italian reds such as Barbaresco or Valpolicella	White & Rose, Chilled; Reds at cool room temperature
Barbecues - Beef & Lamb	Beaujolais, Zinfandel, domestic burgundy	Cool room temperature

FOOD & WINE AFFINITIES   (CONTINUED)

FOOD	WINE	TEMP.
Fish — Poached, grilled, meuniere or simply baked	Medium white Burgundy (Pouilly-Fuisse, St. Veran, Macon Blanc), Alsatian Riesling or Sylvaner, dry Graves, Italian Soave or Orvieto, U.S. Chardonnay or dry Riesling, Pouilly-Fume	Chilled
Fish — more complex, with sauces, etc.	Fuller white Burgundy (Meursault, Chassagne—Montrachet, Puligny—Montrachet, Corton—Charlemagne), U.S. Chardonnay, Fume Blanc, dry Graves	Chilled
Cold meats and poultry	German Rhine or Moselle of Qualitatswein or Kabinett level, Gewurztraminer, Pouilly—Fume, U.S. Fume Blanc or Riesling, light red wines	White — Chilled; Red — cool room temperature
Poultry, roasted, fried or grilled	Fuller white wines as noted in preceding two categories or medium reds (Bordeaux, Burgundy from Cote de Beaune, U.S. Cabernet Sauvignon, Ruby Cabernet or Zinfandel)	White — Chilled; Red — room temperature
Ham or Pork	Semi-dry white wine (Vouvray, German Rhine or Moselle up to Spatlese quality, Chenin Blanc, Rose)	Chilled
Veal, Sweetbreads & other organ meats	Lighter red Bordeaux, Burgundy from Cota de Beaune, U.S. Cabernet Sauvignon, Ruby Cabernet, Zinfandel, Pinot Noir	Room temperature
Lamb	Red Bordeaux, red Burgundy, Cotes-du-Rhone, U.S. Cabernet Sauvignon, Pinot Noir or Petite Sirah	Room temperature
Beef dishes and Steak	Red Bordeaux from St. Emilion or Pomerol, fuller red Burgundy, Cotes—du—Rhone (Chateauneuf-du-Pape, Hermitage, Cote—Rotie), U.S. Cabernet Sauvignon, Pinot Noir, fuller Italian reds (Barolo, Gattinara, Chianti Classico)	Room temperature
Pot roasts, Stews	Full—bodied reds such as Burgundy, Rhone, Bordeaux, Italian or U.S. noted above	Room temperature

FOOD & WINE AFFINITIES   (CONTINUED)

FOOD	WINE	TEMP.
Game — venison or other red meat	Full—bodied Burgundy, Rhone, Bordeaux, Italian or U.S. as noted above	Room temperature
Game — Pheasant, duck, goose	German Rhine wines or Gewurztraminer; red Bordeaux, red Burgundy, more complex red Italian (Gattinara, Barolo, Chianti Classico), U.S. Cabernet Sauvignon, Pinot Noir	White — Chilled; Red — Room temperature
Cheese	Any wines left over from other courses (cheese and wine love one another); otherwise, older, full—bodied red Bordeaux, Burgundy, U.S. Cabernet Sauvignon, Pinot Noir or Cote—du—Rhone	Room temperature
Salad	No wine	
Dessert — pastries	Sauternes or Barsac; German wine of Auslese or higher class	Chilled
Dessert — fruits	In addition to above, Champagne Extra Dry, Asti Spumante Port, cream Sherry, sweet Madeira	Chilled
Nuts & dried fruits	Port, cream Sherry, sweet Madeira	Room temperature

The ultimate correct wine is the wine you prefer with any given dish!

As of 1979 the following bottle sizes will become mandatory in the United States and in the countries of the European Economic Community:

COMPARING THE NEW WITH THE OLD BOTTLE SIZES

New Metric Sizes	Approx. Fluid Ounces	Old U.S. Sizes	Approx. Fluid Ounces
100 ml.	3.4	Miniature	2, 3, or 4
187 ml.	6.3	2/5 pint	6.4
375 ml.	12.7	4/5 pint	12.8
750 ml.	25.4	4/5 quart	25.6
1 l.	33.8	1 quart	32.0
1.5 l.	50.7	2/5 gallon	51.2
3 l.	101	4/5 gallon	102.4

BOTTLE SIZES AND
COOPERAGE IN FRANCE

Until 1978, French bottle sizes were not standardized—some regions preferred 75 centiliters, some 73, and some even 70. From the 1978 vintage onward, however, it will be mandatory that all regular bottles contain 75 centiliters and state this on the label. Half-bottles, magnums, and so forth will be based on this standard measure.

BOTTLE SIZES

WINE	BOTTLES	METRIC CAPACITY	U.S. OUNCES
ALSACE	½ bottle	36.00 cl.	12.17
	bottle	75.00 cl.	25.36
ANJOU	½ bottle	37.50 cl.	12.68
	bottle	75.00 cl.	25.36
BEAUJOLAIS	½ bottle	37.50 cl.	12.68
"Pot"	2/3 bottle	50.00 cl.	16.90
	bottle	75.00 cl.	25.36
BORDEAUX			
Fillette	½ bottle	37.50 cl.	12.68
	bottle	75.00 cl.	25.36
Magnum	2 bottles	1.50 l.	50.71
Marie-Jeanne	3 bottles (approx.)	2.25 l.	80.33
Double Magnum	4 bottles	3.00 l.	101.42
Jeroboam	6 bottles	4.50 l.	152.16
Imperial	8 bottles	6.00 l.	202.85
BURGUNDY	½ bottle	37.50 cl.	12.68
	bottle	75.00 cl.	25.36
Magnum	2 bottles	1.50 l.	50.71
CHAMPAGNE			
Split	¼ bottle	18.75 cl.	6.34
Pint	½ bottle	37.50 cl.	12.68
Fifth	bottle	75.00 cl.	25.36
Magnum	2 bottles	1.50 l.	50.71
Jeroboam	4 bottles	3.00 l.	101.42
Rehoboam	6 bottles	4.50 l.	152.13
Methuselah	8 bottles	6.00 l.	202.84
Salmanazar	12 bottles	9.00 l.	304.26
Balthazar	16 bottles	12.00 l.	405.68
Nebuchadnezzar	20 bottles	15.00 l.	507.10

VINTAGE CHART FOR FRENCH WINES

Explanation of Ratings

20, 19 - exceptionally great	9, 8 - fair
18, 17 - very great	7, 6 - low average
16, 15 - great	5, 4 - poor
14, 13, 12 - very good	3, 2, 1 - very poor
11, 10 - good	

Vintage	Red Bordeaux	White Bordeaux	Red Burgundy (Cote d'Or)	White Burgundy	Red Burgundy (Beaujolais)	Rhone	Loire	Alsace	Champagne
1945	20	19	19	16	20	19	18	17	16
1946	8	7	12	9	10	15	10	10	11
1947	19	19	19	20	19	19	19	19	19
1948	13	13	14	15	9	9	10	12	11
1949	18	18	19	17	19	16	13	16	17
1950	14	15	12	18	12	15	10	8	9
1951	9	6	8	8	7	9	7	9	7
1952	17	16	16	16	16	18	14	14	18
1953	19	17	19	17	19	13	17	17	17
1954	12	9	10	11	10	16	10	11	10
1955	18–19	17	17	18	17	18	18	15	19
1956	12	10	10	14	9	14	12	13	12
1957	17	16	17	18	18	18	18	17	11
1958	11	13	9	17	13	16	15	16	12
1959	18	18	19	18	18	17	19	19	19
1960	13	13	8	15	10	19	14	13	15
1961	20	19	19	19	20	18	17	17	18
1962	17	13	15	16	17	12	16	16	16
1963	8	6	9	11	9	11	9	11	7
1964	17	*	15	15	17	13	15	15	17
1965	11	10	6	11	11	15	10	10	6
1966	18	19	15	16	16	17	15	14	18
1967	16	14	13	15	14	15	14	14	16
1968	9	7	5	6	11	10	10	11	9
1969	13	13	18	16	15	13	15	14	14
1970	18	17	15	17	14	18	16	14	16
1971	17	17	15	16	16	16	16	17	17
1972	13	13	16	11	12	12	12	12	13
1973	15	13	14	15	13	11	13	13	14
1974	15½	†	14	15	13	13	14	13	13½
1975	19	‡	11	15	11	11	16	15	16
1976	18	15	19	16	20	14	16	16	16
1977	15	λ	14	16	12	17	16	14	15

*	10 dry	13 sweet
†	13 dry	7 sweet
‡	13 dry	19 sweet
λ	18 dry	13 sweet

Classification of the Great Red Wines of Bordeaux (1855)

MEDOC

Next to the name of each chateau is the name of its *commune,* or township.

FIRST GROWTHS

Chateaux	Communes	Chateaux	Communes
Lafite-Rothschild	Pauillac	Latour	Pauillac
Margaux	Margaux	Haut-Brion	Pessac
Mouton-Rothschild*	Pauillac		

SECOND GROWTHS

Rauzan-Segla	Margaux	Gruaud-Larose-Faure	Saint-Julien
Rauzan-Gassies	Margaux	Brane-Cantenac	Cantenac
Leoville-Las Cases	Saint-Julien	Pichon-Longueville	Pauillac
Leoville-Poyferre	Saint-Julien	Pichon-Longueville-Lalande	Pauillac
Leoville-Barton	Saint-Julien	Ducru-Beaucaillou	Saint-Julien
Durfort-Vivens	Margaux	Cos-d'Estournel	Saint-Estephe
Lascombes	Margaux	Montrose	Saint-Estephe
Gruaud-Larose-Sarget	Saint-Julien		

THIRD GROWTHS

Kirwan	Cantenac	Palmer	Cantenac
Issan	Cantenac	La Lagune	Ludon
Lagrange	Saint-Julien	Desmirail	Margaux
Langoa	Saint-Julien	Calon-Segur	Saint-Estephe
Giscours	Labarde	Ferriere	Margaux
Malescot-Saint-Exupery	Margaux	Marquis d'Alesme-Becker	Margaux
Brown-Cantenac	Cantenac	Boyd-Cantenac	Margaux

FOURTH GROWTHS

Saint-Pierre Bontemps	Saint-Julien	La Tour Carnet	Saint-Laurent
Saint-Pierre-Sevaistre	Saint-Julien	Rochet	Saint-Estephe
Branaire Ducru	Saint-Julien	Beychevelle	Saint-Julien
Talbot	Saint-Julien	Le Prieure	Cantenac
Duhart-Milon	Pauillac	Marquis de Terme	Margaux
Pouget	Cantenac		

FIFTH GROWTHS

Pontet-Canet	Pauillac	Le Tertre	Arsac
Haut-Batailley	Pauillac	Haut-Bages Liberal	Pauillac
Batailley	Pauillac	Pedesclaux	Pauillac
Grant Puy Lacoste	Pauillac	Belgrave	Saint-Laurent
Grand Puy Ducasse	Pauillac	Camensac	Saint-Laurent
Lynch-Bages	Pauillac	Cos Labory	Saint-Estephe
Lynch-Moussas	Pauillac	Clerc-Milon	Pauillac
Dauzac	Labarde	Croizet-Bages	Pauillac
Mouton-baron Philippe	Pauillac	Cantemerle	Macau

Chateau Haut-Brion, classified in 1855 with the great red wines, is the only one that does not come under the *appellation controlee* of Medoc, since it belongs to the district of Graves.

---

* Reassigned to first growths from second

Classification of the Great White Wines of Bordeaux (1855)

FIRST GREAT GROWTH

Chateau d'Yquem, *commune* of Sauternes

FIRST GROWTHS

Chateaux	*Communes*	*Chateaux*	*Communes*
La Tour Blanche	Bommes	Coutet	Barsac
Peyraguey	Bommes	Climens	Barsac
Vigneau	Bommes	Guiraud	Sauternes
Suduiraut	Preignac	Rieussec	Fargues
		Rabaud	Bommes

SECOND GROWTHS

Myrat	Barsac	Caillou	Barsac
Doisy	Barsac	Suau	Barsac
Arche	Sauternes	Malle	Preignac
Filhot	Sauternes	Romer	Fargues
Broustet	Barsac	Lamothe	Sauternes
Nairac	Barsac		

Chapter 14

Buffets, Table Settings And Napkin Folding

Buffets

Buffets are one of the most popular ways to entertain in this country. It is easier and cheaper to have 24 guests at one party than it is to plan three or four sit-down dinners. A buffet table can be a delight or an absolute disaster, food wise, that is, depending on how it is handled. When you make your plans, just keep in mind my four rules for entertaining. Food must look good, smell good, taste good and be digestible. Observe these rules and you'll never go wrong.

Lets start out with some of the "don'ts". Don't serve food that will not blend with one another. Plan a buffet menu as you would plan any sit down dinner, for most people tend to taste everything that they see. Try to vary both the textures and the tastes of your food. Don't serve two or three dishes with a cream sauce, or flavor everything with tarragon. If you are serving a poached salmon and a mousse for dessert, try also to serve something with a little crunch, unless, of course, all your guests have no teeth.

Don't try to put foods that don't hold up on a buffet table. Hot souffles are definitely out. Remember, also, if you are using a chafing dish or food warmer, the food tends to cook a little from the heat. So please undercook rather than overcook your food, especially vegetables. There is nothing worse than soggy vegetables.

Don't arrange your platters so that the garnish makes it impossible for your guests to serve themselves. It's important to have food look good, but you have to be able to eat it, too. Also, if you are not providing knives, make sure your food is cut into bite-sized portions. Or serve something that can easily be cut with just a fork.

Try to group your food in a logical order. Don't put the desserts first and the dinner plates last. Think of your table as a large rectangle. Staring from one corner, logically plan how you want your meal to progress. Put the dinner plates at the beginning. Then place the food in the order you want it to be eaten.

First, perhaps, your salads and cold platters, then entrees, vegetables and any condiment and relishes, bread and butter. You might want to put your napkins and silverware last, that is up to you. Many people forget to pick up a fork or a napkin and have to run back for one. It might be better to put them at the end in the first place.

If it is possible, put your desserts on a separate table. If people see a lot of food and they only have one plate, they throw everything on together. There is nothing worse than blueberry sauce on Beef Stroganoff! If you want to put all the food out at the same time, provide clean plates for dessert. A pile of small plates next to your chocolate mousse will indicate to your guests that they can come back for dessert and don't have to pile everything on one plate.

It is also a good idea to put your beverages on a separate table, even a card or a bridge table will do. Traffic flows better if people don't have to stop and pour a drink at the same place they serve themselves dinner.

One last suggestion, especially if you have no help. Try to provide an area where your guests can deposit their used dishes. An empty tray somewhere is a good idea unless you don't mind dirty dishes all over the house.

Table Settings

If you sit down to a fully set table and are not sure of which silverware you should use first, just remember one simple rule - you always start from the outside in. If you follow this rule, you will never go wrong. Let's say there are three forks and three knives at your place. Use the fork that is to the far left and the knife that is to the far right of your plate for the first course. Use the next one for your second course and so on. **Illustration 83**. Fish forks and knives are usually smaller in size and different in shape than those knives and forks used for a meat course.

When you finish with each course, leave your knife and fork on the plate, don't put them back onto the tablecloth. Your hostess will not appreciate your dirtying her cloth. Most Americans don't know that if you place your knife and fork across each other on your plate, this is a signal to your waiter (in Europe, at least) that you want more food. If you place your knife and fork together, facing in the same direction, it means you are finished with the course and your waiter can remove your plate.

Sometimes, in a European style restaurant, you will see silverware placed horizontally above your plate. These are put there for your dessert course. Many times there is both a fork and a spoon in this position. **Illustration 84**. If you are served a dessert that has fruit in it, such as a pear half, you hold the fruit with your fork and cut it with your spoon into bite-sized pieces. If there is only a spoon above your plate, it means you will probably be served a souffle or a cream dessert. If there is a fork and a knife, it usually means you will get some sort of torte which has to be cut. You can learn to guess what kind of food your hostess will serve you by what silverware is placed on the table.

When it comes to using glasses, if there is more than one on the table, use the one that is closest to you first and then so on, down the line. **Illustration 85**. If you are not sure which glass to use, don't be afraid to ask your waiter. He will usually be glad to explain to you what is proper.

Try to make your table settings at home as attractive as possible, it's the first thing people see when they walk into your dining room. Add some fresh flowers and some prettily folded napkins. And candles, too, if you like. Just remember, when you set your table, the order in which you will serve your food. Then set your silverware and glasses accordingly, from the outside in.

Illustration 83.

Illustration 84.

Illustration 85.

Napkin Folding

Here are some very impressive ways to fold napkins. They make look complicated, but they are really very simple and very easy to do.

Fan:

Fold the napkin in half, lengthwise.

Then, pretend that you are making a paper fan the way we all did when we were children. Fold the bottom end of the napkin up and over into one inch pleats, like a fan, **Illustration 86.** about two-thirds of the way up the napkin.

Hold the pleats together in your hand and turn the napkin over.

Fold it in half, vertically, so that the folded pleated side is now on the outside. **Illustration 87.**

Fold the top loose end over with a triangular shape, still holding the bottom pleated ends together. **Illustration 88.**

Turn under the extra flap of the triangle to the other side. **Illustration 89.**

Place the napkin down on this back flap and let go of the front pleated end. **Illustration 90.** It will form a fan shape which will be balanced on this back triangle. **Illustration 91.**

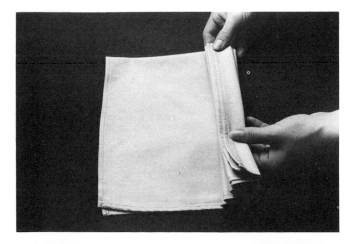

Illustration 86.

Illustration 87.

Illustration 88.

Illustration 89.

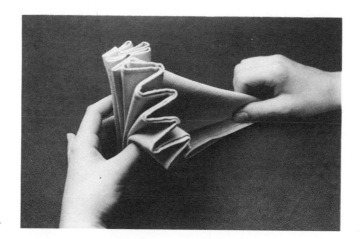

Illustration 90.

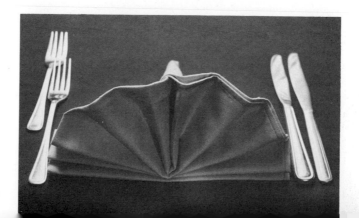

Illustration 91.

Bishop's Hat

Fold the napkin in half, lengthwise, and turn the fold towards you.

Grasp the left top corner and the right bottom corner of the napkin **Illustration 92.** and fold the left side down and the right side up to form two triangles.

The two sides should meet to form a straight line in the center of the napkin. **Illustration 93.**

Turn the napkin over **Illustration 94.** and fold the long side down and in half. **Illustration 95.** The top triangle will remain flat.

With your left hand open out and up the triangular fold to your left side. **Illustration 96.**

Hold the right corner with your right hand and fold this right side half way to the center. **Illustration 97.**

Fold the open left triangle up again. **Illustration 98.**

Turn the napkin over.

Then fold the right side of the napkin into the left side. Do this by holding the right side of the napkin in your right hand and fold it over while loosening the left folded triangular pocket with your left hand enough to slip the right side into place. **Illustration 99.**

Open the center of the bottom of the napkin. Turn it over and stand it up. **Illustrations 100 and 101.**

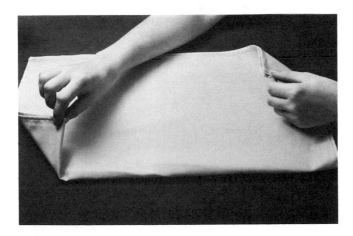

Illustration   92.

Illustration   93.

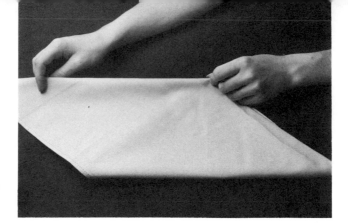

Illustration 94.

Illustration 95.

Illustration 96.

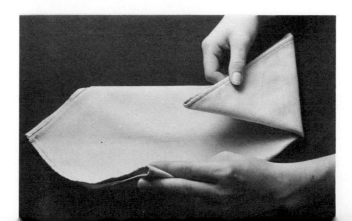

Illustration 97.

Illustration 98.

Illustration 99.

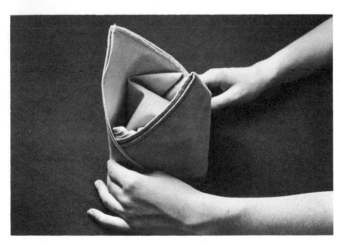

Illustration 100.

Illustration 101.

Buffet Fold:

This is a perfect napkin fold to use for a buffet table. The silverware can be placed into the napkin which then can be picked up easily and carried together.

Fold your napkin in half, lengthwise, and place the folded side towards you. Fold the napkin in half again, from right to left.

Turn the napkin to your left so that the loose edges end up at the top. **Illustration 102**.

You are now going to roll and fold the top layer of the napkin half way, in a triangular shape, beginning with the tip of the napkin. **Illustration 103**. Fold it over and down and continue to make folds, about one inch in size. **Illustration 104**.

Then turn the napkin over and fold in the two sides so that they cross in the center. **Illustration 105**. This fold adjusts how small or how large your pocket will be. The tighter the fold, the smaller the pocket size. **Illustration 106**. Turn the napkin over and place your silverware into the bottom part of the pocket. **Illustration 107**.

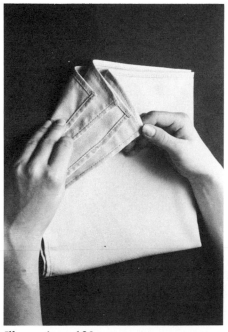

Illustration 102.

Illustration 103.

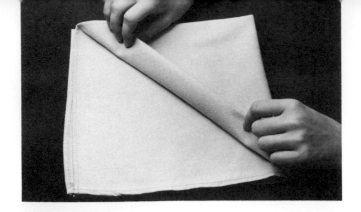

Illustration 104.

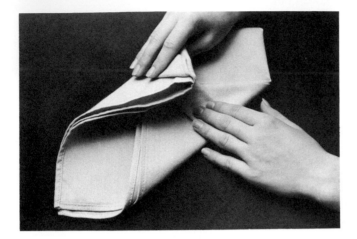

Illustration 105.

Illustration 106.

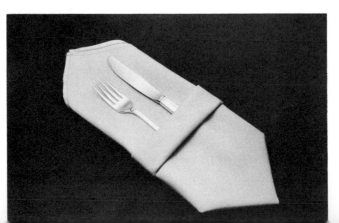

Illustration 107.

Chapter 15
Menus

Brunch And Lunch

1.
Seafood Quiche
Spinach Salad
Strawberries Romanoff

2.
Beef Salad
Sliced Tomatoes
Crepes with Apple Filling

3.
Salad Nicoise
French Bread
Zabaglione with Oranges

4.
Tomato Juice
Farmers Breakfast
Hot Rolls
Fresh Fruit Salad with Kirsch

5.
Cold Cucumber Soup
Spanish Omelette
French Bread
Melon Balls

6.
Fresh Orange Juice
Mushroom Omelette
Tomato and Cucumber Salad
Rolls
Strawberry Tart

7.
Sauteed Fish Fillets
Fettuccine with Pesto
Tomatoes Provencale
Hot Blueberry Dessert

8.
Hot Goulash Soup
Bread and Rolls
Orange Cream Mold

Buffets

Hot
Cream of Cauliflower Soup
Beef Stroganoff
Artichokes Grand-duc
Tomatoes Provencal
Walnut Torte Mexicain
Fresh Fruit Salad with Kirsch

Cold
Cold Fish Salad
Egg Salad
Rice Salad
Ham Rolls with Horseradish Cream
Cold Pork with Prunes and Apples
Chocolate Mousse
Strawberries Romanoff

Dinner Menus

Spring:

1.

Stuffed Cucumbers
Lamb Curry
Rice Pilaf
Cold Vegetable Relish
Fried Bananas
Blueberry Tart

2.

Quiche Lorraine
Baked Stuffed Fish
Stir-fried Vegetables
Hot Blueberry Dessert

3.

Beef Tartare
Curried Chicken
Rice Pilaf
Fried Bananas
Lemon Mousse with Strawberries

4.

Cream of Asparagus Soup
Beef Rouladen
Mashed Potatoes
Vichy Carrots
Fresh Fruit Salad with Kirsch

5.

Salad with Roquefort Dressing
Veal Pojarski
Brown Cream Sauce
Sauteed Zucchini
Glazed Carrots
Chocolate Mousse or
Chocolate Eclairs

6.

Avocado Salad
Swiss Veal Assiette
Pommes Noisettes
Julienned Zucchini
Frozen Banana Souffle

Summer:

1.

Iced Cucumber Soup
Shish Kabobs
Rice Pilaf
Ratatouille
Blueberry Tart

2.

Seafood Quiche
Assiette Diplomat
Pommes au Gratin
Bean and Tomato Salad
Summer Cream

3.

Vichysoisse
Grilled Bluefish
Cucumber Salad
Crepes with Apple Filling

4.

Salad Nicoise
Tarragon Chicken
Pommes Berny
Asparagus
Blueberry Yogurt Cake

5.

Danish Salad
Sauteed Fish Fillets
Asparagus with Hollandaise Sauce
Tomato Rice Pilaf
Strawberries Romanoff

6.

Chicken with Almonds
Fresh Corn Fritters
Grilled Pepper Salad
Hot Zabaglione with Strawberries

Fall:

1.
Cream of Brocolli Soup
Roast Duck
Red Cabbage
Pommes Berny
Apple Tart

2.
Minestroni
Stuffed Chicken Breasts
Rice Pilaf
Brocolli
Brandied Peaches with Ice Cream

3.
Russian Eggs
Chicken with Tomatoes
Buttered Noodles
Spinach Salad
Flambeed Bananas with Ice Cream

4.
Cheese Balls with Pumpernickel
Pork Robert
Buttered Noodles
Ratatouille
Hazelnut Torte with Mocha
       Buttercream

5.
Vichyssoise
Roast Veal Shank
Sauteed Carrots
Pommes Noisettes
Artichoke and Mushroom Salad
Chocolate Mousse
Cookies

6.
Danish Salad
Poisson en Papilotte
Tomato Rice Pilaf
German Applecake

Winter:

1.
Minestroni
Stuffed Breast of Veal
Bread Stuffing
Spinach with Anchovies and Onions
Cauliflower Polonaise
Strawberry Tart

2.
Potato Soup
Veal Birds
Sauteed Spinach
Vichy Carrots
Flambeed Apples with Honey

3.
Poached Eggs with Mustard Sauce
Beef Esterhazy
Pommes au Gratin
Waldorf Salad
Poire Belle Helene

4.
Chicken Soup
Roast Pork Shoulder
Mashed Potatoes
Sauteed Cabbage
German Chocolate Cake

5.
Onion Soup
Meat Loaf
Pommes au Gratin
Leeks with Bacon
Orange Cream Mold

6.
Danish Salad
Szegedin Goulash
Buttered Noodles
Apple Beignets with Vanilla Sauce

7.

Beef Broth with Noodles
Stuffed Cabbage
Sauteed Green Beans
Cauliflower Vinagrette
Wish of a King

8.

Cream of Brocolli Soup
Hot Pork with Prunes
Swedish Apples
Pommes Berny
Cream Puffs

German Dinners

1.

Beef Broth with Noodles
Sauerbraten
Mashed Potatoes
Cabbage Salad
Black Forest Cake

2.

Potato Soup
Roast Veal Shank
Red Cabbage
Sauteed Brussels Sprouts
Frozen Sacher Torte

Holiday Dinners

Christmas

Hot Fish Timbales
Roast Goose
Red Cabbage
Pommes Noisettes
Swedish Apples
Cherries Jubilee and Cookies or
    Buche Noel

Thanksgiving

Cream of Carrot Soup
Roast Turkey
Bread Stuffing
Cauliflower with Sauce
Brocolli
Orange and Cranberry Relish
Lemon Syllabub

Easter

Stuffed Egg Platter
Stuffed Lamb Shoulder
Pommes Boulangere
Sauteed Green Beans
Endive Salad
Frozen cream Puffs with Chocolate Sauce or
    Meringue Easter Eggs

Chapter 16
Staples

Dried And Canned

Apricot Preserves
Achovies, can

Baking Powder
Baking Soda
Bouillon Cubes or Powder
Bread
Breadcrumbs, dried

Catsup
Cereals
Chocolate, semi-sweet
Chutney
Cocoa Powder
Coffee
Cornstarch
Crackers
Current Jelly

Flour
Fruit, canned:
    Figs, Peaches, Pears, Pinapple

Gelatin Powder

Honey

Mustard, Dijon
Mushrooms, dried

Noodles, assorted
Nuts; Sliced almonds, walnuts, etc.

Oil, salad
Olives, green and black

Pickles, dill, jar
Pimentoes, small can

Raisins
Rice, long grain, converted

Salt
Sauerkraut, can
Sugar; brown, confectioners and
          granulated
Syrup

Tobasco
Tea
Tomatoes; canned Italian plum, paste
    and puree
Tuna Fish

Vanilla, beans and extract
Vinegar, wine

Worchestershire Sauce

Miscellaneous:
String for trussing meat
Toothpicks

Optional:
Dried Beans
Canned Ham
Instant Coffee
Lentils
Peanut Butter

Fresh

Bacon
Butter, unsalted
Carrots
Celery
Cheese; cream, cheddar, cottage,
      swiss and parmesan
Cream, heavy
Eggs
Fruits; fresh, apples, oranges,
      lemons, etc.
Fruit Juices
Garlic
Green Peppers

Half and Half
Horseradish
Lettuce
Milk
Mushrooms
Onions
Parsley
Potatoes
Shallots
Spinach, frozen
Sour Cream
Tomatoes

Dried Spices And Herbs

Allspice
Basil
Bay Leaves
Caraway Seeds
Chili Powder
Cinnamon
Cloves
Curry Powder
Fennel Seeds
Ginger
Juniper Berries

Marjoram
Mustard Powder
Nutmeg
Oregano
Paprika
Pepper, white and black
Poultry Seasoning
Rosemary
Saffron
Tarragon
Thyme

Basic Stock For A Bar

Dry Vermouth
Sweet Vermouth
Cream Sherry
Pernod
Campari or Dubonnet
Marsala

Scotch
Bourbon
Canadian whiskey
Gin
Vodka
Rum
Rye

Cognac
Kirschwasser
Grand Marnier
Amaretto
Creame de menthe

Cooking Wines:
red
white

Chapter 17
Substitutions
Equivalents
Conversions

Substitutions

1 teaspoon baking powder   =   1 teaspoon cream of tarter + ¼ teaspoon
                                  baking soda

1 cup buttermilk   =   1 cup whole milk + 1 teaspoon lemon juice
                                  or vinegar

1 ounce chocolate   =   3 tablespoons cocoa powder + 1 tablespoon
                                  butter

1 tablespoon cornstarch   =   2 tablespoons flour

1 cup cream, light   =   7/8 cup milk + 3 tablespoons butter

1 cup cream, heavy   =   ¾ cup milk + ⅓ cup butter

1 cup flour, cake   =   7/8 cup all-purpose flour

1 cup flour, all-purpose   =   1 cup + 2 tablespoons cake flour

1 cup honey   =   1¼ cup granulated sugar + ¼ cup liquid

½ teaspoon herbs, dried   =   1 tablespoon fresh herbs

Eggs, Medium

Whites

1 white = 2 tablespoons
2 whites = ¼ cup
3 whites = 3/8 cup
4 whites = ½ cup
5 whites = ⅔ cup

Yolks

1 yolk = 1 tablespoon
3 yolks = ¼ cup
4 yolks = ⅓ cup
5 yolks = 3/8 cup
6 yolks = ½ cup

Equivalents

Item	U.S. Measure	Cups	Metric
Almonds, whole	4 ounces	¾ cup	115 grams
Almonds, ground	1 pound	2⅔ cup	450 grams
Apples	1 pound, 3 medium	3 cups sliced	450 grams
Bacon, raw	2 ounces	⅓ cup diced	60 grams
Bananas	1 pound, 3 medium	2 cups mashed	450 grams
Beans, dry, kidney	1 pound = 1½ cups raw	9 cups cooked	450 grams
Beans, dry, lima	1 pound = 2⅓ cups raw	6 cups cooked	450 grams
Berries	1 pint	2 cups	473 ml
Breadcrumbs, dry	1 slice	⅓ cup	79 ml
Breadcrumbs, soft	1 slice	¾ cup	178 ml
Butter	¼ pound or 1 stick	½ cup or 8 tablespoons	115 grams
	1 pound	2 cups or 32 tablespoons	450 grams
Cabbage	½ pound	3 cups shredded	225 grams
Carrots	1 pound, 7 or 8 medium	4 cups diced	450 grams
Cheese, cream	3 ounce package	6 tablespoons	85 grams
	½ pound package	1 cup	225 grams
Cheese, hard	2 ounces	½ cup shredded	60 grams
Chicken	3½ pound raw, dressed	2 cups cooked, diced	473 ml
Chocolate	1 square = 1 ounce	4 tablespoons grated	30 grams
Cocoanut, shredded	1 pound	5 cups	450 grams
Coffee, ground	1 pound	40 cups, brewed	450 grams

Item	U.S. Measure	Cups	Metric
Coffee, powder (instant)	2 ounce jar	25 servings	60 grams
Corn	12 ears	3 cups cut	710 ml
Cream, heavy	½ pint or 1 cup	2 cups whipped	473 ml
Flour, cake	1 pound	4¾ cups	450 grams
Flour, all-purpose	1 pound	4 cups	450 grams
Graham crackers	12 squares	1 cup crumbs	237 ml
Lemons	1 medium	2-3 tablespoons juice	30-45 ml
Lemons	1 medium	2 teaspoons rind, grated	10 ml
Meat, beef, raw	1 pound	2 cups ground	450 grams
Mushrooms, dried	3 ounces	1 pound fresh	85 grams
Mushrooms, fresh	10 ounces	4 cups sliced	285 grams
		½ cup duxelles	119 ml
Nuts	1 pound, shelled	3½ cups	450 grams
Onions	1 pound, 1 medium	1½ cups diced	450 grams
Oranges	1 medium	⅓ cup juice	79 ml
		2 tablespoons rind, grated	30 ml
Peas, in pod	1 pound	1 cup shelled	450 grams
Pinapple	1 medium	2½ cups cubed	592 ml
Potatoes	1 pound	3½ cups sliced	450 grams
		2 cups mashed	473 ml
Raisins	15 ounce package	3 cups	420 grams
Rice	½ pound	1 cup raw	225 grams
		3 cups cooked	710 ml
Spinach	10 ounce package frozen	½ cup squeezed, chopped	285 grams

Item	U.S. Measure	Cups	Metric
Strawberries	1 pound	4 cups whole	450 grams
		2 cups puree	473 ml
Sugar:			
Brown	1 pound	2¼ cup packed	450 grams
Confectioners	1 pound	3½ cup packed	450 grams
Granulated	1 pound	2 cups	450 grams
Tomatoes	1 pound	1½ cups peeled, seeded and diced (concassee)	450 grams
Zucchini	1 pound	3½ cups sliced	450 grams
		2 cups grated, squeezed	473 ml

Liquid Measure And Volume, U.S.

3 teaspoons	=	1 tablespoon
2 tablespoons	=	1 fluid ounce
4 tablespoons	=	¼ cup
5⅓ tablespoons	=	⅓ cup
8 tablespoons	=	½ cup
16 tablespoons	=	1 cup or 8 ounces
~~½~~ **2** cup**s**	=	1 pint
2 pints	=	1 quart
4 quarts	=	1 gallon
1 jigger	=	3 tablespoons or 1½ ounces

Measurements For Increasing And Decreasing Recipes

2/3 cup	=	½ cup plus 2⅓ tablespoons
5/8 cup	=	½ cup plus 2 tablespoons
7/8 cup	=	¾ cup plus 2 tablespoons

Liquid Measure Conversions

Cups And Spoons	Liquid Ounces	Milliliters And Liters
1 teaspoon	1/6 ounce	5 milliliters
1 tablespoons	½ ounce	15 milliliters
4 tablespoons = ¼ cup	2 ounces	59 milliliters
5 tablespoons = ⅓ cup	2⅔ ounces	79 milliliters
½ cup	4 ounces	119 milliliters
⅔ cup	5⅓ ounces	157 milliliters
¾ cup	6 ounces	178 milliliters
1 cup	8 ounces	237 milliliters or ¼ liter
2 cups (1 pint)	16 ounces	473 milliliters or ½ liter
4 cups (1 quart)	32 ounces	946 milliliters or 1 liter
4 quarts (1 gallon)	128 ounces	3.97 liters

To Convert:

Ounces to milliliters
multiply ounces by 29.57

Milliliters to ounces
multiply milliliters by 0.034

Quarts to liters
multiply quarts by 0.95

Liters to quarts
multiply liters by 1.057

Can Sizes

Can #	Cups	Ounces
#1	1¼	11
#303	2	16
#2	2½	20
#2½	3½	28
#3	4	33
#10	13	106

Weight
Ounces To Grams

Ounces And Pounds	Approximate Grams And Kilograms	Actual Weight
1 ounce	30 grams	28.35 grams
2 ounces	60 grams	56.7 grams
3 ounces	85 grams	85.05 grams
4 ounces or ¼ pound	115 grams	113.4 grams
5 ounces	140 grams	141.8 grams
6 ounces	175 grams	170.1 grams
7 ounces	200 grams	198.45 grams
8 ounces or ½ pound	225 grams	226.8 grams
9 ounces	250 grams	255.2 grams
10 ounces	285 grams	283.5 grams
12 ounces or ¾ pound	340 grams	340.2 grams
16 ounces or 1 pound	450 grams	453.6 grams
24 ounces or 1½ pounds	675 grams	680.4 grams
2 pounds	900 grams	908 grams
2.2 pounds	1 kilogram	1000 grams
3 pounds	1350 kilograms	1360 grams
3½ pounds	1500 grams or 1½ kilograms	1588 grams
4 pounds	1800 grams	1814 grams
5 pounds	2¼ kilograms	2268 grams
10 pounds	4½ kilograms	4536 grams
15 pounds	6¾ kilograms	6804 grams
20 pounds	9 kilograms	9072 grams
25 pounds	11¼ kilograms	11,340 grams

To Convert:

Ounces to grams
    multiply ounces by 28.35

Grams to ounces
    multiply grams by 0.035

Inches To Centimeters

Inches	Approximate Centimeters
1/16	¼
1/8	½
¼	¾
½	1½
¾	2
1	2½
2	5
3	8
4	10
5	13
6	15
7	18
8	20
9	23
10	25½
11	28
12	30
13	32½
14	35
15	38½
20	50
24	60
30	75

To Convert:

Inches to Centimeters
multiply inches by 2.50

Centimeters to Inches
multiply centimeters by 0.39

Temperatures

Fahrenheit	Approximate Celsius
32°	0°
50°	10°
75°	24°
100°	38°
125°	52°
150°	66°
200°	95°
212°	100°
225°	110°
250°	120°
275°	135°
300°	150°
325°	165°
350°	180°
375°	190°
400°	205°
425°	220°
450°	230°
475°	245°
500°	260°
525°	275°
550°	290°

To Convert:

Fahrenheit to Celsius
    subtract 32, multiply by 5, divide by 9

Celcius to Fahrenheit
    multiply by 9, divide by 5, add 32

Oven Temperatures

250 - 300°F, very low
300 - 325°F, low
325 - 350°F, moderate
375°F, moderately hot
400 - 425°F, hot
450°F and over, very hot

Degrees Fahrenheit

32°	freezing point of water
85 - 100°	lukewarm
165 - 175°	simmer
212°	boiling point of water

Sugar

230 - 234°	makes thread from syrup
234 - 240°	soft ball stage
244 - 248°	firm ball stage
250 - 266°	hard ball stage
320°	liquifies sugar
338°	carmelizes sugar

Chapter 18

Cooking Terms and Definitions

Arrowroot - A finely ground starch made from the root of the plant. Used for thickening.

Aspic - A clear jelly made from meat, fish or poultry stock.

au Gratin - Food covered with a sauce and then sprinkled with grated cheese or breadcrumbs before baking.

au Jus - Served with a sauce made from natural juices.

Bain marie - A water bath or double boiler

Bake - To cook with dry heat, usually in an oven.

Bard - To wrap poultry with thin slices of fat or salt pork.

Baste - To spoon liquid over food while it is cooking.

Beat - To work a mixture until smooth.

Bernaise - A sauce of the Hollandaise family which contains a reduction of vinegar, shallots and tarragon.

Bechamel - A rich white sauce.

Beurre noisette - Butter heated until it turns light brown.

Bisque - A thick soup, usually made out of shellfish.

Blanch - To partially cook by boiling in water and then cooling.

Blend - To mix two or more ingredients together thoroughly.

Bouillabaise - A French fish soup

Boullion - Broth made from cooking meat or fowl with vegetables.

Bouquet garni - Herb mixture used for cooking. Consists of a bay leaf, parsley, thyme and a celery stalk tied together.

Bouquetiere - A variety of vegetables arranged decoratively around food.

Braise - To brown in a little fat, then simmer until tender with a small amount of liquid.

Brine - Liquid for pickling usually containing salt and vinegar.

Brochette - A skewer usually used for broiling.

Broil - To cook directly under a flame.

Brunoise - To cut into fine dice.

Brush - To spread food with butter or eggs, using a brush.

Calorie - A unit expressing the energy or fuel producing value of food. The energy required to raise one liter of water from 14.5° C to 15.5°C.

Canape - An appetizer prepared on a base of bread, toast or crackers.

Caper - The flower bud of the bush, pickled and used for flavoring.

Carmelize - To melt sugar until it becomes liquid and brown in color.

Caviar - Eggs or roe of fish, usually sturgeon.

Cayenne pepper - Pungent red pepper powder.

Chop - To cut food into small pieces.

Clarify - To make clear by adding an agent to remove impurities, usually egg whites.

Coddle - To cook slowly in water just below the boiling point.

Consomme - Very strong clarified broth.

Court bouillion - Broth used for poaching.

Cream - To beat shortening, sugar and eggs until fluffy.

Crepe - Thin pancake.

Croutons - Small pieces of toasted or fried bread.

Cube - To cut into small squares, about one-half inch.

Curry powder - A mixture of several ground spices.

Deglaze - To moisten a saute pan with a liquid in order to dissolve the carmelized drippings in the sauce.

Dice - Cut into small cubes of less than one-half inch.

Dot - To cover the surface of food with small pieces of butter, cheese, etc.

Dredge - Thin coating, usually of flour.

Dust - Coat or sprinkle food with flour or sugar.

Enriched - To make a food product more nutritious by restoring some of the original nutrients destroyed during processing.

Farce - Stuffing or forcemeat.

Farci - Stuffed.

Flake - To separate into small pieces and remove any bones.

Flambe - To pour liqueur over food and ignite.

Fleuron - Puff pastry baked into a crescent shape used for a garnish.

Florentine - With spinach.

Flurries - Same as dot with butter.

Foie gras - goose liver.

Fold - To combine gently.

Forcemeat - Stuffing made of chopped meat and seasonings.

Fortified - Food to which nutrients have been added.

Fry - To cook in a layer of hot fat.

Fumet - A concentrated broth.

Garnish - to decorate.

Gherkins - Small pickled cucumbers.

Glaze - To cover with a shiny coating.

Gratinee - To brown.

Grind - To put through a food chopper.

Gluten - Protein which gives a sticky elastic quality to flour when moistened.

Hors d'oeuvre - Small appetizer served before the main course.

Julienne - To cut into long thin match-like strips.

Knead - To work dough until smooth and elastic.

Larding - Strips of salt pork inserted into meat with a larding needle.

Lardons - Strips of salt pork used for larding.

Liason - Binding agent of cream and egg yolks used for sauces and soups.

Marinate - To soak in an acid mixture before preparation.

Marbling - Flecks of fat within the lean of a cut of meat.

Marrow, bone - Soft tissue found within the cavity of bones.

Mask - To cover completely.

Melt - To heat a solid until it liquifies.

Minced - Chop very finely.

Mirepoix - Mixture of onions, carrots and celery used as a flavoring ingredient.

Mix - To stir until combined.

Papillote - Cooked in foil or parchment paper to seal in the flavors.

Paprika - Spice made of ground dried red pepper.

Parboiling - To partially cook by boiling for a short period of time.

Pare or peel - To cut off the outside skin.

Pate - A spiced meat mixture.

Paupiette - A rolled stuffed slice of meat, fish or poultry.

Petits fours - Small cakes or cookies served with dessert.

Pilaf - Rice sauteed with onions in butter or oil and then cooked with stock.

Pimento - Red sweet pepper.

Poach - Cook in water that bubbles lightly. To simmer.

Preheat - To heat an oven to the temperature needed before using.

Profiterolles - Small cream puffs.

Puree - Food pressed through a sieve or ricer until pulpy. To liquify in a food processor or blender.

Quenelles - Dumplings made of meat or fish.

Ramekin - Shallow baking dish.

Reduce - To lessen volume by cooking down until you have a small concentrated amount.

Roe - Fish eggs.

Roux - Equal parts of cooked fat and flour.

Sabayon - A French whipped egg dessert made with white wine and Sherry.

Saute - To cook quickly in a small amount of fat.

Scald - To heat liquid to just below the boiling point.

Score - Cut narrow gashes part way through food.

Scramble - To mix foods gently while cooking.

Sear - To brown the surface of meat by intense heat.

Shred - To pull into very thin narrow slivers.

Simmer - Slow cooking at just below the boiling point.

Skim - To remove scum or grease from the surface of a stock, soup or sauce.

Sliver -Cut into long, narrow strips.

Squab - Young pigeon.

Steam - To cook in a double boiler without water coming into actual contact with the food.

Steep - To soak in boiling liquid to extract an essence.

Stew - To cook in liquid or sauce.

Suet - Protective fat around kidneys.

Sweetbreads - Thymus gland of a calf or lamb.

Terrine - A container used to cook pate.

Timbale - A small baking mold.

Toast - To brown the dry surface of foods.

Truffles - Fungus-like mushrooms that are found underground, usually wild.

Truss - Tie up so that item will retain its shape.

Whip - To beat rapidly until light.

Zabagilone - An Italian egg dessert made with Marsala wine.

INDEX